THE UNKNOWN CHRIST OF HINDUISM

Towards an Ecumenical Christophany

Revised and Enlarged Edition

Raimundo Panikkar

DARTON, LONGMAN & TODD
LONDON

First published in 1964 by
Darton, Longman & Todd Ltd
89 Lillie Road, London SW6 IUD

Reprinted 1968, 1977

ISBN 0 232 51496 8

British Library Cataloguing in Publication Data

Panikkar, Raimundo
The unknown Christ of Hinduism. – 2nd ed.
1. Christianity and other religions – Hinduism
2. Hinduism – Relations – Christianity
I. Title
294.5 BR128.H5

ISBN 0 232 51496 8

Phototypeset by
Input Typesetting Ltd., London SW19 8DR

Printed in Great Britain by The Anchor Press Ltd
and bound by Wm Brendon and Son Ltd
both of Tiptree, Essex.

CONTENTS

τῷ ἀγνωστῷ Χριστῷ

madhye vāmanam āsīnam
viśve devā upāsate

KathU V, 3

The Spirit[1] whom all the Gods worship
is seated in the middle.

μέσος ὑμῶν στήκει ὅν ὑμεῖς οὐκ οἴδατε

John 1:26

In-between you stands whom
you know not.[2]

1. Lit. 'the dwarf', meaning the *puruṣa* 'of the size of a thumb' who dwells in the heart, cf. KathU IV,12.
2. Cf. Luke 17:21: The kingdom of God is (neither among nor within but) *between* you.
   μέσος : *madhya.*
   In-between, in the middle, in the midst, in the centre: the mediator, the *madhyamaka*, the middlemost.
   It all happens in-between, in the inter-action, in the mutal relationship, i.e. the radical relativity, of all things. And in-between is the One, in the Centre, who makes the interrelation a creative and constitutive intrarelation: the One whom we do not know.

ABBREVIATIONS

Hindu Scriptures		*Christian Scriptures*	
AV	*Atharva-Veda*	Acts	Acts of the Apostles
BG	*Bhagavad-Gītā*	Bar.	Baruch
Bh	*Bhāṣya*	Col.	Colossians
BS	*Brahma-Sūtra*	Cor.	Corinthians
BSBh	*Brahma-Sūtra-Bhāṣya of Śaṅkara*	Ecclus.	Ecclesiasticus (Sirach)
BU	*Bṛhadāraṇyaka Upaniṣad*	Eph.	Ephesians
		Exod.	Exodus
CU	*Chāndogya Upaniṣad*	Gal.	Galatians
IsU	*Īśa Upaniṣad*	Gen.	Genesis
KathU	*Kaṭha Upaniṣad*	Hab.	Habakkuk
KausU	*Kauṣītaki Upaniṣad*	Heb.	Hebrews
KenU	*Kena Upaniṣad*	Isa.	Isaia
MaitU	*Maitrī Upaniṣad*	Jer.	Jeremia
MandU	*Māṇḍūkya Upaniṣad*	Mal.	Malachia
MundU	*Muṇḍaka Upaniṣad*	Matt.	Matthew
PrasnU	*Praśna Upaniṣad*	Phil.	Philippians
RV	*Ṛg-Veda*	Prov.	Proverbs
SB	*Śatapatha Brāhmaṇa*	Ps.	Psalm
SU	*Śvetāśvatara Upaniṣad*	Rev.	Revelation
		Rom.	Romans
TB	*Taittirīya Brāhmaṇa*	Tim.	Timothy
TMB	*Tāṇḍya Mahā Brāhmaṇa*		
TU	*Taittirīya Upaniṣad*	*Other*	
YS	*Yoga-Sūtra of Patañjali*	Denz.	Denziger, *Enchiridion Symbolorum*

PREFACE

vedāham samatītāni vartamānāni cārjuna,
bhaviṣyāṇi ca bhūtāni māṃ tu veda na kaścana.

BG VII, 26

I know, O Arjuna, the beings of the past, the present and the future, but no one knows me.

πότε δέ σε εἴδομεν ξένον καὶ συνηγάγομεν, ἢ γυμνὸν καὶ περιεβάλομεν; Matt. 25:38

And when did we see thee a stranger and welcome thee, or naked and clothe thee?

There has been a fellow traveller on my journeys to the different lands of Man.[1] Child of my own time and environment, I thought I knew well who that companion was in my intellectual and spiritual wonderments of over a half-century ago. There came, however, a critical moment when I reached my ancestral dwelling-place at the peak-period of my life: my companion disappeared. I had often preached about Emmaus, but the settlement I had now reached was my own village. And so, instead of retracing my steps to a City of Peace, to look for and perhaps find my partner again, I proceeded, alone, to a Battlefield ravaged by fratricidal warfare. Shocked and pained, I refused to take a stand and struggle for any of the parties. The Black one wanted to enlist me as a warrior in the Field of Righteousness. The White one wanted me to be a brahman in favour of what seemed to me an unjust *status quo*. Both were my kith and kin, but I remained a conscientious objector, mistrusted by both. Was it that a third great Symbol in the form of Compassion was

[1] Two reasons compel me to write Man with a capital letter: a) to indicate that it means the human being in its totality and thus includes the male and the female; and b) to imply that Man is an irreducible reality standing side by side—with all the necessary ontological distinctions—with God and the world.

taking hold of me? Risking my life in offering my services to everybody without accepting their respective dialectics, I found myself suddenly in the World of Time. And from there the sacredness of everything, even of the secular, dawned upon me. Thus I am at the confluence (*sangam*) of the four rivers: the Hindu, Christian, Buddhist and Secular traditions. This book tells something about this adventure.

Why, in our time of rapid social and individual change, a second edition of a book written a quarter of a century ago? Because of a personal problem of conscience. 'Personal' here is not indicating myself as a particular individual, but my relationship with the world. The most positive way to overcome a tradition is not to step out of it (as if it were a bullock cart) or to cancel one's membership (as if it were a club), but to live that *tradition*, i.e. to 'pass it on', to continue it, to climb to the top where other peaks are visible and/or to descend to the depths where the throbbing of the world is perceptible. I feel that I owe it to many to explain the continuity of my path in spite of the mutation that has taken place both in me and in our world.

I can only be free from a certain type of Christianity or Hinduism (and for that matter from a certain type of Buddhism and Secularism) if I become a better Christian and a better Hindu. If one writes a book with one's life and pays for it with one's blood, if intellectual activity consists of life lived and experience suffered, rather than being a mere secretion of the brain, then what I have written is part of what I was; and what I was cannot be blotted out. It is useless to repudiate it.

Our present time of heightened speed and increased impatience tends to produce ruptures, violent reactions and quick revolutions. Within Christianity we already find extreme attitudes that are falling into the very same mistakes, only in the opposite direction, that they are endeavouring to correct: if God was previously to the right, he is now to the far left. If Christ was a divine idol, now he is just a revolutionary Jew. Within Hinduism we find similar over-reactions: if rituals were previously the backbone of Hindu life for the majority, now they are discarded altogether; if there was once religious inflation, now there is spiritual starvation.

This, then, is my problem of conscience: many people in all walks of life, in both East and West, having gone through a similar process, have either abandoned 'religion' altogether (or a particular religion) or have turned to the 'scientific' study of religion. The young generations also, East and West, seem to run to extremes, completely rejecting their own traditions and/or joining cults and sects of a sacred or profane nature. It is hoped that this second edition may offer an example of transformation without total rupture and of continuity which is not mere prolongation. To offer my personal alternative in response to what I observe to be the plight of many seemed a moral imperative sufficient to justify turning from my many other 'duties' and 'callings' in order to revise this edition.

For revising this book I have been guided by three principles. The present edition has endeavoured 1) to make explicit what was written too cryptically in the first version; 2) to keep from the first edition all that I still believe can truly be said; and 3) to refrain from changing the text completely according to my present vision (this would have meant writing a new book).

The prefaces which were written for different translations from 1957 to 1976 have been reorganized so as to form the first part of the Introduction. The second part is based on scattered notes accumulated over the years as reactions (my own and other people's) to the text. The bibliography has been updated and footnotes added here and there as hints for further study.

My wish is that, just as the first edition contributed towards a more critical Christian self-understanding at a very crucial time, this revised version may offer a new step towards a fuller grasp of our itinerant state. It invites the reader to a contemplative insight into that Mystery that can only be named in the vocative and whose name is a Supername chiselled upon a white pebble that can be properly kept only in the cave of heart—of the World.

I owe gratitude to all of those who have contributed to this second edition in one way or another; especially to Madelon

Bose and Bettina Bäumer, who have helped me in preparing the new manuscript, and to Mary Rogers, who has, once again, revised my language.

R. P.
Santa Barbara
Easter 1979

INTRODUCTION

naiva vācā na manasā prāptum śakyo na cakṣuṣā
astīti bruvato' nyatra katham tadupalabhyate

KathU VI, 12

Not by speech, not by mind,
not by sight can He be apprehended.
Only by him who says: HE IS
can He be comprehended.

ὃς ἐν ταῖς παρῳχημέναις γενεαῖς εἴασεν πάντα τὰ ἔθνη πορεύεσθαι ταῖς ὁδοῖς αὐτῶν. καίτοι οὐκ ἀμάρτυρον αὐτὸν ἀφῆκεν.

Acts 14:16–17

In the ages that are past He
let all the peoples follow their
own ways, and yet He did not leave
Himself without testimony.

1. *TRADITUM*: THE BURDEN OF THE PAST

'God who at sundry times and in divers manners spoke in times past to the fathers by the prophets, last of all in these days has spoken to us by his Son, whom he appointed heir of all things, by whom also he made the World.'[1] From this we may surmise that the Son has inspired not only the prophets of Israel but also the sages of Hinduism, and that he has been present in all the endeavours of Man, for we are certain that 'upholding all things by the Word of his power'[2] he has never forsaken his World. We believe that the Logos himself is speaking in that religion which for millennia has been leading and inspiring hundreds of millions of people. *Vāc*, the Logos,

[1] Heb. 1:1–2.
[2] Heb. 1:3.

is the Firstborn of truth[3] and was with the Absolute from the beginning.[4]

The present study does not claim to unveil this mystery or to dictate the language that the believer in Christ is to use, since only the Holy Spirit inspires the words of his living witnesses, and he takes care to tell us not to think beforehand of what we are to say or of how we are to present it.[5] In this investigation I propose to examine a few ideas regarding three particular aspects of my theme.

The first chapter describes the Hindu-Christian encounter on its ontological and existential level, with the intention of showing that there is in Hinduism a living Presence of that Mystery which Christians call Christ. Now Presence does not necessarily imply historical presence. Christians should find no difficulty in admitting this, for they recognize the same truth in, precisely, the Eucharist, which celebrates Christ's real presence without identifying it with his historical reality. To put it bluntly, Christians do not eat the proteins of Jesus when they receive the Eucharist. The Western world is, by and large, influenced by an exaggerated historicism, as though historicity were the sole component of reality.

Christians in general are well acquainted with the idea that Christ will come at the end of time and that all religions are pointing towards him, who is the expectation of the peoples.[6] This idea, however, should not overshadow the complementary and, in a way, previous truth that Christ is not only at the end but also at the beginning. He could not be the Omega of everything if he were not also the Alpha.[7] Christ, from a Christian point of view, is not only the ontological goal of

[3] Cf. TB II, 8, 8, 5; RV I, 164, 37.

[4] Cf. TMB XX, 14, 2: 'This (in the beginning) was only the Lord of the Universe. His word was with him. This word was his second. He contemplated. He said, "I will deliver this word so that she will produce and bring into being all this world." ' Cf. also BU I, 2, 4–5; I, 3, 21.

[5] Cf. Matt. 10:19–20.

[6] Cf. Gen. 49:10; Isa. 2:2, 11:10, 42:4, 49:6, 55:5, 60:3–5; Luke 2:30–2; Matt. 12:21; Rom. 15:12, etc. It is well known that similar prophecies are to be found in almost all world-religions: of the Coming One, the Centre, the Symbol.

[7] Cf. Rev. 1:8, 21:6, etc.

Hinduism but also its true inspirer, and his grace is the guiding, though hidden, force impelling Hinduism towards its full flowering.[8] He is the 'Principle' that spoke to Men and was already at work before Abraham.[9] He was present in the stone that Moses struck so unbelievingly,[10] and he acted in Moses himself when he chose to share the life of his people.[11] He may have been called by many names, but his presence and activity were always there. The encounter is not an ideological one, but takes place in the deepest recess of reality—in what Christian tradition calls the Mystery.

The second chapter of this study deals with the complementary question of the doctrinal relationship between Hinduism and Christian faith. This means, not that we are comparing two doctrines, but that we are trying to discern what the Christian's attitude should be towards Hinduism understood as a fully-fledged, legitimate and valid religion. Now Christianity understands itself as Catholic, i.e. full and universal, faith or religiousness. In fact, Christianity lived from within does not consider itself as *one* religion among others, or even as *prima inter pares*. Christianity is convinced that it bears a message of integral salvation for Man and thus sees itself as the fullness of all religion and the perfection of each religion. The relationship of Christians, in so far as they are truly Christian, to other religions is not one of simple juxtaposition or total rejection or absolute dominance. It is a *sui generis* relationship, which I shall try to describe in the particular case of Hinduism. This investigation will shed light, I hope, not only on the particular subject of inquiry, but also on the question of the 'salvation' of 'non-Christians' and on the missionary approach to 'non-Christian' religions. I shall let the reader, however, draw most of the conclusions himself. An analogous inverse relationship, i.e. of Hindus to Christianity, also suggests itself, but as it lies beyond the

[8] Cf. John 1:1, 1:9–10, etc.

[9] Cf. the Vulgate rendering of John 8:25, though it does not correspond to the Greek. See also John 8:58.

[10] Cf. 1 Cor. 10:4; Exod. 17:6; Ps. 18:2, etc.

[11] Cf. Heb. 11:24–6. Though 'Christos' here may mean the 'anointed', the author of Hebrews undoubtedly meant Christ.

scope of this study to develop the idea mere mention of it must suffice. It should however be clear from the very beginning that the Christian attitude not only does not contradict the corresponding Hindu attitude, but elicits it in a homeomorphic way,[12] for, just as if I really love you I will have to allow you to love me, so if I want to communicate the best I have to you—even if I want to convert you—I will have to let you also communicate your best to me—even to the point of converting me.

The differences between the two religions, however, are very often complementary. To put it succinctly, if Hinduism claims to be the *religion of truth*, Christianity claims to be the *truth of religion*. Hinduism is ready to absorb any authentic religious truth; Christianity is ready to embrace any authentic religious value. The genuinely Christian attitude is to call forth that 'truth' of Hinduism without destroying the latter's identity. To Christianity, Hinduism in turn offers the authentically Hindu gift of a new experience and interpretation—a new dimension, in fact—of the Mystery. The 'catholicity' of Hinduism calls forth the true 'catholicity' of Christianity, while the truth of Christianity calls forth the truth of Hinduism. The passage from a narrow catholicity and an exclusive 'truth' to a full catholicity and to recognition of the fact that Truth can be neither limited nor monopolized is the Paschal adventure of every religion. A growing Christianity is also a Christianity moving towards greater fullness. This is the mystery of the Cross.

These thoughts should not be misinterpreted. Christianity can be experienced in two ways: either as a religion (and then it cannot claim to be of a different *nature* from the other religions), or as a tangible, historical and thus concrete and dynamic expression of the ultimate Mystery which reveals itself in a faith which will thus be called Christian. That is to say, Christianity may be seen as a concrete embodiment of (Christian) faith. This would apply equally, *mutatis mutandis*, to Hinduism: it may be experienced either simply as a religion

[12] By homeomorphism we understand the 'topologically' corresponding (analogous) function (a functional equivalent) within another setting, Hinduism in this case. Cf. R. Panikkar, *The Intrareligious Dialogue*, p. xxii.

among religions, or as a tangible, concrete and dynamic expression of the ultimate Mystery, through which one may reach the all-embracing transcendent. That is to say, Hinduism may be seen as a concrete embodiment of (Hindu) faith.

It should be made clear from the outset that when we speak of Hindu and Christian faith, we do not refer to a rivalry between two religions, but to the relationship between the deepest faith of the followers of the Vedic tradition and a faith which Christians cannot help but call 'Christian'. This is why the title of the second chapter, Hinduism and Christianity, remains unchanged, in spite of the ambivalence of the expression. We should also stress that throughout this book the adjective 'Christian' does not denote a monopoly of prerogatives reserved for the adepts of Christianity but that it indicates anything endowed with the richness of that reality for which Christians have no other name than Christ.

And rightly so. The great danger today in the study of the encounter of religions lies in either eliminating all differences for the sake of reaching understanding, or in basing such understanding on a minimalistic structure that afterwards proves incapable of sustaining any religious life. Either procedure precludes any truly religious encounter. Certainly there are different symbols and different names. We have several options, which oscillate between two extremes: a) my symbols are the best, they are unique, so yours are inadequate or even wrong; b) each group of symbols and names is mutually incommensurable, though satisfactory for the particular tribe that professes them. The first may easily lead to fanaticism, the second to agnostic relativism. The entire hypothesis of this book is that the power of the symbol may be so enlarged and deepened that each symbol—even if it is primarily and directly meaningful in that environment in which it originated—opens up experiences and realities not (yet) intended in the actual symbol. My contention is that in our present times a Christ-symbol valid only for Christians would cease to be a living symbol, even for Christians—or at least for all those for whom Christian commitment is not understood merely as sectarian religiousness.

Again, the same would apply to Hindu symbols. To want

to keep Hinduism within the ethnic, geographical and cultural limits of an old and immutable tradition would not do justice to the insights of the *sanātana dharma*. The validity of the *sanātana dharma* does not depend upon a rigid and unchangeable social and doctrinal structure, but upon an everlasting claim that it is (the) right *dharma*. Though Hinduism is more flexible in doctrine than Christianity, sociologically or culturally it is more resistant to change.

To put it in a more general way: to speak of Christ seems to some sectarian because of the abuses and misunderstandings attached to that name. Many would not object if instead I were to say the same things about God. Of course others would prefer to speak of the omnipresent Spirit that unites us without distinction. Herein lies the problem. I am reminded of the reaction of an African tribe when they were accused of being polytheist. They replied that the One and only God, supreme Creator of the Universe, in whom we all exist, presents no trouble and needs nothing, whereas the different Gods of the particular spheres require attention, propitiation and worship. Just as there is a peculiar link between God and the Gods, so also there is a subtle relation between the concrete name (whether it be Krishna or Justice or Woman) that we use to express the cosmotheandric mystery and the nameless and utterly transcendent Reality itself. This use of different names is not without consequences, however. We may agree that we all 'mean' the 'same', though from different angles and with different understanding, but this is not convincing, first, because the relationship between the name and the named is in this instance deeper than that which exists between a material thing and its nominalistic label. Second, and more importantly, the sphere of religion is not the realm of pure intentions and lofty ideas, but of daily life's joys and strains, of great decisions as well as of dull routine in the concrete interaction of Men, Earth and Powers. If we speak of the Encounter of Religions we cannot remain in ivory towers or hidden caves: the place for the encounter is properly in the bazaar, the marketplace, the *civitas* and the fields (where the *pagani* live).

The third part of this book deals with a concrete example, namely the encounter of a Vedāntic tenet and a Christian dogma. It endeavours to show, in one particular case, what could well be shown in many others: the presence of a religious truth within more than one religion, and how the unveiling of that truth may be to the mutual enlightenment of all concerned. Now, when a religious truth is recognized by both parties and thus belongs to both traditions, it will be called in each case by the vocabulary proper to the particular tradition recognizing it. If Christians, believing in the truth of their own religion, recognize truth outside it, they will be inclined to say that a 'Christian' truth has been discovered there. In this sense the third part of this book will discover a 'Christian' truth in the Hindu tradition. Similarly, when a Hindu discovers a positive value outside his own religion, he will either try to incorporate it without any 'copyright' qualms or recognize that it was also present, although perhaps dormant, in his own tradition.

* * *

The language of this study has to be understood from its *background*, and with reference to its *goal*:

Its *background* is composed, on the one hand, of the broad scenario of world religions, especially the luxuriant world of Hinduism and, on the other hand, by contemporary problematic concerning general questions of the philosophy and theology of religion.

The *goal* of this study is not to obtain agreement at the cost of fundamental Christian or Hindu principles. On the contrary, it is an attempt to arrive at a certain understanding without renouncing any of the specifically Christian or Hindu truths. This perspective tries not to make the Christian position unnecessarily difficult or complicated, or the Hindu way too exotic or unfairly sectarian. The truths which Christian doctrine, on the one hand, and Hindu doctrine, on the other, propound as universal have often come to be thought of as particular and limited—if not bigoted—points of view, whereas in actuality they are both formulations, necessarily limited by cultural factors, of a more universal truth.

The perspective of this book is clearly one of enlarging and deepening the Christian understanding of the Mystery of

Christ, but another study, which the author has often been asked for, is not here attempted: a book on Christ that Hindus might appreciate.[13] I wonder whether such a book needs to be written at all, because it already exists: the *śruti*, the Hindu revelation. As an introduction to such a study the author sometimes feels tempted to write a volume entitled *The Unknown Christ of Christianity*. He is coming to realize more and more not only that God is a 'hidden God',[14] but also that the thirty hidden years of the life of Christ on earth have been continuing these twenty centuries.[15] The Kingdom of God suffers violence[16] precisely because it is within us,[17] and, unbeknownst to us, our own being is thus the arena of our daily battle.

I would like here to quote the words of an old Christian saint:

> As the physical eye looks at written letters and receives knowledge from them . . . so the mind, when it becomes purified . . . looks up to God and receives divine knowledge from Him. Instead of a book it has the Spirit, instead of a pen, thought and tongue: 'my tongue is the pen' says the Psalm (45:1); instead of ink, light. Plunging thought into light . . . the mind, guided by the Spirit, traces words in the pure hearts of those who listen. Then it understands the words: 'And they shall all be taught of God' (John 6:45).[18]

I need hardly add that Christ will never be totally known on earth, because that would amount to seeing the Father[19] whom nobody can see.[20] It was even good that Christ disappeared and went away;[21] otherwise Men would have made

[13] See Th. Ohm, 'Geben Sie uns ein Christusbuch' in *Der christliche Sonntag*, vol. xiii, no. 39 (1961), p. 306.

[14] Cf. Isa. 45:15; KathU II, 12; MundU II, 2, 1; SU III, 7; III, 11; VI, 11, etc.

[15] Cf. John 7:3–5; Col. 3:3, etc.

[16] Cf. Matt. 11:12; BG II, 37–8.

[17] Cf. Luke 17:21; SU VI, 11–12; CU III, 13, 7; VIII, 3, 2–3, etc.

[18] Gregory of Sinai, *Texts on Commandments and Dogmas* 23 in *Writings from the Philokalia on Prayer of the Heart*, tr. E. Kadloubovsky and G. E. H. Palmer (London, Faber & Faber, 1951), p. 42.

[19] Cf. John 14:9.

[20] Cf. John 1:18.

[21] Cf. John 16:7.

him a king[22] or a God.[23] As for the reason why I still insist on speaking of Christ, I need only quote a Christian mystic who lived in a century in which his sentence might have sounded stranger than it does today: 'A true Christian, who is born anew of the Spirit of Christ, is in the simplicity of Christ, and has no strife or contention with any Man about religion.'[24]

Because introductions are generally written as postludes, the following considerations written for the Italian translation may still be appropriate here.

The Gospel injunction not to put new wine into old skins is more than a simple request for prudence.[25] It means, at least to me, that life in its constant novelty cannot be squeezed into an old framework, that change cannot be measured by an obsolete gauge. It also means that content and form constitute a single thing so that any content which could not create, as it were, its own form, would be a kind of existential lie, just as any form which expresses a content other than its own becomes mere hypocrisy. Truth, the African Augustine used to say, is *sine ulla dissimilitudo*, without disguise.

Nevertheless, if people feel the need for a new wine (a better one)—that is, if life is change and movement—there will be some tension and polarity between content and container, symbol and symbolized, *nāma-rūpa* and *avyakta*. A living content, despite the fact that it depends for intelligibility on its form, will eventually have to break this selfsame form. Likewise, though united with a particular content, a form which is to remain alive will sooner or later fail to satisfy its own content. Yet what appears to be a *vicious* circle is in fact a *vital* circle. As the *Epistle to Diognetes* said long ago, it is not so much that the body contains the soul as it is the soul which contains the body.[26]

Have we not observed all too often how the spirit is suffocated when it is encapsulated, how an ideal is limited when

[22] Cf. John 6:15.
[23] Cf. Mark 10:18; Luke 18:19; Matt. 19:17.
[24] J. Böhme, *Dialogue on the Supersensual Life*, tr. William Law, ed. B. Holland (New York, F. Ungar, n.d.), p. 1.
[25] Cf. Matt. 9:17.
[26] '*Inclusa quidem est anima corpore, sed ipsa continet corpus . . .*' VI.

it is formulated in logical terms and how the message of a prophet is diluted when his vision is transferred to the written page or his call for reform translated into organizations (however necessary such things may be at the time)? Are not books just another form of institution? Yet is it possible to do without them?

When, a quarter of a century ago, I began to write the ideas expressed in this book, I had already lived them in various ways which, though thankfully recalling, I need not now describe. When, however, I began to formulate these intuitions—was almost compelled to do so—my experiences had to be poured into 'old skins', simply because there was nothing else available, either for me or for the public which I was addressing. No wonder they burst the old skins and spilled the new wine.

Since writing this book, I have been engaged in obtaining new 'must' and in procuring new skins, but the human vineyard and the earthen containers remain more or less the same. The process may have been modified and the results may be more accurate, more suited to our times, but the grapes are still ripened by the same sun.

Even now I cannot provide new skins into which the reader could in due course pour new wine. The new skins are being made at the same rate as the must is fermenting into a new wine. This venture of discovering or perhaps even creating new forms of human consciousness—and corresponding new forms of religiousness—requires an intense collaboration. The continuing demand for this book shows that many of us are already committed to the enterprise.

The only thing that I can do here is to point out some features pertaining to the container and the contents. Pursuing the metaphor, I would like, with regard to the skins, to take into consideration the origin of the leather (my original audience) and the method of tanning (the model of intelligibility that is emerging today in relation to this type of problem). As far as content goes, I would like to consider two wines of this new vintage: the significance of catholicity and the significance of identity.

Let me explain these four points briefly. The first two are

'formal', that is, they refer to structure; and the second two are 'material', that is, they refer to content.

The first point (a) is sociological, since it concerns both the cultural ambience of the persons for whom I wrote and even to a certain extent my own situation. The second (b) is epistemological and concerns the theory which underlies understanding. The third (c) is theological, and treats the problem of the universality of a religion. The fourth (d) is philosophical, and deals with the problem of one's own identity.

(a) The *sociological* point is this: although I wanted to help both Christians and Hindus to a better and deeper mutual comprehension, I allowed myself to speak mostly to Christians and in Christian terminology. I wanted in fact to show Christians that the ideas in this book do not dilute the Christian message or evade the 'folly of the Cross' or avoid the Christian 'scandal'. To use the latter as an excuse for condemning others or to stick stubbornly to one's own ideas is not exactly Christian scandal,[27] perhaps, but—to remain in the Pauline context—is prudence of the flesh.[28] On the contrary, I maintained that to pretend to an exhaustive knowledge of the mystery of Christ is to empty the Cross of its power. I still held that the 'old skins' should be taken from the Christian cellars so as to enable Christians to keep their own identity without any alienation, and yet to open themselves up to the understanding and insights of others without misunderstanding, rather than insulting them, as happens not infrequently, with an intolerable attitude of superiority. In a word, I tried to show that there is a way to accept totally the message of Christ without edulcorating it and to remain at the same time open to others, ready to accept them without patronizing or co-opting them.

I wanted above all to say that the truth that we can honestly defend as universally valid, the truth that makes us really free, is an existential truth, not a mere doctrine.[29] Thus, I also maintained that the true significance of orthodoxy does not

[27] Cf. 1 Cor. 1:18–23.
[28] Cf. 2 Cor. 1:12, 17 etc.
[29] Cf. my chapter 'La fenomenologia esistenziale della verità' in *Māyā e Apocalisse*, pp. 241–90.

consist in an objectified interpretation of a 'right *doxa*', understood as doctrine, but in an 'authentic glory' and in a 'considered opinion' (both meanings of the word δόξα), in something closer to an *orthopraxis* than to correct doctrinal affirmations, however true these may be in their own domain.

Such a Christian perspective, nevertheless, has sometimes given—especially to Hindus—the impression that I was being 'too Christian' and thus ultimately unfair, though sympathetic, to Hinduism, that I had still not overcome my innate sense of Christian superiority, and that if there were 'dangerous' Christians today, they would not be the missionaries of the old school, but the more subtle ones like myself who would suck up the living sap of the Hindu *dharma* in order to neutralize its vitality.

Now, it is not sufficient to assert that such was not my intention, since that would only confirm the suspicion that an attitude of superiority was so rooted in Christian thought that it could not be eliminated even from an approach as open and sympathetic as mine. I do not deny that my opinions have evolved and my convictions deepened since then, but I have to stress that from the beginning I have insisted on saying that the relationship between the two religious traditions, Christian and Hindu, is not one of assimilation, or of antagonism, or of substitution (the latter under the misnomer of 'conversion'), but one of *mutual fecundation*. What I do confess, however, is that I have used at times a language that has been ambivalent, sometimes even cryptic, as for example in the preface to the first edition where I wrote that '*the* "book" on Christ (that Hindus might appreciate) already exists', without making it clear that I was not referring to the Bible, but mainly to the *śruti*, the Vedic and the other Hindu revelations.

Now, after this sincere confession, I can add that in practically all my writings, except in my scientific papers, I have made ample use of a linguistic polyvalence. Reality has in fact many layers, and consequently may be expressed by various levels of meaning. Words, when they are not merely algebraic signs (which I call 'terms'), have a constitutive polyvalence which depends not only on various possible contexts but also on the very nature of the reality they express.

My 'wineskins' were certainly made of Christian leather. Should I now write another book for Hindus? Have I trusted them too much or relied on their tolerance to such an extent that I have failed to present the Hindu side adequately? Certainly I am not setting out now to transform this book into something which was never intended, and this for two reasons: in the first place, I am engaged in precisely this task elsewhere and, in the second place, it would not be relevant, for I think that the concern of Hinduism today is not so much to defend its own orthodoxy as to confront the present *kalpa* or aeon without worsening human *karma*. I would say that the question of the existence of other beliefs has never been an *ultimate* problem for Hindus. Hinduism may claim to be superior, but it is not exclusive.

(b) The *epistemological* point is that the process used to tan the hides for the wineskins was also a fundamentally Western method. The principle of non-contradiction served as 'tannic acid' and my intention was to show that if Christ were not the monopoly of Christians, nothing would be lost of his reality, his vitality and truth. The kingdom of God does not come when and where we look for it; in fact, as the Latin Vulgate says, '*non venit regnum Dei cum observatione*' or, the kingdom is not visibly noticeable, nor is Christ himself always recognizable.[30] Identification by differentiation, as I have elaborated elsewhere, is typical of occidental Christianity and gives rise to its own problems.[31] For Hinduism, on the other hand, scarcely any problem arises. It is acceptable to Hindus to be 'anonymous Christians',[32] provided one also admits that Christians are 'anonymous Hindus' (though this expression makes little sense in a tradition which takes polynomy for granted, ever since the famous *ṛgvedic* saying, 'One is he whom the sages call by many names').[33] It is no great wonder, then, if in discussing a specifically Western Christian problem, I

[30] Cf. Luke 24:13–16 ff.; John 20:14.
[31] Cf. e.g. *Kultmysterium in Hinduismus und Christentum*, pp. 127 ff.
[32] Cf. K. Rahner, 'Das Christentum und die nichtchristlichen Religionen' in *Schriften zur Theologie* V, pp. 136–58; 'Die anonymen Christen' in *Schriften zur Theologie* VI (1965), pp. 545–54.
[33] RV I, 164, 46.

have used Western Christian categories. Reducing the epistemological problem to its bare essentials, I have tried to show in this book that though a Christian believes that 'Jesus is the Christ' as more than an abstract affirmation, i.e. as an expression of faith, this sentence is not identical to 'the Christ is Jesus'. Similarly, I have maintained that the assertion 'Christ is the Lord' cannot simply be reversed. It is not necessary, in fact, that the Lord be named Christ or acknowledged by this title, because the saving name of Christ is a supername, above every name.[34]

Of course, the Christian affirms that 'Jesus is the Christ' and that 'Christ is the Lord'. Jesus, who is the Christ for Christians, is more—but not less—than Jesus of Nazareth, prior to his resurrection. A Christian maintains, moreover, that the affirmations 'Jesus is not the Christ' and 'Christ is not the Lord' go against Christian faith and are incompatible with it. The Christian, however, cannot say that 'Christ is *only* Jesus', philosophically, because the *is* does not need to mean *is-only* and, theologically, because in fact the risen Jesus is more (*aliud*, not *alius*) than the Jesus of Nazareth, which is only a practical *identification*, different from personal *identity*. Neither can he say 'the Lord is *only* Christ', because his knowledge of the Lord is not exhaustive. Nevertheless, there are not many Christs, nor are there many Lords. On the contrary, and this is the central argument of this book: 'the Lord *is*' even though his name may not sound like 'Christ' or any of its now familiar expressions. The present work deals with this specific and delicate transplant.

As I have already indicated, every believer sees a tradition from the inside, so that for the believer it becomes a symbol of all that is true. Hence, if some truth is found 'outside', one is led to affirm that one can also participate in that 'external' truth, whether by incorporating it more or less directly into one's own religiosity, or by recognizing that such truth is already present in one's own religion, though in another guise.

Now, entering into the heart of the problematic, a predom-

[34]Cf. 'The Meaning of Christ's Name in the Universal Economy of Salvation' in *Evangelisation, Dialogue and Development* (Documenta Missionalia) (Rome, 1972), pp. 195–218.

inantly analytic mind may have some difficulty in accepting assertions such as 'you too are a Christian' or 'I also am a Hindu', because such a mind gives to these words a restrictive and exclusive meaning ('whatever a Christian may be, he is *not* a Hindu'). Hence, when I maintain that Christ is real and effective, though hidden and unknown, in Hinduism, I allegedly violate the 'sacred' Western canons used to identify Christ, since Christ is seen only in terms of *differentiated identification* instead of in terms of an *identifying identity*.[35]

This is also, of course, a semantic problem. And here I must confess that I have not always made the necessary clarifications and distinctions. When writing 'Christianity' or 'Hinduism', for instance, I should have distinguished more clearly between: 1) the social and historical expression of these religions—that is, Christianity as a particular Church affiliation, or Hinduism as a particular Hindu persuasion, a particular *sampradāya*, or way of religious life; 2) the core of a particular religion, which does not consist merely in its sociological garb but in a faith commitment which is embodied in sacramental or sacred structures that abide through cultural and temporal fluctuations; and 3) the transcendent divine reality (whatever name we may want to give it, and whatever degree of reality we may be disposed to grant it), of which all the rest is but the expression, the manifestation, symbol or creation.

Now in comparing Christianity and Hinduism, as in our case, we should carefully specify which of the three levels or aspects we are dealing with. To be sure, the three are intertwined, so that a believer accepts the lower simply because he believes that it gives concrete expression to the higher; but when crossing the boundaries of a religious tradition we cannot ignore such distinctions. A non-Hindu, for example, who views the caste system and the non-killing of cows as simply sociological or dietary problems misses the point altogether, as does a non-Christian who views the Eucharist as just a

[35] Cf. 'Singularity and Individuality. The Double Principle of Individuation' in *Revue Internationale de Philosophie*, 'Méthode et Philosophie de l'histoire', hommage à Raymond Klibansky, no. 111–12, fasc. 1–2 (Bruxelles, 1975), pp. 141–66.

meagre meal. Obviously, we cannot confront Canon Law with the Upanishads, or the present-day caste system with the Sermon on the Mount, or the Crusades with Advaita.

(c) The third point, regarding the nature of the vineyard itself, concerns the *theological* understanding of catholicity. Synthesizing and simplifying a little, we could say that the concept of catholicity has fluctuated with the political and historical conditions of the times. It is not surprising, then, that during the Colonial and Imperial period of the Christian West, the geographical expansion of the 'Christian' nations was accompanied by the concept of catholicity as a geographical universality. The Catholic religion was in fact considered to be a geographically *universal* religion and thus had the right—even the duty—to spread throughout the entire world. Still, it is not necessary to recall the Greek origins of the word in order to understand that this geographic, extensive and almost quantitative meaning was and is not its only meaning. 'Catholic', in fact, also and perhaps mainly, means 'perfect', complete, i.e. a way of life, a religion, a revelation which possesses in itself all that is necessary to lead Man to Man's goal, by bringing the human being to fulfillment, by caring for every aspect of human existence, and thus providing a way which will enable Man to become what Man is meant to be, *secundum totum*, as St Augustine literally translated it. 'Catholic' is thus, as regards religion, the opposite of 'sectarian', or 'partial'. Here, the *quality* of Catholicism is stressed and, for that reason, its oneness, uniqueness. But a thing is unique precisely because it is in-comparable. If it were comparable, it would cease to be unique; it would be more or less similar to another, not unique.

My *theologumenon*, then, was that the catholicity of Christianity does not need to be interpreted in geographical terms. In point of fact, the modern emphasis on local churches, the mystical comprehension of the sacramental nucleus of Christianity, and also religious pluralism (which now appears to be an obvious necessity), conduce to making the acceptance of this second meaning almost a matter of course. In one sense, there is no catholic (universal) religion; but in another sense, the authentic and true religiosity of every person is catholic.

I would make an analogous statement about Hinduism.

The Hindu concept of universal *dharma* is not a geographical idea. The historians of religion find it difficult at times to understand the existential character of Hinduism which, though it may not be strictly ethnic or historical, is tied to the populace of India.[36] Traditional Hinduism does not proselytize, because *dharma* (religion) comes with the free gift of existence. It is meaningless to want to change a person totally, into something that person is not.

I am well aware that this point needs much more elaboration, but I am also convinced that what I say does not in the least water down the demands of Christianity, nor does it weaken the Hindu position. Today, encounters among religions can no longer follow in the wake of political events; rather, these encounters must condition events. The days of Christian and Hindu empires are over; consequently, it is only fair that the last vestige of Christian 'imperialism' fade completely in order to allow emulation, complementarity and mutual fecundation among religious traditions.

(d) The last point, the *philosophical*, is that the new must that I have tried to ferment in this book, perhaps without sufficient clarification, may be a new consciousness of the unity of Man, not only in the spheres of biology, history or politics, but also, and fundamentally, on the religious plane. As long as the peoples of the world are not considered to be on the same existential level with respect to religion, there can be no firm base for human dignity. To this attitude there is a terrifying corollary which asks whether the religious outsider (infidel, slave, black, *mleccha*, *kafir*, *goy*, etc.) has a human soul or human rights. 'Hell' would be an intellectual aberration if the damned were deemed to have the same human dignity as the elect. If my religion is the epitome of perfection and this perfection is what makes the human being a really complete human being, then it is only too logical that *extra*

[36] Cf. my chapter 'Alcuni aspetti fenomenologici dell' odierna spiritualità indù' in *Māyā e Apocalisse*, pp. 3–32.

ecclesiam nulla salus,[37] that the outsiders do not have the same rights as the citizens. I am not saying that in order to avoid such inhuman consequences there should be just one religion, or that all religions are equal, or that I defend a theory that all races of humankind are equal. Some are doubtless stronger, richer, more beautiful according to one standard, while others are better according to another. I believe, nonetheless, that the equality of every human being *qua* human being cannot logically be upheld if we are not ready to accept the equality, i.e. the parity, of all races with respect to the radical value of 'humanness'. Similarly, religions can differ among themselves, but if they are concerned with the dignity and destiny of Man, if they are different expressions of a constitutive human dimension, they are equal in so far as they are expressions of that same fundamental human religiousness. 'Equal' does not mean equally good (or bad), but that they are on the same level, namely, that which is capable of dealing with ultimate human problems.

A Christian, religiously speaking, is not 'better off' than a non-Christian. On the other hand, we should not toss everyone indiscriminately into the same bag. If, for a Christian, Christ is the ultimate and irreducible symbol and if the Christian really believes in the dignity of Man, then this Christ can also be shared by others.

A similar argument applies to Hinduism. If there are karmic levels, as it were, then it is legitimate to believe that somebody may not be as advanced as you are on the path to *mokṣa*. But ways towards participation in the *paramā gati* or highest

[37] 'Outside the Church there is no salvation.' This opinion is not exclusive to Christians, but exists similarly in almost any religion and is consistent in spite of its possible 'brutality' if interpreted as the exclusive privilege of my 'club'. There are, of course, many ways of getting around it. Cf. Ch. Journet, *L'Église du Verbe Incarné*. Paris 1951. H. Küng seems to abjure it altogether in: 'The World Religions in God's plan of Salvation' in *Christian Revelation and World Religions*, ed. J. Neuner, pp. 67–122. My interpretation is to turn it around and affirm that the statement means that the Church is the locus of salvation, wherever this place may be and however it may appear. Cf. R. Panikkar, 'Salvation in Christ: Concreteness and Universality, the Supername', lecture given at the Inauguration of the Ecumenical Institute of Advanced Studies, Tantur, Jerusalem, 1970, p. 13 ff.

goal must be open to any being in which humanness is actual or potential. Similarly, although the preaching of the *dharma* has different connotations in Hinduism than it has in Buddhism or Christianity, the thrust towards universal peace and fellowship undoubtedly pervades Hindu religiousness.

Here it would seem, however, that one must renounce Christ or one's own symbol in order to remain completely faithful to it, as some Christian mystics suggest, or ultimately sacrifice God, as the example of the Trinitarian 'economy' implies (God the Father sacrificing his Son). But then where does identity lie? Only in differentiation? What makes one reality equal to another, and what differentiates them? Only the external parameters of space and time? Have we not perhaps converted the variety of the World into dialectical differences and then wondered why we cannot find any dialectically convincing solutions? Or, to turn to our problem, where does the identity of Christ lie? If he is already present, what, it is often asked, is the 'use' of Christian missions?

It is not the task of this Introduction to give answers, but only to pose problems in the light of the present work. My first reaction to the specific problem of missions is to call to mind the Gospels on one hand, and the Bhagavad Gītā on the other, in order to learn the meaning of *spontaneity* and of *detachment from all results*, and of acting out of love.[38] To seek to justify Christian missions by counting the number of 'converted' souls would today be both a theological anachronism and a violation of the conscience of contemporary Man. In the second place, the Christian mission—if we still want to use this language—is not finished, nor is that of Hinduism. Human solidarity must impel people to share experiences, and both material and spiritual goods; and this mutual interpenetration may guide us towards building a true family of Man. Whoever has something to share is blessed in the sharing.

In the course of this Introduction I have subjected my book to an almost ruthless critical attack. Let me say in its defence, however, that I have remained true to the title. I speak neither of a principle unknown to Hinduism, nor of a dimension of

[38] Cf. BG II, 47, ff.; John 15:12ff.

the divine unknown to Christianity, but of that unknown *reality*, which Christians call Christ, discovered in the heart of Hinduism, not as a stranger to it, but as its very *principle of life*, as the light which illumines every Man who comes into the World.[39] A Christian master said: 'Anything superior and anything divine, inasmuch as it is superior and divine, is unknown, hidden and veiled.'[40]

I remain faithful not only to the title but also to the reality, to the Mystery, which is the mystery of Christ. Most of the negative criticisms of this book came from a narrow, partial, merely historical point of view—from, precisely, the prevailing microdox conception of that Mystery. But 'Whoever believes in me, does not believe in me, but in Him' (John 12:44); 'I am the vine, ye are the branches' (John 15:5). And as Nicholas of Cusa wrote of the second text: '. . . so that there be Christ's humanity in all Men, and Christ's spirit in all spirits; thus anything at all may be in him, that there may be one Christ out of all'.[41]

A Christ who could not be present in Hinduism, or a Christ who was not with every least sufferer, a Christ who did not have his tabernacle in the sun,[42] a Christ who did not represent the cosmotheandric reality with one Spirit seeing and recreating all hearts and renewing the face of the earth, surely would not be my Christ, nor, I suspect, would he be the Christ of the Christians.

Varanasi-Roma-Santa Barbara
1957–1976

2. *TRADENDUM:* THE CHALLENGE OF THE FUTURE

Cuius vultum desiderat universa terra—'whose face the entire Earth desires'—so sings the Latin Church at Christmas. Now this is the Face, of which the same Liturgy also sings: *Laetentur*

[39] Cf. John 1:9.
[40] '*Omne superior et omne divinum, in quantum huiusmodi, est incognitum, latens et absconditum*' (Meister Eckhart).
[41] '. . . *ut sit una Christi humanitas in omnibus hominibus, et unus Christi spiritus in omnibus spiritibus; ita ut quodlibet in eo sit, ut sit unus Christus ex omnibus*' (*De docta ignorantia* III, 12).
[42] '*Et posuit in sole tabernaculum suum . . .*', Ps. 18:6.

coeli et exultet terra ante faciem Domini, quoniam venit—'let the Heavens rejoice and the Earth delight before the Face of the Lord, for he comes'. Yet in much of Christian consciousness this Face has been objectified. This is one of the side-effects of a pan-scientistic mentality and its invasion of extra-scientific realms. Once the face becomes a picture, the icon an idol, the encounter an idea, Christ an object and reality a thought—once the *Logos* subordinates the Spirit, to put it in traditional theological vocabulary—the dilemma becomes unavoidable: either give up the universality of Christ, for contemporary consciousness cannot accept a single ideology for the entire planet; or give up Christianity, for the very essence of Christian self-understanding is that Christ is the universal redeemer, the single mediator, the only-begotten of God.

The gist of this book is that the concreteness of Christ (over against his particularity) does not destroy his universality (over against his generality) because the reality of Christ is revealed in the personal experience of his uniqueness. This *experience* of the uniqueness of Christ, which is another name for Christian faith, cannot be rendered by the *concept* of uniqueness, which is only a purely formal notion. A concept comes to intelligibility by comparison and discussion. A concept of something which is both a class of its own and a no-class among classes is an impossible concept. Something is unique when it is irreducible, incomparable, incommensurable to any other parameter of understanding. Uniqueness is neither one nor many. It transcends the classical opposition between monism and dualism. One or many saviours, one or many ways are meaningless phrases in the realm of any ultimate human experience. What I propose is both the traditional Advaitic solution and the equally traditional Christian answer: religious truth is existential and non-objectifiable. But I would like to present the thesis without having to adopt either the Advaitic metaphysical or the Christian stance, though the endeavour cannot dispense with a certain spiritual or mystical insight into the nature of reality. Here the symbol of the face may be enlightening. A face is a real face when it is more—not less—than the physiognomy of the human head. It is a face when it is a face for me, with a uniqueness of its own. The face is concrete and not particular; it is that face only for me. It is meaningless to say that you have discovered 'another' face in it. Each face includes your discovery of it. In both cases it is a face when it speaks, responds and is alive with the life that flows also in me.

This is not a new thesis, but one which stresses a dimension that has been neglected in recent times. Could we say that there has been a 'strategic' retreat in Christian theology? A retreat from claiming to be the true, unique and even absolute religion to being just another among many? Yes and no. Yes, in so far as many a Christian believer and theologian have sincerely believed Christianity to be true, unique and absolute. No, however, in so far as that belief was a correct insight expressed in an inadequate and even false manner. The essence of this book is to show a possible middle way between totalitarian exclusivism and libertarian equalitarianism.

This study differs from many of the works that have appeared in recent times by reason of its 'interior' character. It deals with more than phenomenology, with more than an 'external' description of how religions should behave after so many centuries of mutual suspicion and misunderstanding. These approaches are legitimate and urgent, but the character of this book lies elsewhere. It is certainly not a devotional or pious work and yet it emphasizes the interior and personal aspect of religion. It speaks to the *bona fide* Hindu and Christian who are no longer mutually unsympathetic, but who do not wish to dilute their own religiousness or to lose their own identity, in spite of being ready for openness and even change should such be required.

There are ex-Catholics, ex-Marxists, ex-Buddhists and so forth, but I know of no ex-mystic. Once the transformation due to an authentic mystical experience has happened, it is irreversible.

The thesis of this book is a mystical one. It can be expressed in different ways; it needs better and more accurate formulations, but the core remains. I do not say that it remains 'the same': endurance is not the same thing as permanence, nor is continuity the same as conceptual identity.

The Christ of whom this book speaks is the living and loving reality of the truly believing Christian in whatever form the person may formulate or conceptualize this reality.

No believer gives the existential and primal allegiance of his entire being to an idea or a formula, but to a reality that surpasses—not 'denies' or 'refuses', but 'surpasses'—all understanding. And yet names and formulas are not without a bearing on reality itself.

The thesis of this book was and is that the Christian, in recognizing, believing in and loving Christ as the central symbol of Life and Ultimate Truth, is being drawn towards that selfsame Mystery that attracts all other human beings who are seeking to overcome their own present condition. The word 'mystery', though it belongs to a certain tradition, stands for that 'thing' which is called by many names and is experienced in many forms; thus it can be called neither one nor many. The problem of the one and the many appears at the second stage, when the conceptualizing mind starts functioning in a particular way.

I do not defend the naïve and uncritical notion that 'there is' one 'thing' which Men call by many names—as if the naming of the Mystery were simply a matter of attaching such tags as culture or language puts at our disposal. This is, incidentally, not the meaning of the already quoted *ṛgvedic* verse, '(God is) One (though) the sages call it by many names.'[43] Contrariwise, it is suggesting that each authentic name enriches and qualifies that Mystery which is neither purely transcendent nor purely immanent.

In Christian language—which is a legitimate, though not unique, way of true and meaningful discourse—I would say that the paradigm for this Mystery is the *Trinity*. Rather than being a single centre, on which all ultimate human experiences converge in a unity (which ultimately could not avoid a certain monism), the Trinitarian paradigm allows for infinite diversity. The 'persons' of the Christian Trinity are infinitely different—nothing is finite in the Trinity—so that the very name of person (*pace* Aquinas) is equivocal. In this model, the harmony or concord of a non-mathematical Oneness is not broken.

In Indian language, I would say that the paradigm for this Mystery is the *Advaitic* intuition, which refers to something

[43] RV I, 164, 46.

which cannot be called either 'one' or 'two'. The Mystery towards which the religious experience of Humankind tends is neither the same nor different, neither one nor many: it is non-dualistic. It allows for *pluralism*, the modern secular word I would use to express the same issue.

We cannot merely 'talk' about this Mystery in an 'objective' and nominalistic way. Our discourse is not 'about' something that merely 'is' or 'is there'. Rather it is a disclosure of a reality that I *am* and you *are*. The Mystery is not objectifiable because 'you' and 'I' are constitutively part of it. Nor is it merely subjective, because 'we', the subject(s), are not all there is to it.

If the Christian reaches or comes into contact with that Mystery in and through Christ, can I still maintain, and if so how, that there is the hidden and unknown presence of Christ in Hinduism—or in any other religion for that matter? Is not Christ the Way? Does not the traditional Christian liturgy always end: *per Christum Dominum nostrum*, '*through* Christ *our* (and not the universal) Lord'?

Here, perhaps, the thesis of the book is highlighted most strikingly. The Way cannot be severed from the Goal. The spatial metaphor here may be misleading if taken superficially. It is not simply that there are different ways leading to the peak, but that the summit itself would collapse if all the paths disappeared. The peak is in a certain sense the result of the slopes leading to it. Our position distinguishes itself here from the nominalistic one mentioned before. In Christian terms: 'Philip, he who has seen me has seen the Father.'[44] In a certain Hindu parlance the other shore is already here, realization is not 'another' thing, there is nowhere to go: reality *is*.[45] As Buddhism declares: *saṃsāra* is *nirvāṇa* and *nirvāṇa* is *saṃsāra*.[46]

And yet, the goal cannot be identified with any of the ways or means to it. Though Christ is the Mystery in the sense that to see Christ is to reach the Mystery, still the Mystery cannot

[44] John 14:9.
[45] Cf. *Aṣṭāvakra Gītā*, 19, 2ff., 20, 1ff.; Śaṅkara, *Upadeśasāhasrī*, Padyabandha, 10 etc.
[46] Cf. Nāgārjuna, *Mādhyamakaśāstra* XVI.

be totally identified with Christ. Christ is but one aspect of the Mystery as a whole, even though he is *the* Way when we are on that way. Only when we are not walking on them, i.e. when they are mere lines on a map, are there 'many' paths. For the actual wayfarer, there is only one way. Not only is it unique, it is only a 'way' if it gives access to the summit. For the speculative mind, it is a *pars pro toto*, for it is in it and through it that the Christian reaches the Mystery. At this summit, the Christian realizes that he and his experience of the Mystery are inseparable, indistinguishable; thus you discover Christ in all those who have reached the Mystery, even if their ways have not been the Christian one. Likewise you will have to concede that the Hindu who has reached realization, become enlightened, discovered *ātman-brahman* or whatever, has realized the ultimate Mystery. Only for the Christian is the Mystery indissolubly connected with Christ; only for the Vaishnava is the Mystery unfailingly connected with Vishnu or whatever has been the particular form for 'attaining' *mokṣa*. This would also apply for the so-called unbeliever, atheist, humanist; but we do not need to elaborate any further here.

My concern that the Cross of Christ should not be rendered trivial and powerless; *ut non evacuetur Crux Christi* does not arise out of a '*parti-pris*' or sectarian view, but just the opposite. It is because we are on the brink of a mutation in human civilization that, in my opinion, no religious tradition is any longer capable of sustaining the burden of the present-day human predicament and guiding Man in the 'sea of life'. It is important to stress continuity-in-depth and to discover the profound ties that exist between the human traditions which link Men together. Our deepest human fellowship does not occur just because, for example, we all have stomachs or appreciate a comfortable bed, but because we have a common dissatisfaction, uneasiness, desire for joy, thrust towards More. In other words, fellowship arises because we all live by *faith* in spite of the diversity of our beliefs.

I tried to say everything in the title of the book. But was it cryptic or apocalyptic, concealing or revealing? Significantly enough, not many critics pondered the subtleties of the genitive. My main concern was not to speak of a) the unknown

Christ of Hindus who is 'known' by Christians, nor b) of the unknown Christ of Christians who is 'known' to Hindus, under whatever form and name. In both cases the genitive is objective. But my primary intention was to speak c) about the 'unknown' Christ of Hinduism, which can be either unknown, or known *qua* Christ, to Christians and Hindus alike. While in the cases a) and b) the genitive is objective, the title of the book intended to stress c), the subjective genitive.

The author's intention was to state a case which could be interpreted differently by several parties and yet correspond to the basic intentionality of the sentence: There is an x which is unknown, *qua* Christ, to both parties and to which the name 'Christ' could be applied once it is made clear that both sides can make a meaningful use of it. I present the Unknown-Christ *of* Hinduism, i.e. the mysteric aspect which is also present in Hinduism, according to the mystical understanding of the Christian tradition. Directly they come to the belief that Hinduism is recognized as a true religion, Christians will find themselves obliged to call this mysteric aspect 'Christ'. The title does not say *The Hidden Christ*, as though Christians knew the secret and Hindus did not. I wanted to lay stress on the presence of the one Mystery (not necessarily the 'same' Mystery) in both traditions. Now, this Mystery is not a purely transcendent divine reality in which we all worship or recognize, in our different ways, one and the same transcendent 'God'. It is equally immanent and 'this-worldly'; it is also '*saguṇic*' in character and even possesses a historical dynamism. I wanted to stress that we meet not on a transcendent plane where differences matter no longer, where we are no longer in and of this World—but here in this World where we are fellow-pilgrims, where we commune in our humanness, in the *samsāric* adventure, in our historical situation.

If this study, therefore, is so irenic, why did I use the name 'Christ'? Why not Rāma? Or why not a neutral word not so loaded with the burden of history?

I shall briefly answer these questions in order. First of all, I used the name 'Christ' precisely because of the burden of history. Symbols are not created at will, nor are they the product of single individuals. Christ has been and still is one of the most powerful symbols of humankind, though ambivalent and much-discussed. Christ is a historical name and carries with it the heavy reality of history, good and bad. The negative aspects add to its reality as much as the positive ones. That the historical name Christ should not be confined to the thus-named historical Jesus hardly needs mentioning here.

Second, in spite of its ambivalence, the power of that name is highly relevant to the actual problematic that we are here discussing. The living Christ of every Christian generation has invariably been more than a remarkable Jewish teacher who had the fortune or misfortune of being put to death rather young. Any Christ who is less than a Cosmic, Human and Divine Manifestation will not do.

Third, I have not chosen any other name because this study is mainly directed towards deepening and enlarging that particular symbol and no other. The book was, as I have said, intended principally though not solely for a Christian readership.

Fourth, Christ is still a living symbol for the totality of reality: human, divine and cosmic. Most of the apparently more neutral symbols such as God, Spirit, Truth and the like truncate reality and limit the centre of life to a disincarnate principle, a non-historical epiphany, and often an abstraction.

In this book Christ stands for that centre of reality, that crystallization-point around which the human, the divine and the material can grow. Rāma may be another such name, or Krishna, or (as I maintain) Īśvara, or Purusha, or even Humanity. But God, Matter, Consciousness or names such as Future, Justice, Love are not the living symbols that our research required.

The symbol we chose saves us from those pitfalls of pseudo- or one-sided mysticism that Martin Buber, among others, declared invalid. The name of Christ will not permit thought of an apersonal, undiscriminated (ultimately inhuman) unity, nor will it allow for an ultimate duality. The same Christ that 'sits at the right hand of the Father'[47] is the Firstborn of the

[47] Cf. Matt. 22:44, 26:64; Mark 14:62, 16:19; Luke 20:42, 22:69, etc.

Universe,[48] born of Mary;[49] he is the Bread,[50] as well as the hungry, naked or imprisoned.[51]

Within the Christian tradition this Christ is incomprehensible without the Trinity. A non-Trinitarian God cannot become incarnate. A non-Trinitarian Christ cannot be totally human and totally divine. The first case would be a monstrosity, as Jews and Muslims rightly point out when criticizing 'incarnation' in a monotheistic framework; the second case would be a docetistic farce, as Hinduism and Buddhism point out in criticizing the Christian position from a merely historical viewpoint, as theohistorical imperialism. If Christ were an *avatāra* why should one *avatāra* consume all the others?

I am only reflecting the Christian tradition if I consider the symbol Christ as that symbol which 'recapitulates' in itself the Real in its totality, created and uncreated. He is at the centre of the divine processions, being 'originated' and 'originating' (in the consecrated language, being begotten and co-inspiring): at the centre of time gathering in himself the three times and being present throughout in each case in the corresponding way, namely at the beginning, at the end and in between—at the centre of all the realms of being: the divine, the angelic, the human, the corporeal, the material. There is not a single 'type' of reality which is not represented in Christ, as I have shown by quoting not only John and Paul, but the Greek and Latin Fathers, the Scholastics and the Renaissance writers, the representatives of the *devotio moderna*, Spanish and French spiritual writers, the Rhinelanders, Lutherans and modern theologians. Christ is not only the sacrament of the Church, but also the sacrament of the World and of God. Any other conception of the symbol Christ falls

[48] John 1:1, etc.
[49] Matt. 1:20ff.
[50] John 6:35.
[51] Matt. 25:36, etc.

short of what the Christian tradition has overwhelmingly understood this symbol to be.[52]

The thesis of the Unknown Christ is that, whether or not we believe in God or Gods, there is something in every human being that does not alienate Man but rather allows Man to reach fullness of being. Whether the way is transformation or some other process, whether the principle is a divine principle or a 'human' effort, or whether we call it by one name or another is not the question here. Our only point is that this cosmotheandric or Trinitarian, *purushic* or *īśvaric* principle exists.

Christians have called it Christ, and rightly so. My suggestion is that they should not give it up too lightly and be satisfied simply with Jesus—however divinized. It is in and through Jesus that Christians have come to believe in the reality that they call Christ, but this Christ is the decisive reality.

I repeat: it is not that this reality *has* many names as if there were a reality outside the name. This reality *is* many names and each name is a new aspect, a new manifestation and revelation of it. Yet each name teaches or expresses, as it were, the undivided Mystery.

I may venture a metaphor: each religion and ultimately each human being stands within the rainbow of reality and sees it as white light—precisely because of seeing through the

[52] I cannot resist the temptation to quote a text which ties all the mentioned threads together, even historically, since it comes from the transitional period between Past Ages and Modernity: '*Nam et congruum fuit ut qui est imago Dei invisibilis, primogenitus omnis creaturae, in quo condita sunt universa, illi copularetur unione ineffabili qui ad imaginem factus est Dei, qui vinculum est omni creaturae, in quo conclusa sunt universa.*' ('For it was also fitting that he who is the image of the invisible God, the firstborn of all creation and in whom all things in the universe have their foundation – that to him there should be joined in an inexpressible union he who has come into being to express God, he in whom all creation is bound together, he in whom all things in the universe have been summed up.') Pico della Mirandola, *Heptaplus*, Exp. V, c. 7 (*apud* H. De Lubac, *Pic de la Mirandole* [Paris, Aubier, 1974], p. 182, who in previous pages gives generous quotations for the Christian tradition). Erasmus wrote; 'We establish old things, we do not initiate new things'; '*nos vetera instauramus, nova non prodimus*', and De Lubac comments '*instauration n'est pas restauration*', op. cit., p. 241.

entire rainbow. From the outside, as an intellectual abstraction, I see you in the green area and you see me in the orange one. I call you green and you call me orange because, when we look at each other, we do not look at the totality. We do not intend to express the totality—what we believe—but we evaluate and judge each other. And though it is true that I am in the orange strip with all the limitations of a saffron spirituality, if you ask my colour, I say 'white'!

The 'Unknown Christ' remains unknown and yet continues to be Christ. Just as there cannot be a plurality of Gods in the Judaeo-Christian-Islamic conception of God (they would coalesce), there cannot be a plurality of 'Christs' (they would have to be somehow united). Either the Christian will bring *his* conception of Christ to other peoples and religions (as Christians sometimes understood their mission to be, for reasons not to be explained here), or he will have to recognize the unknown dimensions of Christ.

The author has been surprised at the enormous number of book reviews and studies occasioned by the original English version of his book. He has learned from all of them and is grateful not only for the many commendations he received but also for the criticisms. Nevertheless, one thing seems to have been achieved by this study: one can no longer bypass the problem stated by it and go on doing 'missiology' or comparative religion in the 'old' manner. In this sense, whatever merits or defects this book may have, it has done away with many aspects of a certain innocence or self-complacency. At present the writer would be much more radical in his approach, but to preserve intermediate steps in respect for the rhythm of the cosmos and of history is, as always, an indispensable condition for safeguarding the possibility of further progress. In patience we shall save our lives.[53]

Barcelona
15 August 1979

[53] Luke 21:19.

1

THE ENCOUNTER

avijñataṃ vijānatāṃ vijñātam avijānatām.

Kena Up. II, 3

It is not understood by those who understand it;
it is understood by those who do not understand it.

εὑρέθην τοῖς ἐμὲ μὴ ζητοῦσιν,
ἐμφανὴς ἐγενόμην τοῖς ἐμὲ μὴ ἐπερωτῶσιν.

Rom. 10:20[1]

I have been found by those who did not seek me;
I have shown myself to those who did not ask for me.

1. THE SEARCH FOR A MEETING-PLACE

On the encounter between East and West there is nowadays an overwhelming amount of literature.[2] This fact alone proves not only that this question is a vital one, but also that it appears today in an altogether new perspective.

We do not intend to complicate this already complex subject, but only to indicate an answer to the following question: where do Hinduism and Christianity meet? In other words, what is the 'place' of encounter for a real meeting between Hinduism and Christianity? Is there a possibility of dialogue or even eventually of a mutual fecundation? Or are they just two rival religions struggling for the same constituency?

If Christianity, on the one hand, aspires to be the universal religion, what is the meaning of any encounter it may have with Hinduism? Where and how can Hinduism take up the challenge of the nature and presence of Christianity? If, on the other hand, Hinduism claims to be the *sanātana dharma*, the highest 'everlasting religion', how can it start a true dialogue with Christianity? Is there any way for Christianity to cope with such a claim? There is no point in minimizing the

[1] Cf. Isa. 65:1; Rom. 9:30.
[2] Cf. the bibliography given in Chapter 2 and in the Appendix.

issue by speaking about mutual tolerance and peaceful coexistence, if at the core of the two traditions there lies a radical incompatibility.

The meeting of religions is today one of the most profound human problems. Five possible solutions or approaches suggest themselves, each of which is still in existence in a variety of ways. We should not ignore fundamentalist attitudes and fanaticisms of all sorts in all religious traditions. *Corruptio optimi pessima*!

The *first* solution advocates strict segregation. Yet this solution is hardly acceptable any longer because of the technological 'shrinking' of our world. Furthermore, today a proud isolation without care for others would be considered impious egoism and would indeed be the ruination of any religion. We cannot ignore the great contemporary problems common to all races and religions. War, hunger, injustice, lack of human freedom and the like should be issues of central importance to any contemporary living religion.

A *second* solution would be the substitution of one religion for the other. This solution is not only impracticable and utopian; it is also a-religious and wrong and would create only disorder and confusion on both sides. A Christian 'missionary' attitude desirous of undermining the foundation on which Hinduism rests would not only be dishonest and contrary to the principles of Christianity, but it would also be doomed to failure. Similarly, if a Hindu guru undermines or ignores the Christian background of Western disciples he not only violates such fundamental principles of the Hindu tradition as tolerance and openness, but is also doomed to failure. For psychology and history show that such radical (i.e. uprooting) conversions cannot last long unless a certain integration of both traditions takes place.

A *third* solution, the persistent dream of an eclectic unity and idealistic embrace, simply disregards the very real conflicts inherent in the situation. It is thus unrealistic and unrealizable. Such 'liberals', whether Christian or Hindu, who claim that 'we are the same' and that 'ultimately' the two religions are 'transcendentally' one, overlook the concrete and historical religious situation of real people.

A simple peaceful coexistence, on the other hand, *fourth*,

would at first sight seem a likely and practical solution, but it is shortsighted and superficial. Coexistence can only be lasting if there is a 'co-essence' to the two parties. A forced coexistence, adopted in order to avoid trouble, will dissolve the moment that one of the parties is convinced that the values they embody are of greater importance than the 'trouble' in question. It will then appear worthwhile to break the 'peaceful' *status quo*. True coexistence, as we have said, always implies a previous agreement on some form of co-essence. And this is precisely the point we cannot assume *a priori*.

Coexistence, furthermore, will not satisfy the traditional Christian understanding, which is that Christianity embodies the *Mystery* that God has revealed for the whole World.[3] This fourth solution may in the long run become a source of internal corruption within Christianity or may lead to external 'compensations' in the form of violent and illegitimate attacks upon other religions. Nothing is so harmful as what modern psychology would call 'unnatural suppression' and 'pathological repression'. Either Christianity gives up its claim to universality, catholicity, and then coexists peacefully with other religions, or it has to explain its claim with a theory—in the classical sense of the word—that shows the reasonableness and righteousness of such a claim. Otherwise it will bear the burden of being a fanatical and exclusive religion seeking to destroy everything that is not to its particular taste.

Similarly, Hinduism cannot be satisfied with merely coexisting with a militant Christianity such as claims that it has a 'right and duty' (jurisdiction) over the whole world. Even if Christianity were to abandon such a claim, as I am presuming, there would nevertheless persist in the eyes of Hinduism an irritant so long as the rules for coexistence were prescribed by another religion and differed from those set forth by the *sanātana dharma*. In other words, either Hinduism gives up its conviction that it is the 'everlasting religion', at least for the Indian people, or it has to explain how another *dharma* can satisfy the exigencies of its own self-understanding. If it were to coexist with a merely passive Christianity, re-

[3] Cf. Matt. 13:35; Rom. 16:25–6; Eph. 3:8–9; Col. 1:26; etc.

specting the actual *status quo*—being based on the fundamental principle of modern Hinduism, i.e. the relative equality of all religions—this would imply the transformation of Christianity into yet another of the various branches of Hinduism.

It is one thing to exacerbate incompatibilities and foster dissension. It is another to overlook differences and ultimately conflictive views. A good intention towards harmony is certainly a necessary condition for mutual understanding, but it is not sufficient.

If the Christ-event were interpreted as a merely partial disclosure of the Divine and Christianity had thus to abandon its claim upon, or rather its responsibility to, the whole World, most Christians would believe they were betraying their mission. If Hinduism, for its part, ceased to believe itself the religion best suited to Indians, most Hindus would feel it as a betrayal of Hinduism. We have come full circle. It would seem that there can be no encounter between the two, if each is to remain loyal to its essential nature.

To be sure, each tradition, seeing itself from within, considers that it is capable of giving a full answer to the religious urge of its members and, seeing other traditions from outside, tends to judge them as partial. It is only when we take the other as seriously as ourselves that a new vision may dawn. For this we have to break the self-sufficiency of any human group. But this requires that we should somehow have jumped outside our own respective traditions. Herein seems to lie the destiny of our time.

The problem is so acute and so delicate that we cannot ignore it on the pretext that it is better not to disturb an apparent and superficial cordiality. If we do not face it with all humility and sincerity, we will never succeed in overcoming an underlying uneasiness that will emerge only to damage and destroy both sides at critical points in the history of individuals and communities. The example of 'communal disturbances' in India between Hindus and Muslims is a warning of which we should take careful note and is an example of the insufficiency of a merely political or pragmatic 'peaceful coexistence'. Christianity wants the Hindu to become a Christian, although it has not taken sufficient account of the fact that one can be Christian in many different ways.

Hinduism, on the other hand, has no wish to convert Christians, because to the Hindu one cannot become what one *is* not; a Christian cannot 'become' Hindu, but then by the same token a Hindu cannot 'become' a Christian, and thus Hinduism must needs fight 'conversion'.

Is there any way out of this problem? This leads us to the *fifth* solution: interpenetration, mutual fecundation—and a mutation in the self-interpretation of these selfsame religious traditions.

There seem to be three indispensable prerequisites for such an encounter: a deep human honesty in searching for the truth wherever it can be found; a great intellectual openness in this search, without conscious preconceptions or willingly entertained prejudices; and finally a profound loyalty towards one's own religious tradition. In the past, when people lived either in isolation or in subjection, the religious quest was mainly directed towards the unidimensional deepening of one's own religion. But the authentic religious urge of today can no longer ignore a certain thirst for open dialogue and mutual understanding. The religion of my brother becomes a personal religious concern for me also.

Thinking people of all religions are craving mutual help and enlightenment—not only under pressure of exterior events such as the present confrontations between traditional religions, but also for internal motives deriving from an intellectual and existential dynamism. On the intellectual plane, no religion can pride itself on having fully revealed the mystery of Reality; on the existential plane, Man suffers more and more the attraction as well as the repulsion of other religions.

The first step towards a solution of the problem consists in recognizing that an authentic encounter can only take place where the two 'realities' truly meet each other. Every encounter is necessarily reciprocal. I cannot truly meet a cinema artist on the screen, primarily because, though I may somehow come to 'know' her or him, she or he cannot meet me there. Christianity cannot meet Hinduism if Hindus simply ignore Christianity; and, vice-versa, Hinduism will never be able to meet Christianity if Christians will not recognize and step out to meet Hinduism. Any encounter requires a common denominator, a meeting-place. That is to say, the real meeting does not belong to the merely doctrinal level, because we are dealing here with two fully developed and independent social and anthropological entities. The comparative study of religion will not yield any lasting result unless the doctrines are merely considered as starting-points for reaching the reality which underlies them. It is not mainly a doctrinal affair but, as we said, a religious problem.

I shall try to describe now this meeting-place, and, because the perspective of this whole book is that of a Christian reflecting in the presence of the Hindu partner, I shall present the argument as a Christian meditation that aims at understanding its own position without diluting the nature of Christianity and without doing injustice to Hinduism.

2. CHRIST, THE POINT OF ENCOUNTER

The true meeting between two living religions does not occur so much on the doctrinal plane as at a deeper level which could be called the existential, or 'ontic-intentional' stratum.

The two sets of doctrines, although they contain certain undeniable resemblances, are far removed from each other, and yet in a certain sense they possess the same *aim* and pursue the same *goal*. Moreover, they start from the same anthropological situation; they consider the same imperfect and vulnerable human being as he strives to reach fullness and perfection. Neither will contest that the 'ontic intentionality' is the same in both religions: the greatest possible oneness with the Absolute. Certainly, the Christian will affirm that Christian existence is, in the first place, a supernatural gift, a 'new creation'. But he will not deny that this new factor of 'grace' descends upon human existence as it is and is somehow given to all human beings, since God wants the salvation of everyone and without 'grace' there is no salvation. Christianity will also say that its specific goal is already coloured by its own constituents, namely the divinization of Man as Christianity understands it. That is to say, it claims to have a unique knowledge: a 'gnoseological intentionality', namely the *gnosis* that God is Trinity and our union is with God in Christ; but it will not contest the fact that the 'ontic intentionality' may be the same in Hinduism, namely that selfsame oneness with the Absolute.

Words cannot adequately express this ontic intentionality, or goal of existence. Thus, for example, we have used the expression 'oneness with the Absolute', while a certain type of yogin would prefer to say 'pure isolation' (*kaivalya*), while a Buddhist would use the term *nirvāṇa*. Some people will say that there is neither an Absolute with which one could be united, nor any duality to give any such union any sense; and yet the 'ontic intentionality' is one and the same: it is precisely that 'end', that 'final stage', towards which all are aiming from various angles of approach. Thus Christianity and Hinduism meet in a common endeavour, which has the same starting-point and the same ontic intentionality. There is a single *terminus a quo* and one *terminus ad quem* in the ontic order, even though the interpretations of them may differ.

I would like to develop this idea using Christian language. If I choose a Christian point of view, it is not from a prejudice in favour of Christianity. After all, Christianity takes the initiative in encountering Hinduism because Hinduism has so far sought this type of meeting much less, and therefore it is up to Christianity to clarify its own position. There is a tendency in contemporary Hinduism to prefer the fourth solution, namely mutual non-interference. The reason is double: bitter experiences of Christian interference in the past and also the idiosyncratic character of Hinduism in not being too concerned with the socio-historical situation of humankind. Yet in modern India the problem begins to be felt, and very acutely.

Our thesis is simple, though the explanation of it cannot be simplistic: Christianity and Hinduism meet each other in a reality which partakes of both the Divine and the Human, i.e. in what Christians cannot but call Christ. Christ is their point of encounter. It is not possible to prove this statement rationally. But we can try to show that, according to Hinduism as well as to Christianity, if such an encounter is to take place it can only take place in that reality that Christians call Christ.

Were we to take a corresponding Hindu symbol we could not possibly indicate it by one single word. For this difficulty there are two reasons: first, because Hinduism can hardly be called a religion. It is rather a bundle of religious traditions. We should readily understand the instinctive reaction of the people of India against being levelled down to a single 'Hinduism'. Strictly speaking, Hinduism does not exist. In the case of Christianity, however, even if an analogous train of thought should warn us against considering Christianity as a monolithic block, there is nevertheless the central figure of Christ—although diversely interpreted—that justifies to a certain extent this name.

By saying this we have already introduced the second reason. Hinduism has no unifying symbol such as Christianity has. It has not only a plurality of symbols, but no symbol as a rule contains the same pluralistic polyvalence as does the symbol of Christ. Within one single Hindu tradition the name of Rāma would probably be my choice. Rāma in fact is totally human and totally divine, Rāma is material and spiritual, temporal and eternal. But again not all 'Rāmalogies' would agree, as not all Christologies would adopt the stand of this book.

3. INSUFFICIENCY OF DOCTRINAL PARALLELISMS

Obviously, a real and living encounter cannot be limited simply to pointing out certain similarities or common features on the practical or theoretical levels. Christianity and Hinduism are two living religions, not to be confused with mere sets of concepts. Most of the common aspects are in fact common only when they have been separated from their respective contexts and are compared against an abstract and sterilized background as unrelated to one religion as to the other. Furthermore, since the similarities have necessarily to be selected according to the particular criterion of the selector, his syncretic intentionality tends to have an obscuring effect. Whole sections of the 'encountered' may be neglected or ignored simply because they are dissimilar. This is not a naked encounter so much as a sort of wishful thinking. Such similarities have their relative importance, but they do not touch the core of religions as actually lived by real people.

For example, the doctrine of grace in Patristic and Scholastic Christianity meets an analogous doctrine in Śaiva-siddhānta and Kashmir Śaivism. Nevertheless, in spite of many features common to both doctrines, this similarity only offers a meeting-place for a doctrinal discussion between experts in the two theologies. Important as it may be, this or any other doctrinal comparison can never be the ultimate basis of an *integral* encounter between living religions. The decisive point is not whether the Hindu and the Christian concepts of grace tally with each other, but whether the Hindu and the Christian are really 'graced' – according to the other.

Hinduism and Christianity have many analogous concepts and aspirations which offer starting-points for dialogue. But dialectical dialogue only constitutes an intermediary step in the whole endeavour, one which has to be followed by a profound investigation pursued to its farthest consequences, if real encounter is to take place. We should not minimize the importance of theoretical studies. Mutual knowledge is indispensable, but knowledge cannot be severed from reality and must be led by a higher wisdom, for any resultant encounter will ultimately arise from and depend upon such wisdom.

The conclusions drawn from comparative studies of the two religions can be classified according to a simple dialectical scheme: either the two doctrines under comparison will both be found to be fundamentally right or they will not.

In the first case, the identity may be either absolute, if the two doctrines are in fact the same; or it may be simply relative, if both perform the same function within the different doctrinal frameworks. In the latter case, the two doctrines would be equivalent rather than identical. Whether identical or equivalent, we shall have to proceed further until we arrive at the point where the two religions differ, and then seek the reasons for the difference. In spite of all theoretical equalities, we shall reach the point of an historical or rather factual 'otherness', for one religion is not, in fact, any other. Let us imagine for a moment that Śaṅkara's Vedānta is theoretically equal to Thomas Aquinas' Scholasticism. In spite of such a theoretical parallelism the fact would remain that one is a

Hindu doctrine and the other a *Christian* one. They would be the same intellectual garb for different historical realities.[4]

If the two doctrines being studied in a dialectical light are not found to be equally right the less accurate should disappear to make room for the other, or should at least be corrected by the more accurate. But in fact experience proves not only that one will with difficulty be able to convince an opponent in this matter, but also that he will not be able to give up his own doctrine because it is deeply rooted in the core of his own religion, which he holds from supra- and/or extra-rational motives. Imagine a Thomist constrained to admit that his proofs for the existence of God in fact do not prove anything. He should then give up those proofs, but of course he would never easily concede that God's existence cannot be 'proven'. Even dialectics have their limits: in the undeniable existence of the other as a source of self-understanding and in the non-rational factors that play a role in our convictions.

The premises of dialogue are two: the *basic tenets* out of which the doctrines have been developed, and the reality, the *existential truth* which the doctrines try to explain. Both of these dimensions transcend the doctrinal sphere. There is more room at the level of dialogue than for merely doctrinal discussion, for exclusively conceptual thinking. From this, however, it should not be inferred that we are neglecting or underestimating the importance of theoretical studies. It is sometimes only too easy to rely on (existential or mystical) 'experience', while ignoring the far-reaching theoretical implications of every existential attitude. The praxis requires a theory and the theory has to lead to a praxis. Therefore, as we shall see in the third chapter, doctrinal encounter is also necessary for a real and lasting meeting.

4. INADEQUACY OF CULTURAL SYNTHESIS

An encounter in depth between Hinduism and Christianity cannot take place on the profane level of a merely cultural

[4] Cf. R. Panikkar, 'La philosophie de la religion devant le pluralisme philosophique et la pluralité des religions' in *Pluralisme philosophique et pluralité des religions*, ed. E. Castelli (Paris, Aubier, 1977), pp. 193–201.

relationship. It is not about the meeting of two cultures that we speak, but about the meeting of two religions. It is important to stress this point in our times, because there is a tendency, very well-intentioned but misleading, to turn the encounter of religions into merely a question of the interrelation of cultures. The balance between religion and culture is a delicate one.

Hinduism has undoubtedly produced a Hindu culture in which it is intimately interwoven, and in spite of all necessary qualifications we cannot deny the existence of a Christian culture as at least a by-product of Christianity. But the laws of the interrelation of cultures are not the same as those of the meeting of religions.[5] It is by a meeting of cultures on the historical plane that a religious encounter is made possible; on the other hand, questions of religion have a tremendous influence on the cultural problem. For the latter, pragmatic criteria and purely cultural values are decisive; for the former, allegiance to the past and fidelity to oneself, even at the cost of the renunciation of many other values, play an important part.

The interdependence and at the same time independence of culture and religion could be expressed in this way: every religion obviously shapes a culture, but the culture also offers the concrete boundaries within which religion operates. Thus, in a sense, culture makes the existence of a religion possible. So they are neither separable—because there is no religion without a culture nor, in one sense or another, culture without religion—nor can they be identified. In point of fact, one religion may shape, fecundate or influence several cultures, and one culture can host more than one religion. Further, almost every major religion has a transcultural intention, for it claims that it will persist even if its host culture were to be destroyed. Similarly, most cultures have a certain trans-religious validity because they are not necessarily bound up with one particular religion. Kerala Christians and North American Hindus could be cited as two pertinent examples of people who accept one religion and 'live' another culture.

The religious encounter engages the whole Man. Moreover,

[5] Cf. R. Panikkar, *The Intrareligious Dialogue, passim.*

even the encounter between cultures cannot be a purely academic matter; much less so can the encounter of religions. Rather, this must be an encounter of living and loving persons trying to remain faithful to higher values which do not depend on their own will.

It is in a religious spirit that a true encounter between religions takes place. Here the participant dismisses all kinds of partiality towards his own religious tradition and all prejudice with regard to that of others, while at the same time he remains faithful to his own deep convictions. The meeting of religions is not an intellectual endeavour nor a simple practical exercise, but the fruit of experience and religious engagement. Religion only *is* in religiousness, in love for God and fellow-beings, in seeing the Self in all and all in the Self—in a stretching out towards that state which, even in intention, is variously described as 'blessed', as only being realized by, for instance, a second birth or the grace of God. If the encounter does not occur in this spirit it is a meeting not of religions, properly speaking, but of ethical systems, cultural mores, all existing on the conceptual or at least conceptualizable plane. Concepts, even concepts of God, the Ultimate, the Absolute, though unavoidable up to a point, cannot be the heart of religion because ultimacy, whether 'immanent' or 'transcendent', is beyond all human understanding. Religions meet at their common source, not simply on the plane of ideas or ideals, but in the very depth or ground of religion. For the present we cannot develop this point any further.[6]

[6] I once attended a debate on religious problems, in which the dialogue was explicitly syncretistic: it was a matter of emphasizing points of contact. However, everyone was at variance regarding 'tolerance' and 'comprehension': *tot capita quot sententiae!* Though agreeing on a rather vague and liberal framework, everyone had his own opinion within it. Only a Catholic priest and a Buddhist *bhikku*, who held maximalist attitudes, found themselves in real agreement, and theirs were the only two concordant voices in that gathering.

5. THE EXISTENTIAL ENCOUNTER

We have tried to show that the true meeting of religions belongs primarily not to the essential but to the existential sphere. Religions meet in the heart rather than in the mind. By 'heart' we mean not the realm of sentiment but the concrete reality of our lives. The meeting of two differing realities produces the shock of the encounter, but the *place* where the encounter happens is one. This one place is the heart of the person. It is within the heart that I can embrace both religions in a personal synthesis, which intellectually may be more or less perfect. And it is also within my heart that I may absorb one of the two religions into the other. In actuality religions cannot sincerely coexist or even continue as living religions if they do not 'co-insist', i.e. penetrate into the heart of each other.

A Christian will never fully understand Hinduism if he is not, in one way or another, converted to Hinduism. Nor will a Hindu ever fully understand Christianity unless he, in one way or another, becomes Christian.[7] There are, of course, levels of understanding as there are levels of conversion. It is not necessary however for everyone to 'meet' everyone else like this. Certain meetings could be extremely dangerous. Not everyone is able—much less obliged—to incarnate himself in another religion. But if an encounter has to be more than a mere diplomatic move, we cannot escape its exigencies. Since it is not just an individual but a collective and social endeavour, those involved must grasp the dynamics of the history of the encounter up to date, in order to catch and use its momentum and thus continue it in a meaningful way.

Let us first describe this encounter from a general point of view in its fundamental existential dimension. On the one hand, there is Hinduism as a way of life, a path to mysticism, a set of traditions which lead the people of India towards their end, their fulfilment and salvation. 'Lead' may be too strong a word: Hinduism can hardly be described as either commanding or leading. The Hindu will find *mokṣa* (salvation,

[7] Regarding 'understanding as convincement', cf. R. Panikkar, 'Verstehen als Überzeugtsein' in *Neue Anthropologie*, vol. vii, ed. H. G. Gadamer and P. Vogler (Stuttgart, Thieme, 1975), pp. 132–67.

liberation) if he lets himself be led, if he follows his own *dharma*. Needless to say, that fulfilment and salvation may be interpreted in completely different ways. On the other hand, there is Christianity claiming to lead to salvation and hence trying to perform its 'duty' towards the people of Hindu culture and religion. The two religions may agree or differ in details, but the historical, concrete and almost juridical fact remains that on the one side stands Hinduism as an entity, as a way to 'salvation' or 'liberation', and on the other side stands Christianity as an entity with the same claims. The Indian by birth and the converts from both sides are caught inbetween.

The encounter may degenerate into a brutal clash. Let us be blunt. Hinduism follows a certain line of conduct and adopts a certain pattern of life. Christianity, however, intervenes, demanding that the course of Hinduism be continued only in such a way as to reach 'Christian fullness'; thus the Hindu pattern is to be converted into the Christian one, since this is the only one that the Christian can imagine.[8] The initiative comes from Christianity, so it is the duty of Christianity to justify it. What, then, is the internal urge prompting Christians to claim jurisdiction over the Hindu also? Does Christianity really want to destroy Hinduism? Are all its actions just tactics or expediencies to increase its membership by winning over the Hindu to the Christian cause, as Hindus have often felt? We do not seek here some historical justification, explanation or excuse for the fact that Hindus have this impression of Christianity, for the possible abuses of a right or the dangers manifestly inherent in every dynamism are beyond the scope of these reflections.

Our problem, rather, is this: in this encounter is Christianity justified at all in claiming rights over the Hindu or over Hinduism itself? Certain Christians would rather speak

[8] When we speak of 'Christianity' here in a generalized way, we do not forget that most Indian Christians are not militant or aggressively 'missionary', but it would lead us too far afield to introduce here historical distinctions between different forms of Christianity in India. On the other hand, the attitude here mentioned is not confined altogether to foreign missionaries.

of their duties towards the Hindu and Hinduism, but whether right or duty, it ultimately comes to the same thing. Rational proof of such a right or duty can hardly be given. Christianity is convinced that it has certain obligations, a conviction that is inherent in its self-understanding as a logical consequence of its nature; to entertain this conviction, in fact, is practically tantamount to embracing Christianity. It is part of the often tragic tension of history that the encounter between religions is not a peaceful state but a painful confrontation leading either to growth and development or elimination and confusion.

Hinduism and Christianity encounter not in intellectual agreement, but in the ultimate tension or opposition of two living religions. It will be useful, then, to clarify the different positions, exposing the exigencies of this encounter in all sincerity and openness. I shall try therefore to define and describe the ultimate ground of the encounter between Hinduism and Christianity, first according to Hinduism and then according to Christianity. We should not be blind to the brutal facts of the past, but neither should we be deaf to the loud summons of the present.

6. THE HINDU GROUND OF THE ENCOUNTER

Hinduism is such an exuberant and rich religion that it does not have to fear Christianity. Moreover, it believes that it has room even for Christianity within its own multiform structure, though doubtless the Hindu idea of Christianity does not coincide with the consciousness Christianity has of itself. This is why Hindus feel that they are a tolerant people, while Christians, perhaps misunderstanding their attitude, fear that this tolerance may be the subtlest form of intolerance, which consists in allowing others to occupy only that place which it itself assigns them.[9]

Now Hinduism has not always taken the attitude we are about to describe. Though it is a typical Hindu trait, it is especially characteristic of modern Hinduism. Hindu trad-

[9] Cf. Paul Hacker, 'Religiöse Toleranz und Intoleranz im Hinduismus' in *Kleine Schriften*, pp. 376ff.

itions have in the past maintained, each in its own way, that the followers of other faiths are on a comparatively inferior level, while admitting that they are on the path to the same ultimate goal whose final revelation is Śiva or Krishna. The Bhagavad Gītā says that all worship is ultimately directed to Krishna, that it is he who brings all religious acts to fulfilment, even those devoted to other Gods.[10] Thus, if we were to follow these and similar teachings of other schools, we could arrive at a Hindu meeting-point called Krishna or Śiva, but, as we have already said, there is no one universally accepted symbol for all Hindus.

Present-day Hindus however are in general convinced that all religions are good in so far as they lead Men to perfection. Therefore they welcome Christianity as another religion, a younger sister of their own. They would be inclined to accept and even join with it, if Christianity would consent to give up its exclusiveness and its consequent claim to be the definitive religion. If these Hindus claim for their religion a certain wider comprehensiveness, a greater scope, it is in the areas of theological doctrine and of mystical consciousness; but this superiority—as that of the elder sister—is but a secondary feature in the relationship.

What Hindus do defend against Christianity is the right of Hinduism to be their religion, as being the most perfect expression (or expressions) *for them*, of the *sanātana dharma*, the eternal religion. Since Hinduism itself is but a loose compound of many different ways to the ultimate, related theoretically by the tradition of Vedic authority[11] and practically by a set of common beliefs, and since in at least one modern form it recognizes non-Vedic religions as legitimate ways to that same ultimate, it finds almost incomprehensible the fact that other religions cannot accept this standpoint, that they refuse and repudiate the sincere and co-operative attitude that Hinduism offers. According to Christians, Hindus discover, Christianity is *the* way to fulfilment, whereas Hindus

[10] Cf. BG VII, 21ff.; IX, 23–4; 27. These and similar passages would allow for the development of a conception of 'anonymous Hindu (or: Krishna-devotee)'.

[11] Cf. Louis Renou, *The Destiny of the Veda in India*.

affirm 'one way for me, another way for you—our inspiration is the same, our end is the same, but this is necessarily a world of exuberant multiplicity and diversity—accept it as so given in creation, and follow your path to the end.' This is a pervasive attitude, as can be seen in the fact that on the practical plane Indians have created in the caste-system an institution which specifically reflects the different natures of Man. In this (theoretically, at least) every individual fulfils his function in the cosmos by performing the duties most suitable to his nature. This caste-system is, so to say, projected in the encounter with other religions. Every religion is implicitly understood as a separate caste (which for a Hindu has theoretically no negative implications) within which the individual attains his goal by fulfilling his duty. 'Whatever may be our caste and *dharma*, we will all ultimately meet.'

In short, 'we meet either at the end of our journey (all rivers flow into the same sea) or at the very beginning (all receive water from the earth or the clouds or some single source). It is only in the "interregnum" of our earthly pilgrimage that the rivers go their different ways.'

There is, however, a more recent form of Hinduism which, moved by the needs of our times, tends to a kind of syncretism of a characteristically Hindu type. This form of Hinduism would be ready to 'sacrifice itself' as a particular religion, provided that the other religions would do the same, and be thus transformed into a universal—'catholic'—religion without limitations regarding cult, dogmas and other features. We would then all meet in the absolute nakedness of a religion emptied of all contents, in a thrust of Man towards perfection, fullness, happiness. According to this Neo-Hinduism, we should renounce what separates us, anything that would diminish our freedom and the expansion of our being.[12]

For a long time Hinduism, which by reason of the multiplicity of its religious forms has suffered and experienced at least as much as any other religion the imperfections of the human mind and the limitations of the human heart, has dreamed of this universal and boundless religion. We only

[12] Cf. S. Radhakrishnan, *The Hindu View of Life*; R. Tagore, *The Religion of Man*; R. N. Dandekar, *Some Aspects of the History of Hinduism*.

meet in the Absolute; we only meet at the end of our pilgrimage; we encounter one another once we realize that we are one and the same reality. We cannot meet in our differences; we shall only meet in what unites us. We should give up what makes us different and renounce all our ideas, conceptions and practices. Truth, Silence, Love—these would be the only dogmas of this new religion in which all Men would meet.

In summary this would be the position of Hinduism: either we meet as sister-religions striving towards the same end, or we meet by sacrificing our individual ways and coalescing in the mysterious, divine ground of our Origin and End.

7. THE CHRISTIAN GROUND OF THE ENCOUNTER

Christianity accepts the challenge of Hinduism and we hope to show that it will be precisely in the framework proposed by Hinduism that the two will meet. We shall expound first the Christian position and then Christianity's answer to the Hindu point of view.

We may perhaps explain the Christian standpoint like this: Hinduism and Christianity, as two religions believing in God, undoubtedly meet in God. We do not mean that they meet in their respective conceptions of God, but in God, the Absolute, the Ultimate. The Christian elaboration of this meeting-ground does not require the partisanship of the Hindu, but only his understanding.

'We all meet, then, in God. Not only is he omnipresent, but everything is in him, and we, with all our strivings and all our actions, are *of* him, *in* him, come *from* him and go *to* him. (One could just as well have said "it" or "her" in this context.) Now, there is only one link, one mediator between God and the rest, between the one and the many.'

In other words, the meeting-point cannot be only a transcendent platform, divine ground, a disincarnated place, as it were. Ultimately God can be the ideal, the end and goal, but transcendence obviously cannot be the starting-point. We need a concrete meeting-place from the very first, which is more than just an idea or a concept and also more than just humanity with its material needs.

That theandric 'thing', the concrete connection between

the Absolute and relative which all religions recognize in one way or another, we could call 'Lord', but we may also call it 'Christ', for the Christian concept, though of Hebrew origin and connected with the Judaic tradition, has precisely this function. The Christ we are speaking of is by no means the monopoly of Christians, or *merely* Jesus of Nazareth. We may be allowed therefore to call Christ that which we consider to be almost by definition the meeting-point, and which at the same time meets the demands of Christian religion.

This, then, is Christ: that reality from whom everything has come, in whom everything subsists, to whom everything that suffers the wear and tear of time shall return.[13] He is the embodiment of Divine Grace who leads every Man to God; there is no other way but through him.[14] Is not this what Christians call Christ? It is he who inspires the prayers of Man and makes them 'audible' to the Father; it is he who whispers any divine inspiration and who speaks as God, no matter what form a person's faith or thought may have.[15] Is not he the light that illumines every human being coming into this World?[16]

Hence from the point of view of Christianity, Christ is already present in Hinduism. The Spirit of Christ is already at work in Hindu prayer. Christ is already present in every form of worship, to the extent that it is adoration directed to God.[17] The deep-thinking Christian declines to judge Hinduism: God alone judges, through Christ. So long as Men are pilgrims on earth, Christianity has not the right to separate the wheat from the chaff. Rather, in meeting and accepting Hinduism as it is, the Christian will find Christ already there.

Christians and Hindus meet in the depths of death, in the

[13] The following references illustrate something more than merely doctrinal parallelisms, since both traditions put these texts in the context of the quest for the ultimate mystery (cf. TU II, 9,1). Cf. SU II,4; III,3; III,9; III,11; III,16, etc.; BU I,4,7; II,4,5; TU II,6,1; CU III, 14,2.

[14] Cf. KathU II,23; MundU III,2,3; SU I,6; II,4; III,4; III,8; III,20; CU III,15,3; BG IX,23; X,10–11; XVIII,56; 58; 62.

[15] Cf. MundU II,2,2ff.; SU III,12; CU VIII,14,1.

[16] Cf. KathU V,15; MundU II, 2,9–10, etc.; SU III,12; 17, etc.; CU III,12,8–9; III,13,7; III,17,7–8.

[17] Cf. Prov. 8:34–5; John 8:58, etc. Cf. BG IX,24; 26; 29ff.

renunciation of ourselves—including our long-held opinions of others—and in the acceptance of 'new life' which is always there at the heart of true religion. We—Christians or Hindus—can consider ourselves no longer as possessors of truth, but as beings possessed by a truth that is greater than we are and which cannot be known because knowing is possessive, is of the self which must end in order to accept the new life. The Christ who is already present in Hinduism and whom Christians can recognize and revere there has not yet completed his mission here on earth, either in Christianity or in Hinduism. 'If the grain of wheat does not die . . .'[18]

8. CHRIST, THE MEETING-PLACE

The presence of Christ in Hinduism in the above-mentioned sense makes of Hinduism, in the eyes of the Christian, not *another dharma*, but a part or stage of the same *sanātana dharma* that Christianity also claims to be. We have said here *dharma* and not 'religion', as this latter word implies a sociological reality which precludes our perceiving a deeper unity between Hinduism and Christianity.

Hinduism as a whole has no dogmas, no essential contents.[19] Being only the concrete expression of the existential *dharma*, it can take as many forms as people and circumstances require, each form being relative to time and space. The bold Christian claim is that in the historical unfolding of God's revelation there is a kind of pluralistic continuity held together by what they call Christ. Thus the existential *dharma* of Hinduism belongs to what Christians call the 'economy of salvation'.[20] The Christian believes that God, who has spoken through the prophets and the rishis (sages), has sent once for

[18] Cf. John 12:24.

[19] Cf. my chapter 'Algunos aspectos fenomenológicos de la espiritualidad hindú actual' in *Misterio y Revelación*, esp. pp. 26–8.

[20] Cf. W. Bierbaum, 'Geschichte als Paidagogia Theou. Die Heilsgeschichtslehre des Klemens von Alexandrien' in *Münchener Theologische Zeitschrift* 5 (1954), pp. 246–72; J. Daniélou, *Le mystère du salut des nations*. Paris, 1948; K. Rahner, 'Weltgeschichte und Heilsgeschichte' in *Schriften zur Theologie* V, pp. 115–35; A. Darlap, 'Fundamentale Theologie der Heilsgeschichte' in *Mysterium Salutis* I (Einsiedeln, Benziger, 1965), pp. 3–153.

all his living and personal Word—one with him—to fulfil all justice, all *dharmas*.[21]

Christians, however, have always been tempted to extrapolate in an overzealous manner. Already Peter, just because he loved Jesus and was loved by him, thought he could control the relationship between John and Jesus and was rebuked for it.[22] Christians have tended to interpret Christ only in their own terms. Or perhaps we should say, rather, that the Christian context (first Judaism, then European religions, followed by scientific cosmologies which culminated in the myth of history) has been generally taken to be the universal human texture. Other expressions of the human and religious phenomenon have scarcely been taken seriously. When Christians were confronted with a fact outside their horizon, they were tempted to close ranks in a gesture of exclusiveness. This is a common and in-built temptation of almost every religion and culture: 'We are at the centre of the world and possess the paradigms to judge others'; but in the case of Christianity it has been more serious because of the expansionistic thrust within Christian history. However, nowadays Christian reflection begins to be conscious of this shortcoming of the past.

In order to overcome the existing deep-rooted misunderstanding between Hinduism and Christianity one would have to analyse the different approaches to the Centre from which all is sustained and which is also the key to intelligibility. The Western Christian tradition with its theistically charged language has identified it with the historical Jesus, whereas some of the fundamental Hindu intuitions concerning this Centre refer to Brahman, Ātman, *vāc, bindu* and other symbols of the Absolute according to different contexts. The different understandings of this Centre are not irrelevant and the identification of it here or there not without importance. Yet both traditions refer to it and the differences should not blur the identity—nor vice versa.

We could even proceed a step further and say that most of these different understandings—and often misunderstandings—stem from the almost diametrically opposed dynamisms

[21] Cf. John 1:9–17; Heb. 1:1–2.
[22] Cf. John 21:22.

that operate in the actual process of reaching intelligibility. The predominantly Semitic mentality of Christian theology will reach the intelligibility of the ultimately ungraspable Mystery ascending to it from its concrete and visible manifestation: Jesus Christ. Thus, once the identification is made, it will with great difficulty proceed in the opposite direction; if Jesus Christ is the Mystery, any other real name or real manifestation of the Mystery will appear inadequate because it contradicts the Christian understanding. The predominantly Aryan mind of Hindu theology, on the other hand, will reach the affirmation of the ultimately ungraspable Mystery by *descending* to each of its concrete and visible manifestations: e.g. Rāma, Krishna, etc. The identification will never be complete and closed, and thus there will be no difficulty in recognizing several identifications without destroying the identity of the Mystery.[23]

Let me enlarge on this a little more. I would like to submit that both the Christian understanding of catholicity and the Hindu thirst for universality are not contradicted by Christian dogma (as it is termed in theology). A dogma is certainly a consecrated expression considered to be the bearer of an unfathomable truth. Yet faith is not in dogmas, but in the 'thing' expressed in and through them.[24] Dogmas are means, channels, and do not claim to exhaust, let alone to freeze, the truth they try to convey to those who are living in the context of the tradition which has 'proclaimed' the particular dogma. Both Hindus and Christians alike believe in a universal truth in and through concrete ways of expression.

The genuine claim of the Hindu *dharma* is not, strictly speaking, a kind of syncretism—though it often takes this

[23] Popular religiousness offers frequent examples. While an average theologically untrained Christian will not easily accept any other symbol than Christ, the Hindu partner will have no qualms in accepting Christ on what he thinks are, precisely, Christian terms—and is surprised later when he finds that this is not the case.

[24] Cf. the central statements of Thomas Aquinas such as: '*Fides non est de enuntiabilibus*', '*actus fidei non terminatur ad enuntiabile sed ad rem*', etc. Cf. also K. Rahner, 'Was ist eine dogmatische Aussage?' in *Schriften zur Theologie* V, pp. 54–81; R. Panikkar, 'La foi dimension constitutive de l'homme' in *Mythe et foi*, ed. E. Castelli (Paris, Aubier, 1966), pp. 17–63.

form—but it is the voice of catholicity, the very dynamism of the existential *dharma*, leading towards a sublimation of 'beliefs', tending to overcome all exclusivisms in particularity, while maintaining the right of the individual to his particular practices. Similarly, when the Christian says that Christ is God, that Bliss is Heaven, that Perfection is Union with God, that Truth is the Logos, and so on, he does not want to put limitations on the former notions, but endeavours to fill them up with living contents, with a real meaning in order to prevent them from degenerating into mere vague and abstract aspirations that each individual may afterwards interpret in his own peculiar and restricted way. This principle undoubtedly applies to any religious statement or expression of faith.

Likewise the Hindu may bow to the ultimacy of *saccidānanda brahman*, while in his need for the concrete he acknowledges that Śiva (or Krishna or Kālī) is the be-all and end-all of the universe, his 'only way' to ultimacy, repository of that same truth, perfection and bliss which are in fact inconceivable, though he and the Christian both speak of them in their longing. Both agree that universality, catholicity, openness and perfection do not mean vagueness, unbelief, purely abstract intention, nihilism and uprootedness from this earth and our human surroundings, so long as we still dwell here in this world. A Christian dogma or a Hindu tenet is neither an idol nor a limitation nor a definition of faith, nor a place in which to get stuck before attaining the goal. These are just expressions, fit channels through which we may reach the Absolute; just the way—not the end—along which we have to proceed in order to reach fullness.

The Christian welcomes the sacrifice that Neo-Hinduism demands of every religion: that it may be transformed into *the* religion of humanity. Is it not a Christian commandment to deny oneself, to hate one's own life and to die completely in order to rise again to divine life? Is not the mystery of the Cross as symbol of the Resurrection the central core of Christianity?

The Catholic meaning of 'dogma' is not a 'truth' or a 'formula' to which credence must be given; dogma is rather a means to bridle our intellect in order that our higher knowledge may reach, as far as it is possible here on earth, the unfathomable inner nature of Reality. This should not in any way be taken as a subjective interpretation of Christian truths or a relativization of Christian dogmas in a modernistic sense. Dogmas are necessary so long as we are intelligent beings, but we should beware of the danger of 'dogmatolatry'.

What Christianity claims over Hinduism is not a kind of juridical right. Christ does not belong to Christianity; he belongs to his Father only. Christianity and Hinduism both express and unfold their belief in the theandric mystery, though in two different ways.

The encounter of Melchisedech with Abraham[25] and, later, the revelation of Peter at Joppa[26] and the many experiences of Paul[27] are some of the authoritative instances of this Christian attitude and position, in addition, of course, to the living example of Christ and his explicit teachings.

Let me explain again the Christian position, this time using the hypothesis of the relative equivalence of all religions. The Hindu seems to say: 'Because we are all the same, we remain separate; because in the final analysis we are one, let us simply coexist and not strive for a visible unity. We are already the same ocean, our only difference being that you are one stream and we another; because unity is there, let us not pay attention to our present split, since it is only apparent.'

The Christian would like to answer: 'Because we are all the same ultimately, and the differences between our religions may belong only to the realm of appearance, let us see beyond the separation that exists between us as human beings. This separation, though of such great historical breadth, is not necessary. Let us embrace one another and not keep aloof any longer; let us discover—uncover—our deep unity, realize and make manifest the depth of that identity of which you are convinced and for which we yearn. If there are still some differences, they will disappear like the difference between levels of liquid in two vessels, once the vessels are connected.

[25] Cf. Gen. 14:17–20.
[26] Cf. Acts 10.
[27] Cf. Acts 9, etc.

He who has more will spontaneously give if the other does not refuse the gift.'

The encounter of the two great streams may produce some passing waves or some sudden whirlpools, but the enrichment and growth will be mutual. Christianity claims to be catholic, but logically it is not complete (i.e. 'catholic') until that unity has been realized. The confusion lies in mistaking *religious unity*—for which we plead—for the *unity of religions*. We are not self-sufficient monads, but fragments of the same, unique religious faith. 'That all may be one': this is what drives Christianity to realize this oneness, which of course does not mean uniformity. 'Because, as you say, we *are* the same, let us really *be* the same!' Christianity does not want assimilation or dominion, does not want to destroy; it only shares with Hinduism the fundamental urge towards unity.

I would dare to say more: this thirst for unity, this prayer for oneness is so fundamental in Christianity that it conditions everything else. Obviously unity which is not based on truth is not unity at all; a oneness which is not the real one—willed by God, the Christian would say—is not oneness at all. This amounts to saying that no human compromise is a way towards union, that this union is not the result of sitting down together and framing a liberal religious constitution, but of praying and struggling together to discover the Will of God, as regards realizing this unity. This means also that though Christians may be convinced of the contents of their faith, they do not know what the further developments in their Church may be, they do not have access to the plans of divine providence, they should in truth and honesty not cling to a fixed scheme or to a frozen faith. New dogmas, renewed formulations of old ones, real evolution and progress are constant features of Christianity. Nobody knows how Christianity will look should the present Christian waters unite with those of other religions to form a bigger river where the peoples of the future will quench their thirst for truth, for goodness, for salvation.[28]

There is little sense in discussing, in this context, what

[28] Cf. R. Panikkar, 'Ṛtatattva: A Preface to a Hindu-Christian Theology' in *Jeevadhara* 49 (Jan.–Feb. 1979), pp. 6–63.

Christianity considers definitive and what changeable.[29] There is and there will be a continuity, but it is not for the theologian to pontificate; it is not even for the pontiff to silence the prophet, to rule the future. Follow me, Christ said to the first head of his Church, and do not bother about John. 'Sufficient unto the day is its own burden!'[30]

Finally, we will add a word for the Hindu about Christ himself, since at first sight it really looks ridiculous if not preposterous from a Hindu point of view to say that the encounter takes place in Christ. We are not making any kind of apologetic or trying to dispel the many misconceptions about Christ, perhaps given to Hindus by Christians themselves. These are very important points, but beyond the scope of this study. Our only objective is to clarify the issue as it stands.

We have already said that Hinduism and Christianity both meet in God and that God is working inside both religions and transcends them. The Christian claim is that God and Christ have a unique relation, that they are indivisible and inseparable, though without mixture or confusion, and that where God is at work in this World, it is always in and through Christ that he acts. Hindus would not find much difficulty in accepting this aspect of God and would perhaps call it Iśvara (Lord) or Bhagavān. The statement made above about Christ as the place of encounter makes sense, at least for the Christian, and can be made understandable—if not acceptable—to the Hindu also, if an equivalent (homeomorphic) statement is made about Śiva or Krishna or Kālī. The equivalence is not complete since the theological frameworks are different, but it may contribute to an existential understanding of the Christian statement.

The major obstacle appears when Christianity further identifies, with the necessary qualifications, Christ with Jesus, the

[29] A little more than a decade ago many theologians, in their desire to be open, used to view the question with a list in mind of all the 'concessions' one could make and the 'non-negotiable' or 'firm points' that a Christian must strictly preserve. I maintain that this is methodologically an inaccurate approach and theologically a rationalistic posture.
[30] Cf. Matt. 6:34.

son of Mary. It is precisely this identity that characterizes the Christian belief. The Hindu can only respect, without sharing in, this 'theohistoriological' aspect of Christianity.

9. THE ENCOUNTER

We are led to a point which seems to render impossible even the 'formal' mutual agreement that we have been seeking. If Christ is the point of contact, yet only Christians can fully accept his necessary identity with Jesus, we cannot hope for a very fruitful dialogue.

At this juncture we would like to propose an important consideration which may help to overcome the impasse but which, had it been made sooner, would have been too easily misunderstood by both sides. We are referring to the Spirit of God as the place where the encounter, if at all, takes place. It is only in the Holy Spirit that prayers meet, intentions coalesce and persons enter into communion.

We needed first to clarify this question of the confession of *Christ* as universal saviour, because to the Christian it is so vitally important. Also, without having previously mentioned the concrete, theandric Christ, talk of the Spirit would have amounted to saying that we all profess belief, in a vague and amorphous way, in a certain spirit of truthfulness and sanctity. This is by no means false, but a general commitment to truth and sincerity, *necessary* as it is for every real encounter in any realm, is not *sufficient* to constitute the ground for a truly religious, and not merely ethical, understanding. Now we can say that if Christ in Jesus as the culminating point of God's self-disclosure seems too specifically Christian a view to be accepted by a Hindu, then the Spirit of God—which Christians will consider the Holy Spirit or the Spirit of Christ, and which the Hindu will interpret as the Divine *śakti* penetrating everything and manifesting God, disclosing him in his immanence and being present in all his manifestations—this Spirit of God provides the real ground for an authentic religious communication and dialogue at a deep level.

Whoever really prays does so in the Spirit, and ultimately it is the Spirit which prays. While Christ as the Incarnate Son of God is a specifically Christian figure, the presence and reality of the Spirit is an element common and important to both Hinduism and Christianity. Only because the Spirit dwells in our hearts and in the World was it possible for the Logos to become flesh and establish his dwelling among us. In other words, we meet in the Spirit, the Spirit of God, which for the Christian is the Spirit of Christ. Let me clarify immediately that we are not dealing here with a mere semantic quibble. It is not a question of whether this Spirit is God's or Christ's or Śiva's. It is a matter of agreeing on the fundamental nature of this Spirit.

We must not linger any longer on this subject lest I be obliged to make a complete study of its implications and consequences. I wish, rather, to add a few reflections of a pastoral character. The Christian encounter with Hinduism, as we have said, is essentially neither a doctrinal dialogue nor the mutual comprehension of two cultures. It is a historical encounter of religions in the concrete meeting of Men in society. This encounter can really take place, because it is an encounter in the Presence of the one who is already present in the hearts of those who *in good faith* belong to one or the other of the two religions.

Mutual understanding is absolutely necessary: it is an ineluctable condition. However, knowledge alone is not enough. It not only lacks the warmth necessary for a full human encounter, but it tends to produce reactions of an almost antagonistic sort, for human knowledge in fact always entails an egocentric movement. The 'thing' known (doctrine, person) comes to *me*. I am at home, I am the host: I receive, welcome and assimilate the 'things' that I know—I possess. I enrich myself.

Only an outgoing mutual love overcomes that egocentricity of knowledge. When I love, I go out, I give up, I am the guest, I am no more at home, I am received and possessed. Purely intellectual knowledge commits an offence against whatever it does not choose to assimilate, whatever is left behind. I may reach some synthesis in an intellectual victory over my opponent, but I bring only the spoils of the confrontation back to my system. Śaṅkara, let us say, is overcome or 'understood', but the Śaṅkarites remain outside, unconvinced. This love requires from both sides an asceticism, a mystical life, a detachment from all categories and formulae, from both prejudices and critical judgements. This should not be taken as a denial of orthodoxy but as its implementation and integration into 'orthopraxis' (right action).

An authentic Christian encounter with other religions requires a special asceticism: the stripping off of all externals, of 'garb' and superficial form, and a lonely vigil with Christ, the naked Christ, dead *and* alive on the Cross, dead *and* alive in those Christians who dare to come to such an encounter with their brethren. This asceticism entails real mysticism, an immediate contact with Christ which carries the Christian beyond—not against—formulae and explanations. Only then is it possible to discover Christ where he is, for the moment, veiled; only then is it possible to help unveil or reveal the mystery hidden for long ages in God. Few indeed, except by some special grace, are capable of such a stripping, are able to remain with the naked Christ living within them, to perform this existential imitation of the incarnation of Christ.

The Hindu encounter does not require just a certain degree of purity and a few attempts at non-attachment (*asakti*). We must rid ourselves of all pride and self-congratulation that we have understood the Mystery and realized the Truth. We have to accept our *karma* and our *siddhis*, our limitations as well as our gifts. We need to swim in the stream of history without ceasing to fly in the air (*ākāśa*) of the timeless. We need incarnation as much as transcendence, and we should take our *iṣṭadevatā*, the manifestation for us of the Divine, as a real symbol, something more than a mere sign.

The consequences of all this reach far and augur the ultimate failure of the merely comparative study of religions. The study has to be done, but it must also be transcended. A meeting of spiritualities can only take place in the Spirit. The aim of encounter is not to give rise to a new 'system', but to give birth to a new *spirit*, which is both ancient and ever new. Spiritualities are not there to be 'studied' (they are not properly 'objects' of study) but to be lived, authentically experienced.

The meeting of religions should be a *religious* act, an act of incarnation and redemption, an encounter in *naked Faith*, in *pure Hope*, in *divine Love*—and not a conflict of formulae, in the expectation of 'winning the others over' (—to what?).

In *naked Faith*: I believe, *credo*! But faith is not a matter of reifying the living expression of a mystical or 'supernatural' act into a belief in some crystallized and disconnected formulations. The act of faith is a gift of God, through which I participate in the divine knowledge that God has of himself and, in himself, of everything else; it is a simple, vital act which needs only a minimum of intellectual explicitness. 'I believe, Lord!': this act alone is a saving one. I believe—in the only thing which requires this higher and supreme act—in the unthinkable Absolute, in God, the Mystery, the Void. I grasp it vaguely and with unclear vision, yet I am fully convinced and already somehow 'taste' him: God who, as my faith explains it, is Trinity—Father, Logos and Holy Spirit. And faith in turn allows me to enter into the ineffable heart of Divinity, there to discover, to understand that this Father is omnipotent, creator; and that the Logos is Man, and that the Spirit is the living breath of his People and of the universe: 'I believe, Lord!' I cannot put it into words, or, rather, many expressions will leave me equally happy and yet unsatisfied. I believe in the invisible, the transcendent and immanent at the same time, in *ātman-brahman*, or in Vishnu, the Supreme, or Śiva, the Absolute. But all these 'articles' of faith are only expressions, manifestations, explicit examples of the mystical act of faith, which has no fixed points, no adequate intellectual expression, and can only be imperfectly translated into human words. All of this might be summed up in the spoken and lived attitude of the devotee, whether Hindu or Christian: 'Not I, not I but thou, thou, O Lord.' It is in this faith that Christian and Hindu encounter as brethren.

In *pure Hope*, in the desire for liberation (*mumukṣutva*) or in the consciousness of being already possessed by God, of being possessed so as to be (in) his fullness one day, in the expectation of the manifestation and glory of the Absolute: in this, the Christian is almost one with the Hindu. How can either exclude anyone who is already pervaded by the same hope of liberation and union?

In *divine Love* the encounter is not only implicit but also explicit. The Christian and the Hindu not only share the same hope, not only meet others in faith, but each actually embraces his 'ideal', whether it be God, Christ or his chosen *iṣṭadeva*, and communicates with him in the person of his brothers and sisters, the Men of this earth, without distinction of race, creed or condition. If he really loves them, he discovers the Christ or his *iṣṭadeva* already in them. It is Christ himself (Christ the Unknown) who has awakened that love, and neither the Christian nor the Hindu will be able to explain how he came to be inflamed by it. Love unifies, makes one.

This religious encounter is in reality much more than a meeting of two friends; it is a communion in being, in the one Being which is much more intimate to both than they are to themselves. It is communion not only *in* Christ but also *of* Christ. No condescension, no paternalism or superiority is to be found in the true encounter. Whether one's role is one of teaching or learning matters not at all in the unity of love. He who has the higher intensity, the richer knowledge of a certain area of spirituality will spontaneously dispense what he has, share it with the other, his neighbour.

Only when a Man is completely empty of himself, is in a state of *kenosis*, of renunciation and annihilation, will Christ fulfil his incarnation in him. Only *kenosis* allows incarnation, and incarnation is the only way to redemption. Only the *naiṣkarmya* attitude, the renunciation of the fruits of any good action, only the ego-less action in which the *ahaṃkāra* has been overcome, leads Man to his true Self and allows him to serve and liberate the whole World.

2

HINDUISM AND CHRISTIANITY

ye yathā māṃ prapadyante tāṃstathaiva bhajāmyaham,
mama vartmānuvartante manusyāḥ pārtha sarvaśaḥ

BG IV, 11

In whatsoever way Men approach me, even so do I reward them; for it is my path, O Pārtha, that Men follow in all things.

οὐκ ἔστιν προσωπολήμπτης ὁ θεός, ἀλλ' ἐν παντὶ ἔθνει ὁ φοβούμενος αὐτὸν καὶ ἐργαζόμενος δικαιοσύνην δεκτὸς αὐτῷ ἐστιν.

Acts 10:34–5[1]

God is not a respecter of persons, but in every nation he who fears him and does what is right is acceptable to him.

1. *STATUS QUAESTIONIS*

a) An Ecumenical Problem

One of the most encouraging phenomena of our times is the widespread and sincere desire for mutual understanding, which is coupled with a real thirst for universality.[2] Geography and history are becoming ever more global, leaving behind the limited dimensions of the past.[3] Hardly any individual or group—whether nation, race, culture or religious

[1] This text not only means that personal good will is acceptable, but also contains a definite cultic reference: God accepts the 'sacrifices' of other religions.

[2] We are dealing with so vast a problem that we can only dedicate one or two sentences to questions that require full development. In order to indicate the wider context of our approach, we give further references in the notes and refer the reader to the bibliography. These are meant as a kind of orientation in the dense jungle of relevant modern literature.

[3] Cf. A. Toynbee, *A Study of History.* 10 vols, O.U.P 1934–54; F. Heer, *Quellgrund dieser Zeit.* Einsiedeln, Johannes Verlag, 1956; idem, *Europäische Geistesgeschichte.* Stuttgart, Kohlhammer, 1953; C. Dawson, *Dynamics of World History.* London, Sheed and Ward, 1957; and the classical works by P. Hazard, A. V. Randa, C. J. Burckhardt, Pirenne, etc.

confession—wants to be shut off from the rest of the world, locked up as it were in particularism, nationalism, regionalism, isolationism or in any other 'ism' that denotes a lack of universality.[4] This need for universality appears in many seemingly antithetical but actually convergent movements, in which people of our times are beginning to see the danger of mere abstractions, generalizations and uprootedness and are becoming increasingly aware of the value of the concrete, of the person, and of our earthly roots.[5] If we could develop the urge for universality without neglecting the concrete, a prospect full of promise would undoubtedly open out before us.[6] Of course it must be admitted that this trend towards a global perspective is still the privilege of minorities all over the world. On account of socio-political and economic factors, most of the peoples of the earth are still absorbed in their own urgent local needs. Yet at the same time they long for a liberation such as may usher in not only justice but also universality.

The Christian ecumenical movement is a prime example of this general trend, and an important one for the shaping of the future.[7] Christians are becoming more and more aware that their divisions and divergencies are untenable and are sincerely trying to overcome them. At the same time they are at pains to avoid facile compromises, which are so easily the

[4] See for instance UNESCO, *Interrelations of Cultures: Their Contribution to International Understanding* 1953; UNESCO, *Traditional Cultures* (Proceedings of the Seminar organised by the University of Madras). University of Madras 1956; UNESCO (comp.), *Freedom and Culture*. London, Wingate, 1951. Pax Romana, *La Culture et les Cultures* (Assemblée Générale et Session d'Études de Beyrouth, April, 1956). Beyrouth, U.C.I.L., 1956. *Der Kongress für die Freiheit der Kultur, Wissenschaft und Freiheit* (Internationale Tagung). Hamburg-Berlin, Grünewald, 1954. *The Great Scriptures* (Papers presented at the first Seminar of the Union for the Study of the Great Religions), ed. T. M. P. Mahadevan. Madras, G. S. Press, 1956.

[5] Cf. the works and the significance of E. Mounier, R. Guardini, T. Steinbüchel, G. Thibon, M. de Corte, S. Weil, E. Massis, G. Marcel.

[6] Cf. F. Heer, *Begegnung mit dem Feinde*. Recklinghausen, Paulus, 1955.

[7] See the article by J. Corbon, 'Pour un oecuménisme intégral' in *Proche Orient Chrétien*, 1959, no. 4. Cf. also A. Kardinal Bea, *Der Ökumenismus im Konzil*. Freiburg, Herder, 1969; H. Fries, *Ökumene statt Konfessionen? Das Ringen der Kirche um Einheit*. Frankfurt, Knecht, 1977.

fruit of indifference to others' convictions and lack of loyalty to one's own.[8]

In an attempt to reach a deeper and more authentic Christian unity, Christian ecumenism seeks a truthful middle path which will permit dialogue and encounter between different Christian confessions without imposing solutions in anticipation of the problems or compelling disloyalty to concrete personal faith. In other words, true ecumenism is not minimalist, i.e., it does not try to establish unity by relying on a minimum of indisputable points held in common, but maximalist, i.e., it attempts to affirm unity at that higher level towards which all aspire. The danger of minimalism is clear: matter is in fact the one thing common to all.[9] Between two different sets of convictions uniformity on the conceptual level is at best provisional, for the more that concepts are elaborated by successive persons, the more likely they are to diverge. However, unity on the level of the mystery, of the unmanifest, must almost by definition be an authentic unity, since it cannot be conceptualized. There is more difference between, for instance, Saint Francis and Saint Dominic, two Catholic saints of the same century, than between a lukewarm Roman Catholic and a lukewarm Methodist. There is more unity, however, between the former pair, though there is less uniformity. In fact, the higher the being on the scale of beings, the more it is differentiated from others. Let us remember that the differences between the Persons of the Trinity are infinite—nothing can be finite in God—and yet their unity is absolute. But all this is only by way of introduction.

A similar movement is detectable in contemporary Hinduism, although the historical and 'theological' situation is quite different. There has never been such a thing as 'Hindu unity' or 'unity of the Indian religions', because Hinduism has no founder and even the Vedas are not universally recog-

[8] See, regarding ecumenical problems, Y. Congar, J. Vajta *et al., Vocabulaire oecuménique*. Paris, Cerf, 1970.

[9] This should be sufficiently proved by the unreal and peculiar conception of 'natural religion' of the eighteenth and nineteenth centuries in Europe—which should also be a warning for those who are at present discussing 'natural law'.

nized; but in spite of great differences there has been a certain consciousness of unity like that of plants growing in the same soil. The challenges which modernity presents to traditional religions and the coming closer of the different religions, sects and schools on all levels—due to means of communication, social and political life—are contributing to a general trend towards universality, both among the different traditions of Hinduism as well as *vis-à-vis* other religions. A number of *sampradāyas* not only collaborate on the socio-political level, but also come together, for example, for the celebration of festivals and pilgrimages. On the other hand, they all try to respond to present-day problems and changing situations by transforming and opening themselves. By way of example one can mention the movement which has led to the opening of certain temples to Harijans and in part to Non-Hindus, thus permitting members of other religious communities to participate in ceremonies and worship. In this way even texts which were reserved to the initiates of a particular community are taught to outsiders.[10]

This ecumenical movement detectable within different religions is now in the process of being widened and deepened into an *ecumenical ecumenism*, if the expression is permissible. I mean by this an ecumenism that is really ecumenical, catho-

[10] A most striking and recent example of this 'Hindu ecumenism' has been the Second World Hindu Conference held in Allahabad in January 1979. The heads of religions and sects which had been fighting one another for centuries not only met peacefully, but even requested the Dalai Lama to inaugurate the Conference, in spite of the fact that until recently Buddhism had been considered one of the greatest enemies of Hinduism. Significantly enough, each one of these religious heads (including Sikhs and Jains) stressed repeatedly their unity on the basis of their common heritage and in the face of the challenges with which religion is confronted today. These traditional *jagadgurus* even unanimously agreed to abolish untouchability and caste distinctions in all practical religious matters (by law they were already abolished, but so long as the traditional religious leaders and the faithful continue to practise these distinctions, the law cannot be enforced). Yet in spite of the open, fraternal and universal spirit it was quite clear that the different traditions did not intend to give up their own identity for the sake of a 'mixed Hindu syncretism'. The relation between faithfulness to one's own tradition and openness seems to be not an exclusive one but, rather, inclusive.

lic, engaged not only in a dialogue and encounter between Christian confessions or Hindu *sampradāyas*, but between religions as well. It is certain that this catholic ecumenism would be of great help to inter-Christian ecumenism as well as in solving other specifically Christian problems.[11] Latin-Greek disputes look almost like family quarrels confined to the Mediterranean horizon, if they are compared in scope to, say, the encounter between Christianity and Hinduism.[12] Observation of this fact, though it should not minimize the importance of the Latin-Greek tension, can certainly put it in its proper perspective. We must, of course, not lose sight of the fundamental differences between the problems that arise in encounters between Christians and those that arise in encounters between believers of different religions.[13]

In this chapter I would like to speak further and more specifically of the relationship between Hinduism and Christianity in this wider ecumenical atmosphere, confining myself however to the formal aspect of their relationship and not venturing further into concrete problems.

b) The 'And' of the Relationship

The present study of the relationship between these two religions constitutes just a small chapter in the philosophy,

[11] Likewise, the present concept of philosophy suffers a challenge in the meeting with Eastern 'philosophies'. Similarly, discussions for or against a 'Christian philosophy' could draw some inspiration from encountering other 'philosophies'.

[12] J. Corbon quite rightly points out that 'an ecumenical vocation which limited itself solely to the reunion of the baptised would not be faithful to the call of Christ within history'. 'Ecumenismo e Mistero' in *La Missione* 28, 1960, p. 22. Christian ecumenism is really universal, inserted in the very dynamism of history, or it is not true ecumenism.

[13] See, for the expression and for the ecumenical attitude, the article by O. Karrer 'Ökumenische Katholizität' in *Hochland* IV, 1959, pp. 297–314; and for an authentic ecumenical spirit, the remarkable writings of the German Protestants belonging to the 'Sammlung' (H. Asmussen, M. Lackmann, R. Baumann, W. Stälin, etc.) in *Istina I*, 1959, pp. 93–106. Cf. also Y. M.-J. Congar, *Divided Christendom: A Catholic Study of the Problem of Re-Union.* London, G. Bles, 1939.

or rather the theology, of religion.[14] Hence we presuppose a knowledge of what both Christianity and Hinduism are from ancient as well as modern sources.[15]

It seems useful to examine the value of the conjunction 'and' that relates Hinduism and Christianity. Needless to say, a simple 'and' may be of the utmost importance; we may recall that Eastern and Western Christian traditions have already had long discussions about the meaning of another 'and' in relation to the *filioque* controversy. However, our main concern now is Hinduism, and we wish to keep in mind both its Indian cultural context and the general issues that emerge in any encounter of religions.

First I shall express the situation in purely Christian terms[16] before attempting any kind of interpretation: Christ is the

[14] Any believer will experience a salutary feeling of uneasiness in giving a mere list of books as an introduction to his belief, because living faith cannot adequately be expressed in any written form whatsoever. He knows his faith and lives by it and will only refer to one book or another according to the special circumstances in which he finds himself or in which he believes his partner in dialogue to be. We are also taken aback when asked about literature on Hinduism or on Christianity. This remark should be kept in mind for the following notes.

[15] In such an endeavour certain generalizations are unavoidable. While speaking of 'Hinduism' and 'Christianity' we do not forget that these are two complex religions, concerning which many differentiations are required. What we are analysing here is their formal relationship.

[16] Since the time when this book was written, the ideas expressed here regarding the relationship of Christianity to the other world-religions in the universal economy of salvation have been generally accepted and have been developed in some detail by many theologians. We do not intend to rewrite these pages completely since they represent, so to say, a historical moment in this new theological understanding. For literature on this subject see e.g. K. Rahner, 'Das Christentum und die nichtchristlichen Religionen' in *Schriften zur Theologie* V, pp. 136–58; H. R. Schlette, *Die Religionen als Thema der Theologie*; idem, 'Einige Thesen zum Selbstverständnis der Religionen' in *Gott in Welt*, Bd. 2 (Freiburg, Herder, 1964), pp. 306–16; J. Heislbetz, *Theologische Gründe der nichtchristlichen Religionen*; H. Küng, 'The World Religions in God's Plan of Salvation' in J. Neuner, ed., *Christian Revelation and World Religions*; H. Waldenfels, 'Zur Heilsbedeutung der nichtchristlichen Religionen in katholischer Sicht' in *Zeitschrift für Missionswissenschaft und Religionswissenschaft* 53 (1969), pp. 257–78; H. Bürkle, *Einführung in die Theologie der Religionen*, and the bibliography given there.

universal redeemer.[17] There is no redemption apart from him.[18] Where there is no redemption there is no salvation. Therefore, any human person who is saved—and we know by reason and by faith that God provides everybody with the necessary means of salvation—is saved by Christ, the only redeemer.[19] This amounts to saying that Christ is present in one form or another in every human being as he journeys towards God.[20]

Though the Church in the mystical sense may thus be considered as the locus of the action of Christ in all the World, Christianity itself, or the Church as an institution, is a concrete religion that claims to be the normal and ordinary place of Christ's redeeming power and saving action.[21] What role does Hinduism play, if this is the state of affairs?[22] There are

[17] See Eph. 1:3–14ff.
[18] See Col. 1:13–22ff.
[19] Cf. M. Schmaus, 'Gott der Erlöser', *Katholische Dogmatik* II, 2. München, M. Hueber, 1955, which will spare us from further references. See also section 5c) in this chapter.
[20] Cf. K. Adam, *The Christ of Faith*. London, Burns & Oates, 1957.
[21] Cf. M. Schmaus, 'Die Lehre von der Kirche', *Katholische Dogmatik* III, 1. München, M. Hueber, 1958; H. de Lubac, *Catholicisme*. 5th edn. Paris, Ed. du Cerf, 1952.
[22] Cf. E. W. Thompson, *The Word of the Cross to Hindus*. Madras, CLS, 1956. We should make reference here to several articles which appeared in *Light of the East* by G. Dandoy and P. Johanns. Some of the articles by Johanns were published in book form: *To Christ Through the Vedānta*. Cf. also H. J. D'Souza, 'Catholicism Meets Hinduism' in *World Mission* VIII, 2 (Summer 1957), pp. 64–80. (We do not fully share the optimism he expressed in vol. ix, n. 44:62–74 of the same journal.) Since the first edn of this book, Vatican II has for the first time in the history of the Church expressed a positive and explicit evaluation of other religions in which Hinduism is expressly mentioned. See the 'Declaration on the Relationship of the Church to Non-Christian Religions' (*Nostra aetate*) in *The Documents of Vatican II*. (London, Geoffrey Chapman, 1966), pp. 660–71. Cf. also the commentaries, e.g. in *Lexikon für Theologie und Kirche, Das zweite Vatikanische Konzil . . .*, Bd. 2 (Freiburg, Herder, 1967), pp. 405–95; R. Panikkar, 'Church and the World Religions' in *Religion and Society*, vol. xiv, no. 2 (Bangalore 1967), pp. 59–63; idem, 'Christianity and the World Religions' in *Christianity* (Collective work) (Patiala, Punjabi University, 1969), pp. 78–127; P. Schreiner, 'Die Heiligkeit der Religionen und die Dokumente des Zweiten Vatikanischen Konzils' in *Zeitschrift für Missionswissenschaft und Religionswissenschaft* 56 (1972), pp. 108–22.

only two possible kinds of answer:[23] either Hinduism is not a channel for any possible action of Christ whatsoever (i.e. Christ would then save good Hindus in spite of and against their Hinduism), or *somehow* Hinduism is incorporated into the universal economy of salvation by God through Christ.[24] The second alternative does not deny, of course, that salvation is always a personal affair, nor, on the other hand, does it imply that the whole of Hinduism as a concrete historical religion has saving power[25]—neither, for that matter, has the whole of Christianity. However, the question remains whether Hinduism as such has any place in the (Christian) economy of salvation.

In Hindu terms, Christianity, like other major religions, will lead its faithful to liberation to the extent that it imparts to their hearts the three central truths of the *sanātana dharma*, the eternal religion: namely, that God is, that he can be realized, and that the purpose of life is to realize him. This realization, this liberation, is *homeomorphic* with what the

[23] This problem was felt in Christianity from the very beginning. Cf. the following text of the second century:

> Here we have the following alternatives: either the Lord cares not for all men—which might arise from incapacity (but this it is forbidden to say, for incapacity is a mark of weakness), or from want of will on the part of one possessed with power (but such an affection is incompatible with goodness . . .)—or he has regard for us all, which also beseems him who was made Lord of all. For he is the saviour not of one here and another there, but to the extent of each man's fitness, he distributed his own bounty both to Greeks and to barbarians, and to the faithful and elect . . .

Clement of Alexandria, *Stromata* II, 6, tr. J. B. Mayor, J. E. L. Oulton and H. Chadwick in *Alexandrian Christianity*, The Library of Christian Classics II (London, SCM, 1954), pp. 96–7.

[24] See O. Karrer, *Das Religiöse in der Menschheit und das Christentum*. Cf. the articles on concrete topics by J. Monchanin, 'Yoga et hesychasme, Apophatisme et Apavāda'; and A. Bareau, 'L'Absolu dans le bouddhisme', *Entretiens*. Pondicherry, Institut Français d'Indologie, 1955; F. König, ed., *Christus und die Religionen der Erde*, 3 vols. especially the last study by the editor, 'Das Christentum und die Weltreligionen', III: 731–76; B. Kelly, 'Notes on the Light of the Eastern Religions' in *Dominican Studies* (1954), pp. 254–71.

[25] We shall return to this problem. See p. 90ff.

Christians call salvation.[26] The 'relationship' of religions is scarcely a problem when all are seen as forms of the eternal religion.

The present study, however, tackles the problem from a Christian perspective because through the centuries Christians have felt the problem more acutely. Relationships with other religions have been problematic to the highest degree because of exclusivistic interpretations of the action of Christ. Our thesis attempts to formulate just one aspect of the second Christian alternative mentioned above, namely finding a way of integrating the Hindu and the Christian 'economies' by means of the conjunction *and*. This is the whole problem *in nuce*, since the expression 'Hinduism and Christianity' itself does not seem immediately significant or problematic. In other words: is there really any 'and' that links the two, and, if so, in what sense does it do so?

2. FIRST APPROACHES

I shall start the discussion negatively, by eliminating interpretations of the relationship that are inadequate or untrue; then I shall offer positive suggestions for a way to view the relationship which will neither contradict the doctrines nor (I hope) offend the sensibilities of Hindus or Christians.

Most of the missionary studies of today are beginning to reconsider the theological justification of missions.[27] The negative part of the discussion may therefore seem outdated and no longer necessary in these days of changing attitudes. But those older views are still alive and form the concrete historical background of our discussion, since they were the views which created the conditions for Christianity's encounter with other religions. They must therefore be taken seriously into account, if only to show the evolution of Christian thought.

The relationship between Hinduism and Christianity finds in the conjunction *and* a more or less adequate expression, in that *and* itself, being neutral, does not favour either of the two

[26] Cf. M. Dhavamony in *Studia Missionalia* 29 (1980) on *Salvation*, pp. 209ff.
[27] Cf. e.g. G. Evers, *Mission—Nichtchristliche Religionen—Weltliche Welt*; J. Schütte, ed., *Mission nach dem Konzil*. See Bibliography I.

terms. Hence the polar opposites such as falsehood-truth, darkness-light, sin-sanctity, damnation-salvation and even natural-supernatural are not implicit in the simple conjunction, though they were long used among Christians to characterize Hinduism and Christianity respectively. After years of contact, another kind of characterization, mutually more sympathetic, began to be considered more satisfactory, namely dynamic pairs such as potency-act, seed-fruit, forerunner-real presence, symbol-reality, desire-accomplishment, allegory-thing in itself, and even the specifically Christian dynamism of death and resurrection.[28]

The relationship under study, however, is a relationship *sui generis*, a peculiar one which differentiates itself from and cannot be included in any other.[29] For understanding's sake, however, it has traditionally been expressed by *analogy* with other pairs, as in the sets of oppositions and dynamisms listed above, even though it cannot adequately be classified under any of them.[30] Herein lies the problem.

Before stating what I now feel to be the true relationship of the two religions, let us systematically explore the implications and limitations, in today's world, of the two kinds of characterizations that have been considered valid in our recent past.

3. SIN AND SANCTITY; ERROR AND TRUTH

The relationship between Hinduism and Christianity cannot be one of opposites, as past missionary approaches main-

[28] I agree with K. Klostermaier (*Kristvidya* [Bangalore, Christian Institute for the Study of Religion and Society, 1967], p. 11) that 'the *actus-potentia* scheme' would not lead us very far, but it may be a starting-point for a certain habit of thinking.

[29] For the praxis of the Church in this matter, see A. V. Seumois, *La papauté et les missions au cours des six premiers siècles* (Eglise Vivante). Paris, 1951; G. Bardy, *La conversion au Christianisme durant les premiers siècles*. Paris, Aubier, 1949.

[30] See the first Christian treatise on the salvation of non-Christians, written about 450: Prosper of Aquitaine, *Duo libri de vocatione omnium gentium*, especially the translation and study by P. de Letter, *St. Prosper of Aquitaine, The Call of All Nations*, Ancient Christian Writers 14. London, Longmans, 1952.

tained, as if the one embodied sin and the other sanctity, the one falsehood and the other truth.

First, these opposites are too static. From sin to sanctity, from darkness to light—or between any two such hermetically sealed concepts—no possibility is allowed or envisaged of a bridge or over-pass or any form of transit. To call a religion a sinful religion or a vehicle of darkness (or damnation or falsehood) amounts to saying that in fact it is not a religion at all. Every religion deals with the salvation or liberation of Man, which means union with God, divinization of our being, the acquisition of truth, sanctity, light, and of freedom from the bonds of injustice, slavery, the passions of worldly existence, and so on. To characterize a religion as sinful or dark would be to call it a non-religion, a would-be religion lacking the power which belongs to the phenomena that we call religions.[31]

Further, since very few human minds would choose falsehood over truth, darkness over light, and hence sin over sanctity, or damnation over salvation, if they truly saw them as false, dark or sinful, it is safe to say that if anyone knew his religion to be falsehood, he would not trouble to follow its injunctions or to hold its beliefs. If Hinduism is in fact darkness, it is clear that its followers do not recognize that it is. This, then, is a one-sided judgement which must be justified by those who make it. However, this is also theologically impossible.[32]

Furthermore, if Hinduism were adjudged by Christianity to be utter error and sheer falsehood, a Hindu would not only be wholly repelled by such a preposterous attitude but indeed

[31] This inner conviction manifests itself in the theologies of K. Barth and H. Kraemer which are thus led to condemn all religions as the impotent work of Man and to absolve the Christian movement or faith from being a 'religion'. Cf. K. Barth, 'Gottes Offenbarung als Aufhebung der Religion' in *Kirchliche Dogmatik* I/2, 17 (Zollikon-Zürich, 1938), pp. 304–97; H. Kraemer, *Religion and the Christian Faith* and *The Christian Message in a Non-Christian World*. (See Bibliography I.)

[32] This is the ground of the once accepted hypothesis that God saves those who are in a (for them) unsurmountable error!

ought not on theoretical grounds to accept it.[33] Is he to believe that a loving God and merciful redeemer, such as the Christian affirms him to be, has been so fanciful, if not so cruel, as to leave him, up to the time of his encounter with Christianity, in total darkness and falsehood? Even if he were prepared in all humility to recognize his personal sins, could he believe that all the glorious saints of Hinduism—perhaps some of them his ancestors—were mere impostors, both deceivers and deceived, or rascals and damned? He would justifiably come to the conclusion that such a Christian God must be highly partial, indeed not much better than the jealous God of some passages of the Old Testament, and that the Christian concept is certainly inferior to the sublime concept of God in the Indian tradition.

4. THE NATURAL AND THE SUPERNATURAL

Another paradigm which does not help is the alleged distinction between Hinduism as a natural and Christianity as a supernatural religion. I do not wish here to enter into purely Christian theological discussions which have already challenged the validity of this distinction except in the epistemological realm (for in fact 'natural-supernatural' primarily designates two modes of knowing).[34] To apply these terms to two distinct historical religions would be an illegitimate extrapolation. However, I discard this hypothesis also on other grounds.

First of all, if true religion is considered to be 'supernatural', a 'natural' religion is a contradiction in terms. Either it is religion, i.e. a way of life that leads to the attainment of Man's goal (however it may be conceived) and then it is 'supernatural' (it breaks through the barriers of the factual human situation), or it is no religion at all. For salvation is precisely the transit, the passage from the natural to the supernatural; the transformation or radical mutation from

[33] See S. Radhakrishnan, *An Idealist View of Life*. London, Allen and Unwin, 1927.

[34] See First Vatican Council, Session III (Const. *de fide*), especially chap. 4 (Denz. 1795, etc.). Cf. also H. de Lubac, *Surnaturel*. Paris, Aubier, 1946; idem, *Le mystère du surnaturel*. Paris, Aubier, 1965.

natural Man to the supernatural, divinized person; the rupture of planes, a breach in the distinctions matter/spirit, nameable/nameless, the transcending of selfness/otherness.

Christianity may be supernatural in a specific sense, but Hinduism cannot be called natural religion in the sense of being just a product of nature. This would debase it to being a mere projection of the human mind.[35] The term 'natural' also retains too many reminiscences of the naturalism of past centuries. Even if we were to affirm that Hinduism was the creation of the human mind, where is the human mind which is not enlightened by God, 'the Light illuminating every Man that comes into the World'? It would not be simply a 'natural' mind, but rather a fallen mind which, like every existing mind, is already experiencing the call of Christ, for he died for the whole of Mankind.[36] The human being may therefore be either fallen or redeemed, but not simply 'natural'. Or, to be more precise, Man's 'existential condition'[37] is not simply 'fallen', because the mystery of the Cross has a universal efficacy; yet it is not simply 'redeemed' or supernatural either, since the effects of redemption have not yet been fully ac-

[35] See the remarkable, though sometimes still too dualistic, collective vol. by A. Chavasse, J. Frisque, H. Denis, R. Garnier, *Église et Apostolat* (Église Vivante). Paris, Casterman, 1953.

[36] See chapter IV of the Synod of Quiercy: '*Christus . . . sicut nullus homo est, fuit vel erit, cujus natura in illo assumpta non fuerit, ita nullus est, fuit vel erit homo, pro quo passus non fuerit . . .*' ('There is no man and never has been or will be whose nature has not been assumed in Jesus Christ our Lord; similarly there is none nor has been or will be for whom he has not suffered his passion, even though not all are redeemed by the mystery of his passion.') Denz. 319. Cf. a traditional text: '*Sed sicut in Adam omnes moriuntur, ita et in Christo omnes vivificabuntur* (cf. 1 Cor. 15:22). *Itaque sicut primitiae mortis in Adam, ita etiam primitiae resurrectionis in Christo omnes resurgent. . . . Omnes quidem resurgent, sed unusquisque, ut ait Apostolus* (ibid., 23), *in suo ordine. Communis est divinae fructus clementiae, sed distinctus ordo meritorum.*' ('For as in Adam all die, so also in Christ shall all be made alive [cf. 1 Cor. 15:22]. Therefore, as the first-fruits of death are in Adam, so also the first-fruits of the resurrection are in Christ, in whom all will rise again. . . . All indeed will rise again, but, as the Apostle says [ibid., 23], each in his order. The fruit of the divine goodness is common to all, but the order of merits is different.') Ambros., *De fide resurrectionis* (*apud Brev. Rom., lect.* V, *dom.* V *p. Pascha*).

[37] See R. Panikkar, 'Freiheit und Gewissen' in *Neues Abendland* 10 (1955), n. 1, pp. 25–32.

cepted or acknowledged.[38] Let us not forget that we are now dealing with the *human spirit* facing ultimate religious problems, not just technical or mathematical questions of the natural realm wherein the 'natural' *human mind* has its *ontonomy*.

Finally, the dichotomy natural-supernatural and its subclasses of opposites are not applicable to Hinduism and Christianity respectively, because the proper place of these distinctions is, instead, within each human being—Hindu or Christian—who is in the process of conversion from merely 'created' structures to the living God who calls him to share his own Life.[39]

5. THE INADEQUACIES OF THE SUPERIORITY APPROACH

We do not want to exclude out of hand the possibility that, from a particular viewpoint, one of the two religions may be better than the other. Obviously this point of view will be relative, i.e. dependent upon a certain set of convictions or doctrines which will require critical examination. Even this, however, in no way justifies a superiority approach, as if the sociological complex called Christianity were actually superior to the other socio-religious complex called Hinduism.

Three sets of considerations prevent us from adopting such an attitude: a) the psychological/pastoral: a superiority approach is contrary to religious honesty as well as to what may be called the 'Christian spirit'; b) the historical: history provides no evidence for it; and c) the theological: the superiority approach is not consistent with Christian theology.

[38] Cf. the distinction between an 'objective or potential' and a 'subjective or actual' redemption in U. Lattanzi, *Il primato universale di Cristo secondo le S. Scritture* (Rome, Lateran, 1937), p. 57.

[39] '. . . Whatever concerns man's exit from God may be called the natural order; and whatever has regard to man's return to God may be called the supernatural order.' G. M. Dupont, *Foundation for a Devotion to the Blessed Trinity* (Calcutta, The Oriental Institute, 1947), p. 132. Cf. Thomas Aquinas, *In I Sent.*, d. 14, q. 2, a. 2.

a) Psychological and Pastoral Inadequacy

Whoever maintains that Christianity and Hinduism are to be assessed on a comparative basis (true/less true, superior/inferior) automatically shuts the door to any communication and any understanding.[40] Nothing could be more distant from the Christian spirit.

Christ, certainly, came to teach: he is the Master.[41] He taught, however, by his own example and by parables, by being open to the exigencies of the truth and by serving instead of being served[42]—not by preaching 'at' people and claiming to 'have' the truth. Nothing is so dangerous in the Christian apostolate as the paternalistic attitude and false security of one who thinks he is in full *possession* of the truth.[43] The true Christian (as also the true Hindu) possesses nothing, not even the truth. Rather, he is possessed by the truth, as Thomas Aquinas points out.[44] He knows God because he is known by him.[45] This makes the truly religious Man uncompromising in his attitude towards error. He cannot yield an inch[46] from a truth of which he feels himself to be the servant, yet he does not feel that he belongs to an 'exclusive bourgeois club' which sits comfortably on the 'true way' and condescends to point out the path of salvation to others.[47] Rather, he is a pilgrim seeking his way, trying to pass in at the narrow gate,[48] going with fear and trembling,[49] humbly checking his beliefs and acts so that he himself may not be 'a castaway' even while preaching the true doctrine to others, as Saint

[40] See J. Levie, *Sous les yeux de l'incroyant,* 2nd edn. Paris, Desclée, L'édition universelle, 1946.
[41] See John 13:14ff.
[42] See Matt. 20:28; Phil 2:7.
[43] Cf. H. Duméry, 'La tentation de faire du bien' in *Esprit,* Jan. 1955, pp. 1–34.
[44] *I Metaphys* 3 (Nr. 64).
[45] Gal. 4:9; cf. 1 Cor. 8:3.
[46] Cf. the typical utterance of Tertullian—which has to be rightly understood in its context: 'After one has believed there is but one thing more to believe, namely that there is nothing more to believe.' *De praescriptione haereticorum* 9.
[47] Cf. Matt. 23:1ff.
[48] Luke 13:24.
[49] Phil. 2:12.

Paul himself feared.[50] He is aware of the perilous nature of spiritual life, knowing that the fact of having eaten and drunk in the presence of the Lord,[51] or of having cried 'Lord, Lord',[52] or even of having performed miracles in his name,[53] will not save him. His example,[54] service to others,[55] and 'service of the Word'[56] by which he imparts the doctrine which he has received[57] and of which he has no power to modify so much as an *iota*,[58] is what the Christian offers to the World. The privilege of the Christian faith, if we wish to term it thus, is only a vocation to a special service.[59] The Christian way is always one of co-redemption.[60] It is a way of friendship, according to the example and the explicit teaching of Christ himself, and friendship presupposes mutual communication, confidence and a certain equality.[61] Where this does not exist, no communication is possible and without it there is no *kerygma*, no proclamation of the Word, no transmitting of faith.[62] And where communication does not arise, communion is not possible. Hence even from a psychological point of view such an attitude of superiority and exclusiveness is incompatible with the Christian duty of apostolate.[63]

Further, a religion is an organic set of beliefs and practices which can only change through natural growth from within and not by merely external imitation or artificial imposition. It has often been remarked that Hinduism, despite having an excellent relationship with Western Christianity, does not like

[50] 1 Cor. 9:27.
[51] Luke 13:26.
[52] Matt. 7:21.
[53] Matt. 7:22–3.
[54] Matt. 5:16ff.
[55] Luke 10:37.
[56] Acts 6:4.
[57] Matt. 28:18–20; Mark 16:15–16.
[58] Matt. 5:17–20.
[59] See John 13:13–17.
[60] Cf. R. Panikkar, 'The Relation of Christians to their Non-Christian surroundings' in *Christian Revelation and World Religions*, ed. J. Neuner, pp. 143–84.
[61] See John 15:14ff.
[62] Rom. 10:17.
[63] Cf. John 10:1 ff.; Matt. 10:16 ff.

to be imitated. It makes a stand against so-called Christian adaptation because, on the assumption that Christian missionaries really believed Hinduism to be falsehood, such adaptation could only be an expedient for ushering in foreign beliefs in a familiar guise. It amounts to hypocrisy and even dishonesty to appropriate the shell of a religion without knowing its kernel, which is the *raison d'être* of the shell. This is what alienates the Hindu and makes him dislike intrusion, imitation, adaptation.[64] Even if Christians express interest in assimilating the positive values of Hinduism, it is seen as robbery by the orthodox Hindu because these Christians are not likely to know Hinduism from within, to know the heart, the core from which those same values grew.[65] Similarly it would be futile and merely superficial if Hinduism were simply to adopt certain characteristic features of Christianity, if those features had not evolved out of the heart of Hinduism nor were an expression of a deep experience of the reality of Christianity. Yet we can learn from each other.[66]

b) Historical Experience

The superiority approach cannot in any sense stand the test of history. Even the most elementary history seems to prove

[64] Nothing is more delicate than collective psychology. Cultures and religions have a psychological component but cannot be reduced to psychological factors. For an acquaintance with Indian mentality, cf. the works of R. Kipling, Mahatma Gandhi, R. Tagore, R. K. Narayan, M. R. Anand, A. K. Coomaraswamy, C. F. Andrews, G. M. Carstairs *et al.*

[65] See G. Dandoy, *Catholicism and Natural Cultures*. Light of the East Series, no. 27, Calcutta, 1939.

[66] It would be worthwhile to make a study of the deep meaning of idolatry, showing how it could impart a richer meaning to the Christian ideas of presence and adoration. On a parallel issue, see the inspiring book by J. Lacroix, *Sens de l'athéisme*. Tournai, Casterman, 1958. Hints can also be found, for instance, in M. Éliade, *Patterns in Comparative Religion*. (London, Sheed & Ward, 1958), pp. 25–30; and in his *Images et symboles*. Paris, Gallimard, 1952. See also: A. K. Coomaraswamy, *Figures of Speech or Figures of Thought* (London, Luzac, 1946), pp. 216–46; G. van der Leeuw, *L'homme primitif et la religion*. Paris, P.U.F., 1940; A. le Roy, *La religion des primitifs*. Paris, Beauchesne, 1925; S. Lévi, *La doctrine du sacrifice dans les Brāhmaṇas* (Bibl. Hautes Études). Paris, E. Leroux, 1898; cf. R. Panikkar, 'Eucharistischer Glaube und Idolatrie' in *Kairos*, 1961, n. 2; idem, *Le mystère du culte dans l'hindouisme et le christianisme*.

beyond any doubt that the history of Christian nations and even that of Christianity itself have not always been models of righteousness and virtue, nor has the relationship between Christians and non-Christians throughout history been a charitable and merciful encounter.[67] If it had been so, the difference between the history of Christian peoples and that of other cultures would have been so strikingly clear as to leave no doubt about the superiority of Christianity. But the fact is that history cannot be accounted a witness in favour of Christianity.[68]

Moreover, it is inappropriate in this context to cite the unworthiness of individual Christians in order to save the 'worth' of Christianity,[69] because the question is not so much whether Christians are good or bad Christians according to a theoretically pure Christianity, but whether Christianity as a whole—including its history—stands with regard to Hinduism as a whole in such a superior position that the analogy of the positive-negative pairs mentioned above is an accurate characterization of their relationship.

Certainly, some forms of popular Hinduism may be full of superstition, degraded features and impurities. But the history of Christianity also is not exempt from such features. Furthermore, an impartial history would find it hard to deny that Hinduism also presents miracles and stupendous facts such as are recorded in the history of Christianity. It is an accepted

[67] See Cardinal Tisserant, *Eastern Christianity in India*. Bombay, Orient Longmans, 1957. For a systematic survey, see *Histoire universelle des missions catholiques*, 2 vols., ed. Delacroix. Paris, Grund, 1956–7. Cf. also the following general works: J. T. Addison, *The Medieval Missionary*, Studies in the World Mission of Christianity 11, New York, I.M.C., 1936; J. Glazik, 'Die russisch-orthodoxe Heidenmission seit Peter dem Grossen' in *Ein missionsgeschichtlicher Versuch nach Quellen und Darstellung*. Münster, Aschendorff, 1954; K. S. Latourette, *A History of the Expansion of Christianity*. New York, Harper, 1937–45.

[68] See, as typical examples, S. Radhakrishnan, *Eastern Religions and Western Thought*; K. M. Panikkar, *Asia and Western Dominance*. London, Allen & Unwin, 1955. Cf. also, in a different line altogether, T. Ohm, *Asiens Nein und Ja zum westlichen Christentum*; idem, *Asiens Kritik am abendländischen Christentum*. München, Kösel, 1948.

[69] See N. Berdyaev, *De la dignité du christianisme et de l'indignité des chrétiens*. Paris, 1931.

Christian idea that the History of Christianity presents undeniable proofs of a very special providence, especially as regards the prophecies before Christ and the miracles after him.[70] But nowhere in Christian doctrine is it said that in order to extol the merits of Christianity we should hide, minimize or deny the merits of other religions.[71]

The spiritual history of Hinduism is full of instances parallel to that of Christ finding in the non-Jewish woman[72] or in the Roman officer[73] more faith than in the house of Israel.[74] The spiritual history of both past and present Hinduism records instances of true virtue, real sanctity, authentic mysticism, undeniable miracles and true charity.[75] If any Western Christian should read these lines with a touch of scepticism I would invite him to consider for himself the life-witness of other religions.[76] 'Where do you dwell, Lord?' 'Come and

[70] Cf. *Conc. Trid.* III, 3 (Denz. 1798), and *Sacrorum antistitum*, 1 January, 1910 (Denz. 2145).

[71] See Exod. 22:28 (though it could be interpreted along the lines of Acts 23:5).

[72] Matt. 15:28.

[73] Matt. 8:10; Luke 7:9.

[74] The last word of Matins on the last day of the liturgical year in the Latin rite seems to be a rebuke of Israel and an acceptance of the 'peoples':

> *Non est mihi voluntas in vobis, dicit Dominus exercituum, et munus non suscipiam de manu vestra; ab ortu enim solis usque ad occasum magnum est nomen meum in gentibus et in omni loco sacrificatur et offertur nomini meo oblatio munda, quia magnum est nomen meum in gentibus, dicit Dominus exercituum.* Mal. 1:10 (*Mat. Sabbat infra Hebdom.* V *Novembris, lect.* 3).
>
> I am not pleased with you, says Yahweh Sabaoth; from your hands I find no offerings acceptable. But from farthest east to farthest west my name is honoured among the nations and everywhere a sacrifice of incense is offered to my name, and a pure offering too, since my name is honoured among the nations, says Yahweh Sabaoth (Jerusalem Bible).

[75] Cf. J. Monchanin, H. Le Saux, *Ermites du Saccidānanda*, 2nd edn. Paris, Casterman, 1957; Abhishikteśvarānanda, 'Le monachisme chrétien aux Indes' in *La Vie Spirituelle* supp. 38 (15 Sept. 1956), pp. 288–316. Cf. also S. N. Dasgupta, *Hindu Mysticism*. New York, Frederick Ungar, 1927. For Śaṅkara's biography see M. Piantelli, *Śaṅkara e la rinascita del brahmanesimo*. Fossano, Editrice Esperienze, 1974.

[76] See Abhishikteśvarānanda, 'L'hindouisme est-il toujours vivant?' in *La Vie intellectuelle* XI (1956), pp. 2–40; the entire issue is dedicated to Hinduism. See also vol. xii, 1956, on 'Vitalité des religions non-chrétiennes'.

see!'[77] Only then, after having seen, can we tackle the theological problem of grace and mysticism outside Christianity or within Christianity itself.[78]

Though salvation ultimately takes place in the unfathomable depths of the human person, the normal divine preparation for this ultimate step uses the more tangible channels of the established religions.[79]

c) Theological Reflection

The superiority approach—and *a fortiori* that which views the relation between Christianity and Hinduism as one of opposition between two poles—is contradicted even by the principles of Christian theology.

Two propositions are universally accepted by Christian theology:[80] one, salvation comes exclusively through Christ;[81]

[77] John 1:38–9.

[78] Cf. a single reference which embraces the Old and the Middle Ages: '*Et Augustinus 1. VII Conf.* (c. 9, n. 1) *dicit se in libris Platonis legisse in principio erat verbum et magnam partem huius primi capituli Johannis.*' ('And Augustine 1. VII Conf. [c. 9, n. 1] says that he has read in the writings of Plato *In the beginning was the word* along with a great part of this first chapter of John.') M. Eckhardt, *Expositio in Ioan.* (initium), no. 2 (Quint's Critical Edn, p. 4). Cf. also '*Dubitandum non est et gentes suos habere prophetas*!' ('It is not to be doubted that the nations also have their own prophets!') August., *Contra Faustum* XIX, 2 (P. L., 42, 348).

[79] Cf. W. Bierbaum, 'Geschichte als Paidagogia Theou—Die Heilsgeschichtslehre des Klemens von Alexandrien' in *Münchener Theologische Zeitschrift* V, 4 (1954), pp. 246–72.

[80] The Hindu reader will, I hope, excuse the theological technicalities of the following paragraphs, which are unavoidable in any dialogue with contemporary Catholic theology.

[81] This does not mean at all that those who psychologically do not know Christ should be damned. The following quotation is typical of this misunderstanding (it obviously does not agree with the orthodox Christian doctrine):

> Augustine's teaching that only a small fraction of humanity, the elect, are destined to bliss while the many are 'reprobate', predetermined to everlasting damnation, is contradicted by the law of *karma* which affirms that by doing what is in our power we can dispose the mind to the love of the Eternal and attain salvation. Man's instinctive sense of justice is bewildered by the bland relegation of a large part of humanity to everlasting torment. S. Radhakrishnan, *The Brahma Sūtra*, pp. 196–7.

As a matter of fact, most of the traditional religions of the world have believed that only a small portion of humankind reaches salvation, *mokṣa, nirvāṇa, satori* and the like.

and two, God does not condemn anybody.[82] Now, this second proposition amounts to saying that God provides every Man coming into existence with the *means* of salvation.[83]

We have mentioned God's universal will to save.[84] Now if he created Men for union with him, then surely he also provided them with the means whereby to attain this end.[85] If these means were exclusively in the visible Church or in 'official' Christianity, other people could not be saved, but this, in fact, is not so.[86] If it be true that 'outside the Church there is no salvation', this 'Church' should not be identified with a concrete organization, or even with adherence to Christianity.[87] The problem has been so explicitly stated that we need not do anything more than simply recall it.[88]

The ultimate reason for this universal idea of Christianity, an idea which makes possible the catholic embrace of every

[82] Cf. the theological dictum: *facienti, quod est in se Deus non denegat gratiam* (God does not deny grace to those who do what they can).

[83] Cf. the *rejection* by the Catholic Church of the doctrine which says that 'sanctifying grace'—i.e. the ultimate instrument for salvation—is what makes the difference between a Christian and a non-Christian (against Quesnel, see *vgr.* Denz. 1379); or defending that the non-Christians have no influence of Christ whatever (Denz. 1295) or that Christ performed his saving sacrifice only for the 'believers' (Denz. 1294); etc.

[84] 1 Tim. 2:3–4; cf. R. Lombardi, *The Salvation of the Unbeliever*. London, Burns & Oates, 1956; M. Seckler, 'Das Heil der Nichtevangelisierten in thomistischer Sicht' in *Tübinger Theologische Quartalschrift* 140,1 (1960): 38–69 and K. Rahner, art. cit. (note 16).

[85] Cf. A. P. Arokiasamy, *The Doctrine of Grace in the Śaiva Siddhānta*, Pont. Kandensi-Diss. ad Lauream. Trichinopoly, S. Joseph's, 1935; C. B. Papali, 'Il concetto della Grazia nella Teologia Indù' in *Il Fuoco* 1 (1963), pp. 3–8; R. Otto, *India's Religion of Grace and Christianity Compared and Contrasted*. New York, Macmillan, 1930; P. de Letter, *The Christian and Hindu Concept of Grace*, Light of the East Series 51, Calcutta, 1958.

[86] See the document by Pius IX, *Quanto conficiamur munere*, 10 Aug. 1863. Cf. Denz. 1677.

[87] Cf. C. Journet, *The Church of the Word Incarnate*, vol. i. London, Sheed & Ward, 1954. See also the recent literature in the Bibliography I.

[88] See a short review of some relevant literature in *Herder Korrespondenz* IX, 7 (April, 1955), pp. 321–7; and Y. Congar, 'Salvation and the Non-Catholic' in *Blackfriars* VII–VIII (1957), pp. 290–300; and another bibliographical review in *Parole et Mission* II, 4 (1 Jan. 1959), pp. 142–6. Cf. the rather negative J. C. Fenton, *The Catholic Church and Salvation*. London, Sands, 1958.

people and religion, lies in the Christian conception of Christ: he is not *only* the historical redeemer, but *also* the unique Son of God, the Second Person of the Trinity, the only ontological—temporal and eternal—link between God and the World.[89]

However, when the mystical insight into the theandric nature of Christ weakens and is replaced by a merely historical understanding of the human actions of Jesus, then this Christian position appears untenable. When the myth of history begins to take hold of Western Christianity, Jesus Christ becomes the embodiment of the supreme Imperium. Incarnation becomes just a little slice of history and 'evangelization' consists in 'civilizing' others and incorporating them into one 'Christian' (and post-Christian) world-order.

The theological problem that our question raises concerns the *means* of salvation that God provides for non-Christians, that is, in our case, for Hindus.[90] Undoubtedly, salvation being a supernatural act (for it is union with God), it is always a gratuitous divine act, and there are no proportionate 'natural' means here on earth for attaining participation in divine life. Yet the normal procedure of divine providence in dealing with the whole creation, not excluding Mankind, is not one of anarchical interference, but rather follows a pattern which is evidenced in what we call the physical and the historical order. This happens in such a perfect way that very often it appears as though God's personal and individual care for each of his creatures is somehow left to cosmic or historical laws far removed from his concrete love for each of us, which even extends to the numbering of every hair on our head.[91] In other words, his providence, even in the 'supernatural'

[89] See the 70 pages of bibliography on Christology in B. M. Xiberta, *Tractatus de Verbo Incarnato* II. Madrid, C.S.I.C., 1954; and the 40 pages in M. Schmaus, *Katholische Dogmatik* II, 2.

[90] Cf. the problem posed by H. R. Schlette, 'Die "alten Heiden" und die Theologie', *Hochland* 52/5 (June, 1960): 411. Cf. his book, *Towards a Theology of Religions* (see Bibliography I).

[91] Matt. 10:30; Luke 12:7.

sphere, follows ordered and ordinary ways.[92] And in this sense he provides normal, natural means for leading peoples and individuals to himself.[93]

The normal and ordinary means within the Christian Church are the sacraments, which are different aspects, 'signs', symbols, of the one and only sacrament of the New Testament, which is the Church as a whole and ultimately Christ himself.[94] By virtue of their divine institution those sacraments, when received with the proper dispositions confer the divine grace that they symbolize.[95]

I shall not linger on the doctrine of the 'Cosmic Sacraments', but this much may be said in order to clarify my thesis. If we take the concept of sacrament not in the restricted sense used by the Church when she speaks of the sacraments of the New Law[96]—to distinguish them from *other* sacraments—but in a more general sense, as applied by Christian Scholastics when speaking of the sacraments of the Old Testament and of the *sacramenta naturae* (sacraments of nature),[97] then we may well say that *sacraments* are the ordinary

[92] As for the people of Israel, see: W. Eichrodt, *Theologie des Alten Testaments*, 4th edn. Göttingen, Vandenhoeck & Ruprecht, 1961; L. Bouyer, *La Bible et l'Evangile*, 2nd edn. Lectio divina 8 (Paris, Cerf, 1953), p. 33; F. Spadafora, *Collettivismo e individualismo nel Vecchio Testamento*. Rome, 1953; L. Cerfaux, *La théologie de l'Église suivant saint Paul*. Paris, Cerf, 1948; A. Gelin, *Les idées maîtresses de l'Ancien Testament*, 4th edn. Paris 1952.

[93] Cf. R. Garrigou-Lagrange, 'La volonté salvifique chez saint Augustin' in *Revue Thomiste* 35 (1930), pp. 473–86; F. Stegmüller, *Die Lehre vom allgemeinen Heilswillen in der Scholastik bis Thomas von Aquin*. Rome 1929; L. Caperan, *Le problème du salut des infidèles*, 2nd edn. Toulouse 1943; J. Ratzinger, 'Die neuen Heiden und die Kirche' in *Hochland* 51/10 (Oct. 1958), pp. 1–11; K. Rahner, 'Der Christ und seine ungläubigen Verwandten' in *Schriften zur Theologie* III (Einsiedeln, Johannes, 1956), pp. 419–39, and his other works quoted above.

[94] Cf. Eph. 1:4–9; 3:3–6; Col. 1:26; 2:2. Cf. H. de Lubac, *Méditation sur l'Église*, 'Le sacrement de Jésus-Christ', 3rd edn (Paris, Aubier, 1953), pp. 175–203. See also *The Documents of Vatican II*, The Church (op. cit. pp. 9–106).

[95] Cf. A. Amaldoss, *Do Sacraments Change?* (Bangalore, Theological Publications in India, 1979) for a theological reflection on the nature of the sacraments in an Indian context.

[96] Cf. Conc. Trident., Sess VII, *De Sacramentis* (Denz. 844 sq.).

[97] See Thomas Aquinas, *Sum. Theol.* I–II, 9.102, a.5; and III, q. 60 and 61.

means by which God leads the peoples of the earth towards himself.[98]

No true sacrament is magical.[99] Nevertheless the sacraments have a special causative strength because of their extrinsic connection with the will of God. Thus the efficacy of the Christian sacraments does not reside in themselves as isolated elements or actions, but depends on the action of Christ within them as instruments of grace.[100] One may or may not assume that the same efficacy is conferred upon all other sacraments, *qua* sacraments.[101] Yet it remains true that Christ may be active and at work in the human being who receives any sacrament, whether Christian or any other.[102]

Further, because the human person is not just an individual,[103] but also has a sociological, historical and cosmological dimension, salvation, though an inner and personal process, is prepared and normally carried out by external and visible means which we call sacraments.[104] The good and *bona fide* Hindu as well as the good and *bona fide* Christian are saved

[98] 'R.d.q. *Sacramenta sunt necessaria ad humanam salutem . . .*' Thomas Aquinas, *Sum. Theol.* III, 9.61, a.1; also *ante Christum*, a.3.

[99] Cf. R. Panikkar, *Kultmysterium in Hinduismus und Christentum*, pp. 72f., 84f., etc.

[100] 'The sacraments when presented scientifically can appear as mechanical instruments of grace (*ex opere operato*) instead of the personal acts of Christ using this means to unite mankind with the Father by the loving power of the Holy Spirit. (The term *ex opere operato*, properly understood, means *ex opere operantis Christi*).' E. Zeitler, 'Our Liturgical Programme' in *The Clergy Monthly* 5 (July 1959), p. 175.

[101] Traditional Christian doctrine emphasizes the distinction between the sacraments of the New Covenant and all other sacraments (cf. Denz. 845; 857) and points out that those of the Old Law did not cause grace (cf. Denz. 695) but just foreshadowed it: *figurabant, praesignarunt*. (Cf. Denz. 711.)

[102] For the Hindu sacraments, see R. B. Pandey, *Hindu Saṁskāras, A Socio-religious Study of the Hindu Sacraments*. Banaras, Vikrama Publications, 1949.

[103] Cf. R. Panikkar, 'Sur l'anthropologie du prochain' in *L'homme et son prochain*, Actes du VIII Congrès des Sociétés de Philosophie de Langue Française (Toulouse, P.U.F., 1956), pp. 228–31, and also 'Singularity and Individuality. The Double Principle of Individuation' in *Revue Internationale de Philosophie, art. cit.* on p. 15. Cf. K. Rahner, 'Das Christentum und die nichtchristlichen Religionen', art. cit, pp. 148ff., etc.

[104] Cf. Thomas Aquinas, loc. cit.

by Christ—not by Hinduism or Christianity *per se*, but through their sacraments and, ultimately, through the *mysterion* active within the two religions.[105] This amounts to saying that Hinduism also has a place in the universal saving providence of God and cannot therefore be considered as negative in relation to Christianity.[106]

As we have seen already, it is not just the Hindu's personal conscience that is concerned: the Hindu religion as such has also an important role to play, because only through its mediation can the Hindu attain his goal. In fact, in India, as in many other cultures of both past and present, the individual, i.e. the individual's separate consciousness such as is assumed in the West today, is hardly conceivable. Hençe a private, personal relationship with God cannot be postulated as the normal and common way for everybody. This means that the hypothesis of *direct* and *immediate* action by Christ on an individual's conscience without a particular religion as a medium, i.e. without 'sacraments', is, to say the least, psychologically very difficult and improbable in the majority of

[105] By sacraments in Hinduism we do not mean exclusively the *saṃskāras*, which have been losing momentum in modern Hinduism, but also other means, signs and symbols provided by Hinduism. The powerful influence of Tantrism with its basically sacramental approach on most of the branches of Hinduism, besides the almost universally accepted customs like bathing in sacred rivers etc., could be mentioned by way of examples.

[106] See the Patristic idea of a Church since the beginning of the World. For a collection of such texts, see M. Schmaus, *Katholische Dogmatik* III, 1, sec. 167 b, pp. 60–75; J. Beumer, 'Die altchristliche Idee einer präexistierenden Kirche' in *Wissenschaft und Weisheit* 9 (1942), pp. 12–22; Y. Congar, 'Ecclesia ab Abel' in *Festschrift für Karl Adam: Abhandlungen zur Theologie und Kirche*, ed. M. Reding (Düsseldorf 1953), pp. 79–108; A. M. Dubarle, 'Les conditions du salut avant la venue du Sauveur chez saint Cyrille d'Alexandrie' in *Revue des sciences philosophiques et théologiques* 32 (1948), pp. 359–62; Ch. Journet, 'L'univers de création ou l'univers antérieur à l'Eglise' in *Revue Thomiste* III (1953), pp. 439–87ff. Cf. also the astonishing and yet traditional text by Paul of Samosata in Mansi, *Amplissima Collectio Conciliorum*, vol. i (Paris, Leipzig, 1901–27), 1033–40; cf. G. Bardy, *Paul de Samosate* (Louvain, 1929), pp. 13–19; and see the 'Declaration on the Relationship of the Church to Non-Christian Religions' of Vatican II (op. cit.).

religions.[107] The purely individualistic attitude of nineteenth-century Europe is *still* unthinkable for the Indian people. It is difficult to find in India a concept identical to that which we mean by 'individual conscience'. In Hinduism, Man is still immersed in collective consciousness, he still has cosmic instincts which lead him through life with more certainty than a 'modern' Man may possess through his own 'private' reason.[108] This does not mean that the *kaivalya* ideal is not present in Hinduism. On the contrary, in few religions has the desire for salvation through absolute detachment been given more importance than in Hinduism, but even there 'isolation' implies universalization and not 'individualization'.

The fact that Christ speaks to the whole Man means that he does not speak to an abstract and common nature, but to persons whose very being is intermingled with and inseparable from their beliefs, customs, ways of thinking, feeling, and so forth.[109] Man is constitutively a historical and social being with cosmological dimensions, and Christ does not overlook this human dimension—he himself in his time walked and spoke as a Jew.[110]

[107] See, besides other works already mentioned: J. Pepin, *Mythe et Allégorie, Les origines grecques et les contestations judéo-chrétiennes*. Paris, Aubier, 1958; J. Cazeneuve, *Les rites et la condition humaine*. Paris, P.U.F., 1958 (with ample bibliography); A. W. Watts, *Myth and Ritual in Christianity*. London, Thames and Hudson, 1953; L. Malevez, *Christian Message and Myth*. London, SCM Press, 1958.

[108] Cf. J. J. Bachofen, *Der Mythus von Orient und Occident—Eine Metaphysik der alten Welt*, ed. M. Schroeter. München, Beck, 1956. Cf. remarks on this important work in G. Söhngen, 'Tiefe und Wahrheit des Mythos' in *Münchener Theologische Zeitschrift* 10/2 (1959), pp. 137–40. For the myth as a source of tradition even in a Christian sense, see valuable hints in J. Pieper, 'Über den Begriff der Tradition' in *Tradition im Industriezeitalter* (Düsseldorf, Pädagogischer Verlag Schwann, n.d.), pp. 25–7. See for bibliography and the problem itself, R. Panikkar, *Le mystère du culte dans l'hinduisme et le christianisme*.

[109] See the whole chapter 'La liturgia e la legge della salvezza in comunità' in C. Vagaggini, *Il senso teologico della liturgia* (Rome, Ed. Paoline, 1957), pp. 211–30: '. . . le relazioni tra Dio e l'uomo sono tutte impostate sulla legge dell' oggettività', p. 214.

[110] That is why the approach 'I do not preach the Gospel to Hindus, I preach the Gospel to men' (C. F. Andrews) will not do if those 'men' happen to be Hindus. Cf. B. de Kretser, 'Christianity and the Renascence of Non-Christian Religions' in *National Christian Council Review* 89/9 (Sept. 1959), pp. 306–14.

Individual conscience may be a purely historical evolution of Mankind, but the fact remains that if God looks after the salvation of the Hindu people, it cannot be through purely personal-individual action, which would have very little meaning; it has rather to be something collective, sociological and mythical. This again is the reason that Hinduism has a true place in the economy of salvation[111] and cannot be equated with 'sin', 'falsehood' and the like.

My purpose is to recall and emphasize that, according to Christian doctrine, the Father in heaven makes his sun to rise on the good and on the evil, and sends rain on the just and on the unjust,[112] that Christ is the expectation of the peoples,[113] that his spirit is at work among non-believers,[114] that he is already found by those who did not seek him,[115] and that he is a hidden God[116] who has sometimes hidden himself either in an unknown God[117] or in the hearts of Men of good will.[118] Christians often need reminding that Christ himself

[111] The case of the people of Israel has received a special treatment in the Christian economy. But it must be emphasized that God's election of the 'chosen' people is a positive and particular act which does not mean at all a rebuke or rejection of other nations. For the problem of the Old Testament, which provides an *analogy* to our question, see: A. Landgraf, 'Die Gnadenökonomie des Alten Bundes nach der Lehre der Frühscholastik' in *Zeitschrift f. kath. Theologie* 57 (1933), pp. 215–53; G. Philips, 'La grâce des justes de l'Ancien Testament' in *Ephemerides theol. lovanien.* 27 (1947), pp. 521–56, and 24 (1948), pp. 23–58; A. F. Hofmann, 'Die Gnade der Gerechten des Alten Bundes nach Thomas von Aquin' in *Divus Thomas* 29 (1951), pp. 167–87; W. Baumgarten, *Israelitische und altorientalische Weisheit.* Tübingen 1933; K. Thieme, *Biblische Religion heute.* Heidelberg, L. Schneider, 1960; H. U. von Balthasar, *Einsame Zwiesprache.* Köln, J. Hegner, 1958; H. L. Goldschmidt, *Die Botschaft des Judentums.* Frankfurt, Europäische Verlagsanstalt, 1960; M. Vereno, 'Israel und Kirche' in *Kairos* 1/1962, pp. 32–6, and the whole number dedicated to Israel.

[112] Matt. 5:45. Śaṅkarācārya utilizes the old image of Parjanya, the rain-giver, helping with his rain the different growths of the most varying seeds (which should explain how men grow differently due to personal *karma*). *Brahma-sūtra-bhāṣya* II, 1, 34.

[113] Gen. 49:10.

[114] Rom. 15:21 quoting Isa. 52:15.

[115] Rom. 10:20; cf. Isa. 65:1.

[116] Isa. 45:15.

[117] Acts 17:23.

[118] Cf. Luke 2:14.

taught Peter not to call profane or impure anything that God has made clean,[119] for he already has other sheep which are not following the visible flock[120] and other disciples who work miracles and are not acknowledged by his visible followers.[121] It was Christ also who sent a non-Jewish woman not to sow but actually to reap where others (non-Jews) had toiled, reminding his closest disciples of the meaning of this action.[122] In ancient days God spoke to our fathers in many ways and by many means;[123] now in recent times he has spoken to us through his own Son,[124] in whom everything is summed up,[125] for he is the atonement not only for our sins, but for the defilement of the whole World.[126]

It is important to note that Christian theology can no longer ignore Hinduism—or any other religion—when taking seriously into account, in its own doctrines, the exigencies of our times.[127]

6. THE RELATIONSHIP

To avoid egalitarian syncretism and also bland denial of the validity of polar analogies, a second kind of analogy evolved.

[119] Acts 10:15.
[120] John 10:16.
[121] Mark 9:37.
[122] John 4:38.
[123] I.e. not just by the prophets of Israel, as the Old Testament itself corroborates. See Job 4:12; Jer. 49:7; Baruch 3: 22–3; Hab. 1:5, etc. Cf. also J. Daniélou, *Les saints 'païens' de l'Ancien Testament*. Paris, Le Seuil, 1956; S. Grill, 'Die religionsgeschichtliche Bedeutung der vormosaischen Bündnisse' in *Kairos* (1/1960), pp. 17–22.
[124] Heb. 1:1.
[125] Eph. 1:10.
[126] 1 John 2:2.
[127] See J. Neuner, 'Das Christus-Mysterium und die indische Lehre von den Avatāras' in *Das Konzil von Chalkedon*, vol. iii, ed. A. Grillmeier, H. Bacht (Würzburg, Echter, 1954), pp. 785–824 ('. . . so bringt die übernatürliche Bestimmung des Menschen den Mythos hervor . . .', p. 822). Often, however, due to objective difficulties in understanding a complex religion like Hinduism and the lack of a proper hermeneutic, many of the theological studies of world-religions in general and Hinduism in particular are one-sided and not sufficiently balanced. Cf. e.g. H. Küng, *On Being a Christian* (London, Collins, 1977), pp. 98ff.

This second model characterized Hinduism and Christianity respectively as potential-actual; seed-fruit; forerunner-real presence; allegory-thing in itself; desire-accomplishment; symbol-reality; or the specifically Christian dynamism of death-resurrection. This attitude was called 'fulfilment theology'.

In this view, Hinduism is the desire for fullness, and that fullness is Christ, hence Hinduism is already pointing towards the same mystery as does Christianity—already contains, indeed, the symbolism of the Christian reality. Hinduism has the prior place by right of its age, while Christianity is a certain culmination, not just because of its historical position, and not just as a continuation or merely natural prolongation of an earlier religion, but as the actual new and decisive step towards fullness. Inasmuch as Hinduism is recognized in this model as belonging, at least potentially, to the economy of salvation, as aiming, we might say, in the right direction, this kind of analogy is more fair to it, albeit still somewhat patronizing. That is, it admits that Hindus have access to genuine ultimacy. However, these analogies suffer from shortcomings similar to those that afflict the static polar analogies.

The justification for viewing the relationship of Christianity and Hinduism according to the analogy of these dynamic pairs is the belief that Christianity embodies the fullness of God's revelation and that no other religion has that fullness, which is the presence of the ultimate on earth (in the Eucharist), the immanence of the transcendent as Man. Thus, people of other religions *reach for* the infinite, whereas for the Christian it is here now as Christ in Man. But objections to the implications of such a scheme outweigh the possible insights it might afford us.

1. An obvious objection to the analogy desire-accomplishment is that teleological evaluations of collectivities are unwarranted over-interpretations. That Hinduism embodies Man's yearning to experience the theandric reality certainly

cannot be denied;[128] but to say that the accomplishment of that desire *is* Christianity would be to put a very special interpretation on the word 'Christianity' in which case the analogy would not serve to show us the relationship between Christianity and Hinduism, because the special definition of Christianity removes it from the plane of the ordinary definition of Hinduism.

2. A second objection is theological: if Christianity alone offers the fullness of the theandric reality to Men on earth, and no other religion possesses that fullness, but only reaches towards it—as the potential does towards the actual, a forerunner to real presence and allegory to reality—the proper theological place of Hinduism in the economy of salvation is once more denied. If the *raison d'être* of religion—including Hinduism, as we saw in the previous section—is salvation, and salvation is union with God (or in even more Christian terms, incorporation into Christ), either this theandric dimension, the immanence of the transcendent as Man, is central to the matter of salvation, or it is irrelevant. Now this theandric dimension is in fact the essence of salvation, and since Hinduism does have a place in the economy of salvation according to Christian theology, there is no justification for the belief that only Christianity has the fullness of God's revelation and saving power.

3. A third objection to such dynamic analogies is a matter of terminology: if a thing is only a potential, how can it function? That is, if Hinduism were only potentially the fullness of religion, or only potentially offered to disclose the theandric mystery, then it could never belong to the actual economy of salvation, i.e. God's saving action in universal history. This, however, has already been shown to be untrue.

If, on the other hand, Hinduism is accepted as belonging to the universal plan of salvation, but only in its function as potential, the terms 'potential' and 'actual' would be nothing more than arbitrary labels not corresponding to reality, since Hindus do continue nonetheless to be saved.

[128] The word 'theandric' (both divine and human) of Christian Patristics corresponds to the *puruṣa* concept of the Vedas (cf. RV X, 90) and of later speculation, as well as to the *nara-nārāyaṇa* motif.

As for the analogy of seed and fruit, if 'Christianity' is a name for the fullness of religion, for the realization of the theandric mystery, then Hinduism as a concrete religion may indeed give rise to it, in which case the seed-fruit analogy would have a certain validity. But, just as in the first objection, this means defining Christianity in a way that does not refer to historical phenomena. The analogy then no longer characterizes the (horizontal) relationship of two concrete entities, but rather the (vertical) movement within Hinduism. The cyclical, reproductive character of seed and fruit does not apply to the relationship in either case, except as a possible analogy for the teacher-disciple relationship in the mystical life—which is quite beside the point of the present discussion.

4. Psycho-pastoral objections to the potency-act model are the same as those to the positive-negative model: the idea not only appears patronizing on the part of Christians and hence distasteful to Hindus but also fails to produce valid argumentation. The Hindu reaction may be of two kinds. Either they will say that the boastful claim of Christianity is not true, because all religions are equal and more or less equivalent, or they will turn the Christian statement the other way around, affirming that Hinduism is the end and fulfilment of Christianity. Here again, 'fulfilment' refers to the heart of religion, so that in this case 'Hinduism' is given the same special interpretation. In both cases the name 'Christianity' or 'Hinduism' only indicates the culturo-temporal background of those who are claiming the completeness of their realized vision and bears a highly charged, specialized meaning.

All forms of 'actuality' (fruit, reality, accomplishment, thing-in-itself, real presence) are in fact contained in Christianity or Hinduism only in so far as they are personally realized. The above-mentioned dynamic analogies are valid within each person only, that is to say, vertically, in the movement from Man to God, not horizontally, in the relationship between two entities such as Hinduism and Christianity.

In the potency-act model, Hinduism was to have become a fuller religion, a fuller phenomenon as it moved in the direction of 'Christianity', or of the knowledge of the cosmotheandric reality. But the only way that Hinduism will become fuller is to be composed principally of people who have mystically realized that fullness of Man. Christianity itself is not statistically any 'fuller' in this respect. The same is therefore true of it: it must become 'filled' with people who have experienced the cosmotheandric reality.[129]

One could also speak of a mutual fecundation taking place. It is natural that he who loves more, who has experienced more, may have more to offer. The result may be a new creature. Christians should recall that the Spirit makes all things new,[130] that in Christ we are a new creation,[131] and that this does not happen once and for all, for we die every day.[132] Also Hindus should recall that only at the end of many transformations does true realization come.[133]

Moreover, the symbol-reality analogy, though it may be a useful way to view Hinduism and Christianity, is not a dynamic analogy with some kind of horizontal distinction or movement from one to the other. Rather, the symbol is the appearance of the reality—and, as such, a symbol is as true a manifestation of concrete Christianity as it is of concrete Hinduism. Again, the reality is to be known through and in the symbol by the *person*.

The death-resurrection analogy needs to be understood in its proper context. The real intention behind the analogy is not to say that Hinduism should become Christianity, but to point out that there is within Hinduism itself a dynamism which leads it towards that peculiar movement of death and resurrection in which we detect the work of the *antaryāmin*, the inner guide, which Christians call Christ. The individual must die to himself, to his previous limiting beliefs concerning

[129] Cf. R. Panikkar, 'Colligite Fragmenta: For an Integration of Reality' in *From Alienation to At-oneness*, Proceedings of the Theology Institute of Villanova University, ed. F. A. Eigo (The Villanova University Press 1977), pp. 19–91.

[130] Cf. Rev. 21:5.

[131] Cf. 2 Cor. 5:17.

[132] Cf. Rom. 8:36.

[133] Cf. BG II, 22; II, 72, etc.

the nature of Man, and be 'resurrected' in true knowledge of the cosmotheandric reality.

Of course with the passage of time the encounter of religions and cultures will bring about the death of religions as we know them. They will be 'resurrected' in new forms, having perhaps new life which we would hardly recognize. But if the very nature of life is change, who is to say when, at exactly what point, Hinduism or Christianity has 'died'? Only a sizeable temporal distance permits that kind of judgement, whereas we are caught up now in the ongoing process.

It will not perhaps be out of place to recall that because we are dealing with the meeting of religions, the encounter is not merely rational, but is an encounter of two different sets of beliefs. It is therefore in the depths of the dark, and yet more sure, knowledge of faith that the two spiritualities can meet. It is there that real change, real conversion may take place on both sides.

The call for radical transformation that the dynamic pairs suggest, namely, a transformation into the fullness of what each religion is, into a 'better' form of itself, has to find a response within the human race. The hope that such a transformation may happen can be neither substantiated nor enforced. Still, we may surely attempt to convince existing religions that they should not stay closed and static, but rather follow their own rhythms, their own dynamisms, lest they simply disappear through stagnation, by turning in a sterile fashion to their own present or past structures.

The call is for growth, but it could as well be called avoidance of stagnation. What is wanted is something to jolt each and every person into finding and living his deepest reality. Perhaps the shock of encounter might produce this effect, perhaps the shock of existential predicament.

If the analogy of static polar pairs was misleading, historically untrue, psychologically inadequate and theologically contradictory; and if the analogy of dynamic pairs was ambivalent by definition, psychologically disappointing and theologically misleading—how then are we to define the *and* of Hinduism and Christianity? It cannot be translated by an optimistic 'towards' or by a pessimistic 'versus'. Simply to shift the alleged horizontal movement of the dynamic analogy and to turn it into a vertical movement within each tradition may be a valid observation of the real nature of this phenomenon of religion, but it sidesteps the present issue of the relationship between two very different concrete religious realities and tends to equalize or ignore their differences. Differences are not by nature undesirable. It is the fear that a facing of our differences may involve us in conflict that has caused us to overlook entirely the possibility that such a confrontation may reveal to us certain hitherto unsuspected aspects of truth.

There is probably no single analogy that will adequately characterize the relationship of Hinduism and Christianity in all its complexity. Perhaps each religion is a dimension of the other in a *sui generis* co-inherence or co-involvement, just as each human is potentially the whole of Mankind, though each one develops and actualizes only a finite number of possibilities in a limited way.

Each religious orthodoxy might be considered a map of the religious territory, keeping in mind that the map is not the territory. Maps may be more or less accurate and may vary in scale and in the aspect of the territory that they delineate. Sometimes roads, mountains and rivers may be enough to orient the traveller; at other times urban agglomerations may suffice. Topographic maps, maps of vegetation, micro-climate or soil type will orient initiates of different persuasions—each one complementary, each revealing a different aspect of reality. Perhaps Christianity is the 'historical map' of Man's religious territory, of the eternal, while Hinduism is an ancient, polyvalent, a-historical map. But will the map analogy help us to see what happens when the major active fault shown on the geographer's map literally shifts the micro-climates on the meteorologist's? Maps are made according to established facts; the reality of the encounter and consequent change in different human awarenesses of ultimacy is an ongoing contingent and dynamic occurrence in today's world. Our attempt to understand, to catch the pattern of this contingency, is a part of the actual dynamism of the encounter of religious traditions.

There is a link between Hinduism *and* Christianity, and we have tried to describe it as clearly as we could. But we might also say that on a higher plane there is no link from below between these historical entities—only one from above, inasmuch as the truly transcendent call manifests itself as an immanent longing in all. The *and* then is not only ambivalent but transcendental, similar to the copulative that links the Father *and* the Son *and* the Holy Spirit in the Trinity.

In other words—though on this level we should put all words aside—the nature of our *and* is a mystery. We do not know the plan of God, nor can we decipher the secret of history. We have tried to describe a relationship, but at the ultimate level, so far as it is given to us to surmise the divine will, we are bound to recognize that this *and* should not merely be interpreted in the sense of integration, assimilation or conversion, but in a higher way which does not deny these earlier ideas, but gives to all our thoughts a lower, humbler meaning and a higher harmony. Unfortunately, it seems that the musical score was lost in Paradise, and at present we can but stumble through our separate melodies in the hope that one day we may hear the full symphony.

3

GOD AND THE WORLD ACCORDING TO BRAHMA-SŪTRA I,1,2

yato vā imāni bhūtāni jāyante,
yena jātāni jīvanti,
yat prayantyabhisaṃviśanti,
tad vijijñāsasva.

TU III,1[1]

That from which truly all beings are born,
by which when born they live
and into which they all return:
that seek to understand.

πάντα δι' αὐτοῦ ἐγένετο

John 1:3[2]

Everything has been made through him.

1. PRELIMINARY REMARKS

The existential character of the first chapter and the historico-sociological aspect of the second chapter should not overshadow the intellectual and doctrinal dimension of this third chapter. The study of philosophical aspects of religion is certainly not enough to trigger a fruitful dialogue, but it is a necessary condition for a lasting and effective encounter. In this sense this third chapter completes, by means of one single example, what has been suggested in the two previous ones. Corroboration for our vision is not dependent upon just one single case, but the following paragraphs study in detail one concrete instance which serves to illustrate the dialectics of the relationship.

Yet this concrete example has a special value. We could have chosen more experiential texts like the many utterances of the Upanishads. This would have been perhaps more in-

[1] This text is the scriptural basis of BS I,1,2.
[2] *Omnia per ipsum facta sunt.* Cf. also 1 Cor. 8:6; Col. 1:16.

teresting and less controversial. The Upanishads as mystical texts can speak to anybody capable of reaching the heights of a certain spiritual experience. But we are not dealing with the mystical core of two religions. We are concerned with the whole complex of two living religious traditions. Our text, as we shall see, is taken from an Indian scholasticism that is already crystallized. It purports to disclose a real experience, but it claims also to express a theoretical truth capable of sustaining a doctrinal system and 'theological' speculation. The encounter between Hinduism and Christianity, I repeat, cannot be reduced to a well-intentioned desire for mutual understanding. It has also to face the exigencies of theoretical speculations. The chosen example does not claim to sustain the burden of an entire theory, but it may have the value of a paradigm.

a) A Philosophical Dialogue

There are three things I do not intend to do: I do not propose to write a complete *bhāṣya*, a commentary on a *sūtra* of the *Brahma-Sūtras* following the traditional canons of Indian philosophy. Though the temptation has been great and the effort would prove worthwhile, I have no intention of adding a new commentary to the existing line of rich and famous commentaries on this central point of Vedānta. To do such a thing in a sensible way I should be obliged to expose, comment on and criticize all of the Indian philosophical tradition that has a bearing on the subject.

The second thing that I do not intend to do is to write an essay on apologetics. Apologetics are good in their proper place. They are justified not only subjectively by the good intention of the writer, but also objectively by the nature of the subject matter. However, this study is not apologetics, otherwise I should have to go into problems that I expressly leave aside. I do not enter into the Christian tradition and show how Indian thematics fit or can be fitted into it, how and to what extent Indian concepts and answers are compatible or incompatible with it. Apologetics either take a defensive stance in trying to prove that the Christian answers make sense and can refute the arguments framed against

Christianity, or they take the offensive and try to fit the questions and answers of the other religious traditions into the Christian framework. Both attitudes are alien to the spirit of this book.

Third, its goal would be misunderstood if this essay were to be regarded merely as a comparative study. I do not intend to compare one philosophy with another, or to check the answer given by one tradition with a parallel answer of another, much less compare God the Father with Brahman, or Īśvara with Christ. I am sincerely concerned with a contemporary philosophical or theological problem, one to which I feel called to address myself through a personal philosophical endeavour. I cannot, however, express this problem without using words and concepts—and these are pregnant with meanings and nuances given them by the history of human thought. I must therefore choose those existing formulations most suited to express my thoughts. In studying these various formulations, I accept guidance from the philosophical traditions of Mankind that have already reflected deeply on such perennial philosophical problems. It is through the confluence of two of these traditions that this essay may make some contribution to our present question.

I should like to make a philosophical study on a subject that belongs neither to the East alone nor to the West and, while drawing heavily on the Indian philosophical tradition, explain it in a manner intelligible to Western thought. This subject is the philosophical problem of God and the World—a problem that we discover with our minds and agonize over in our inner beings. Before making any observation of my own, I feel obliged to study what the thinkers of this earth have *thought* or *meant* through what they have *said* or *written* on the subject. A variety of perspectives and different solutions reveal themselves in this way. I do not set about harmonizing them or finding a higher synthesis; I simply feel a deep concern for the misunderstandings and fundamental differences between the several visions of reality. I sometimes think that not all oppositions are irreducible. Keeping in mind the basic problem stripped of accretions, I should like to suggest an essay of translation even at the price of sometimes transposing the actual truths. Moreover, this transplant of truths—that is, the placing of them in a wider context or a different framework—though a very delicate operation, may prove to be not only fruitful to the transplanted truth, but also of service to the 'host' philosophy. A living seed may germinate in a neighbour's field also.

The meeting between East and West, or more precisely the encounter between Hinduism and Christianity or Indian and Western philosophy, has amounted in past centuries to hardly more than a superficial communication and mutual misunderstanding, though there have been valuable but rare exceptions. It is an indisputable fact that there has been no merging of the two traditions to form a more universal stream. Certainly, the West has done some useful work of discovery and rehabilitation of Indian culture, but the *approaches* have been too much characterized by either pro- or anti-Western bias that has made real dialogue and mutual fructification very difficult. Until now, the meeting has not gone much beyond a more or less accurate mutual knowledge, and has so far not achieved any reciprocal inspiration or stimulation. Orientalism is still a specialization—the renaissance that Schopenhauer was expecting from Western contact with India has not been perceptible though we may be coming now to a new period.[3] To this intricate problem the present study does not claim to bring a solution, but simply hopes to be a contribution towards mutual understanding and cross-fertilization. It aims to be a commentary not on a *text*, but on a theologico-philosophical problem *based* on a text rooted in one philosophical tradition and relevant to the other tradition. It intends simply to open the door for a sincere dialogue by finding out the underlying or transcending reality to which both traditions refer.[4] Whatever further opinions we may hold, and whatever the answers we may find convincing, a dialogue requires *common* ground first of all, even if we have to abandon it later in our pursuit of truth. It may be, for instance, that

[3] Cf. M. Eliade, 'Crisis and Renewal in History of Religions' in *History of Religions* 1 (1965), 2. Cf. also E. W. Said, *Orientalism*. New York, Random House, 1978.

[4] *Cuiuslibet rei tam materialis quam immaterialis est ad rem aliam ordinem habere*, says Thomas Aquinas, *De veritate* XXIII,1.

a relation between Īśvara and Christ is not only dangerous but completely beside the point. There are nevertheless two different levels on which the dialogue can be both feasible and fruitful: the intentional level and the analogical level.

By *intentional level* I mean the underlying *existent* reality that a concept intentionally 'means', that which lays bare the intentionality of the concept. When two pious and sincere persons of different religions intend to pray together despite their divergent ideas, when they in fact address the Divine, either there is 'something' to which these two existential attitudes refer, or there is nothing in one or both cases. That 'something', if we accept it, must ultimately be *intentionally* the same. If we think that this reality can be reached through only one of the two attitudes, then the second person is not praying at all, but addressing an illusion, though the intentionality remains. If, taking an atheistic attitude, we reject the existence of this reality completely, then both persons are on the same level and we can rightly compare the two concepts of divine reality which we presuppose to be lacking a referent though possessing the same intentionality. In all cases the intentionality remains.

The *analogical level* refers to the *essential* realm. For instance, Christians call Christ 'the Lord', just as Hindus call Īśvara 'the Lord'. The meaning they give to 'Lord', however great the difference may be, cannot be so absolute as to transcend all analogy. The word 'Lord' is an analogous one and has several not altogether different meanings. What is the *primum analogatum*, the primordial principle that enables us not only to call the Lord by separate names, but also to refer to him by two different concepts?

On both the intentional and the analogical levels we discover a common ground on which dialogue can proceed. To deny *a priori* the possibility of such common ground is to condemn oneself not only to isolation but also to fanaticism and stagnation. On the other hand, the recognition of this common ground on the basis of transcendent existence or immanent analogy does not allow us to ignore all the differences which arise out of our differing cultural worlds and ways of life on earth. The Divine Reality is the ontological point of attraction of any philosophizing, but it is not necessarily the psychological starting-point. Indian mentality has, in fact, been inclined to the latter attitude,[5] as did also for the most part early Christian philosophers, but this tendency was counterbalanced by the Scholastic effort of the thirteenth century to such a degree that European thinking after the seventeenth century was characterized by the opposite tendency. But neither attitude—neither one which explains the World by starting from a concept of God, nor one which attains a certain concept of God by starting from knowledge of the World—can be made absolute. They are, in fact, complementary.

I do not intend to tackle the entire problem of the relationship between God and the World, but only to offer an example of how clarification may be sought. I shall try to do justice to the opposing tendencies from a philosophical standpoint—a procedure which may help to overcome the historical and cultural East-West dichotomy. We therefore approach the problem keeping both traditions in view and try to clear a common path, or perhaps even a sizeable road, which will take us quite some distance before we reach a parting of the ways.

b) The Living God of Our Research

We shall speak throughout this study about God, the Absolute, Brahman, the Trinity. In order to make our terms clear from the start, we should like to outline briefly some dialectical implications which follow if in fact this God exists.[6] This is not to say that these implications will necessarily be recognized by all schools of thought. However, most schools when speaking about God refer to that 'thing' which we shall now try to characterize. These remarks should not be understood as defending a particular theological or metaphysical doctrine, though since they speak a concrete language they are invested with unavoidable connotations. The most central of my assumptions is based on the conviction that, whatever God may be or mean, any talk about God refers to a *sui generis*

[5] Cf. R. Panikkar, *Máyá e Apocalisse*, pp. 83–6.
[6] These short reflections were published in *The Vedanta Kesari*, Madras, December, 1956, under the title 'If God Exists'.

'thing' that cannot be included in any other category. I am not attempting a phenomenology of God, but only clarifying the meaning of this word in a way at least congruous to the two traditions we are considering.

If there is a God, the rest of reality, down to the smallest and most hidden entity, as well as any kind of human activity, cannot be independent of or even indifferent to that fact. The recognition of God's existence is in itself not a neutral statement, but a truth which pervades everything. I shall therefore now formulate, not the consequences following from this assumption, but some of the implications that necessarily precede it.

If there is a God, this implies *ipso facto* some *epistemological* presuppositions. If God exists, this fact does not depend on my affirmation or negation of it; it is independent of my opinion. I may demonstrate the existence of God or I may deny the possibility of any proof, or even reject his Being; but that does not affect the fact that God is. Moreover, not only my possible negation but also my affirmation of God has no *existential* effect *vis-à-vis* the Divinity. If God exists, this fact is independent of my knowledge of it. This statement, incidentally, is valid even if we consider, as is possible, that our conception of God changes or modifies him for us. Even if God were a creation of our mind he would have to fulfil the role of creator of that same mind—if there is a God.

If there is a God, he cannot be comprehended by any human intellect, but must transcend all human forces and capacities since, if he exists, he is more than Man. He can be transparent, fully knowable, only to himself. For us he is a mystery in the real sense of the word. A comprehensible, a plainly *under-standable* God would not be God at all, for I would then be his ground and not he mine, the very source of my *under-standing*. No human formula, therefore, can give an adequate expression of God.

If there is a God, on the other hand, though he transcends reason—and Man—and his essence is incomprehensible, yet that material-spiritual being that is Man must have a conscious existential approach to God, an approach which is obtained not as a result of lofty and arduous intellectual development, such as only a few learned, highly cultured people can attain, but which must be *given* along with the normal maturity of a human being. In other words, there must be an existential, normal and simple way to realize God's presence—if there is a God.

If God exists, his existence must have not only epistemological precedence, but also *ontological* priority: God is the Ground, the Absolute, the Principle—of all. Man and the World depend on God, and even if some vice-versa relation is admitted, the former relation has a peculiar priority. God's Being may be cognizable to us through our fellow-men and through the World about us, and we may thus obtain some analogical knowledge of him; but in fact both Men and the World are themselves based on God, are related constitutively to him. Man can ascend epistemologically to God only because God has descended ontologically to us.

If there is a God, his being Ground and Principle is not to be taken only as origin or commencement, but also as end and achievement. He is the timeless and pure ontological foundation of everything. God is not only in the ontic beginning of the universe, but also at its termination and consummation. God is not only the inspiring and originating force and source of all, but at the same time the attracting term and conclusion of all being and activity. God is the fullness towards which each particle of being aspires and each movement tends. God is the goal of the World as well as the destination of history.

If there is a God, there is nothing above him, nothing outside or even below him. There is nothing independent of God. Nothing exists without being an existence, an outcome, an effect (*factus*) of God. Nothing is disconnected from him. All that is, is in, from, for, God. All beings not only proceed from God and go to God but also *are* in God.

If God exists, this fact involves some specific *anthropological* connotations: God cannot be just an 'it' but must appear to me as a Person. An 'it' is not conscious and is not perfect; moreover, God cannot be a He or a She—God must be an 'I'. Furthermore, God must be not *an* I, but *the* I. God is the One-who-is, the I-who-is, the I-am, the I-am-who-am, the *aham*. We are God's *thou*. God is the I, and we are the *thou*, if God exists. God has absolute priority. We may have to speak of God as 'he', but if there is a God, *God* speaks first, speaks *us* out—and so we come into existence. God is the I who speaks and each of us is a spoken 'thou' of God, not, properly speaking, an 'I', but more exactly a 'thou', and this we *are* to the extent that God—the I—utters our being as his 'thou'. We are God's—and this is the reason for our dignity and our limitation, both in one. We *are* the 'thou' of God—and only to this extent do we have any *being*. Every one of us is the 'thou art' uttered by the 'I am'.

If there is a God, his relation with me cannot be an abstract, 'universal' one, but must be real, concrete, definite, constitutive and existential. That is to say, my relation with God is not numerical, quantitative, as if I were a 'case' or a 'number' as regards *the* Absolute, *the* Being, but must be a personal, intimate and particular one, having God as *my* source, *my* Being, *my* maker, *my* sustainer, *my* utmost self, *my* father. My approach to God cannot therefore be simply 'generic' or purely intellectual, but must be integral, total, involving body and soul, intellect and will, and also knowledge, service and love—and all this in a personal, unique and unchangeable way.

If there is a God, human society as well as human culture is not and cannot be a-religious, i.e. non-linked (the word religion being derived from *religare*, to bind, connect), independent and disconnected from God, as if God were not. This does not mean a restriction or a diminution of the proper autonomy—or better, ontonomy—of society, but rather a correct enlargement of religion. If God exists, Man has duties primarily, rather than rights. His rights are a consequence of his duty to be a Man, that is, a person, a reflection of the divinity, with an unalienable and irrefusable ontic mission.

Briefly, if God exists, this hypothesis is not irrelevant to anything, is not superfluous in any action of the cosmos, but is in very truth the hypothesis or underlying support of the whole universe along with all our being and acting.

2. THE TEXT

a) Background

We have chosen as a starting-point (*prasthāna*) for our reflection one aphorism of the *Brahma-Sūtras*. Before proceeding to analyse it, it may be useful to give in short the historical background of this text.

The *Brahma-Sūtras* of Bādarāyaṇa[7] (probably fourth century A.D.) are one of the three basic texts of the Vedānta school (called *prasthāna-traya*), the other two being the Upanishads and the Bhagavad Gītā, both sacred texts, the former being a formal part of the *śruti* and the latter considered equally as 'revealed'. Like the *sūtra*-texts of other philosophical schools (e.g. Mīmāṃsa-Sūtras, Yoga-Sūtras), they constitute a concise summary of the teachings of the Upanishads (hence also called Vedānta-Sūtras). Every philosopher claiming to be a Vedāntin was supposed to write a commentary (*bhāṣya*) on each of these three texts. The most prominent commentators are Śaṅkara[8] (around 700 A.D.), who expounds an Advaitic interpretation, and Rāmānuja[9] (around 1100 A.D.), whose school has been termed 'qualified non-dualism' or Viśiṣṭādvaita. The main exponent of a dualistic interpretation (*dvaita*) was Madhva[10] (thirteenth century). In addition to these famous commentators, the Brahma-Sūtras have also been commented upon by Bhāskara, Vācaspati Miśra, Ānandagiri, Govindānanda, Padmapāda, Vallabha, Śrīkaṇṭha, Nimbārka, Vijñānabhikṣu, *et al.*[11]

[7] Cf. S. Radhakrishnan, *The Brahma Sūtra*; B. N. K. Sharma, *The Brahmasūtras and their Principal Commentaries*, vols. i and ii.

[8] Cf. Works of Śaṅkarācārya, vol. iii: *Brahmasūtra with Śaṅkarabhāṣya. The Vedānta-Sūtras with the Commentary by Śaṅkarācārya*, tr. G. Thibaut, Pt. 1 and 2; Paul Deussen, *Das System des Vedānta nach den Brahma-Sūtras des Bādarāyaṇa und dem Kommentare des Çaṅkara über dieselben.*

[9] Rāmānuja, *Śrībhāṣyam; The Vedānta-Sūtras with Rāmānuja's Śrībhāṣya*, tr. G. Thibaut.

[10] Madhva, *Brahmasūtrabhāṣya*; cf. S. Siauve, *La voie de la connaissance de Dieu (Brahma-jijñāsa) selon l'Anuvyākhyāna de Madhva*, id., *La doctrine de Madhva.*

[11] Cf. *The Brahmasūtra-Shānkara-bhāshyam* with the commentaries Bhāshya-Ratnaprabhā, Bhāmatī and Nyāyanirṇaya of Shrīgovindānanda, Vācaspati and Ānandagiri.

Although the terse *sūtra*-style often makes it difficult to ascertain the exact meaning which the author of these Sūtras wanted to convey, one assumes nowadays that Śaṅkara's most famous interpretation does not in fact reflect the opinion of the *sūtrakāra* and that Bādarāyaṇa must have been closer to a philosophy of 'difference-and-non-difference' (*bhedābheda*).[12]

b) Analysis

This renowned summary of Indian wisdom says in its laconic second aphorism: 'Whence the origin etcetera of this.'[13] The meaning of the text is obviously: 'Brahman is that from which the origin, etcetera, of this World proceeds.'[14] A further grammatical analysis of the text only serves to strengthen this interpretation.[15] Tradition agrees in saying that the 'etcetera' of the *sūtra* refers to several texts beginning with 'origination' and adding preservation, dissolution, and sometimes also growth, decrease, transformation and the like.[16] This would

[12] Cf. Klaus Rüping, *Studien zur Frühgeschichte der Vedānta-Philosophie*, Teil I (Wiesbaden, Franz Steiner, 1977), p. 1.

[13] *Janmādyasya yataḥ*, or, splitting the words: *janmādi asya yataḥ*, the meaning being: Origin etc., of this, whence, respectively.

[14] All commentators agree that *janmādi* = *utpattyādi; yataḥ* = *yaddhetukam; tad* = *brahma*; and *asya* = *jagat*: i.e., the production, etc. for *janmādi*; that which acts as cause, that is Brahman for *yataḥ*, and World for *asya*.

[15] *Janmādi* is a bahuvrīhi compound of the type *tadguṇasaṃvijñāna*, meaning *janma utpattiḥ ādi asya tat*, i.e. that which has *janma* (origin) for its beginning. The root *jan-* means to generate, to beget, to produce, to create, to cause, to be born and is connected with the Greek γίγνομαι and the Latin *(g)nascor*. It could also be brought into relation with '*natura*'. Cf. R. Panikkar, *El concepto de naturaleza*, 2nd edn (Madrid, 1972), pp. 55 ff. *Asya* is the genitive form of the demonstrative pronoun 'this' in its neuter or masculine form: 'of this'; *yataḥ* is a conjunctive particle meaning 'whence', but also 'because', 'since', 'for'.

[16] Cf. the several edns and commentaries for further scholarly details about this question. In order to give an idea of the concept used we may remember that Yāska (cf. the Bhāmatī in h.l.) speaks of six modifications, namely *jāyate* (being produced), *asti* (continuous existence), *vardhate* (grows), *vipariṇamate* (changes, transforms), *apakṣīyate* (decays) and *naśyati* (is destroyed) in *Nirukta* I,2. For Yāska, cf. Siddheshwar Varma (with assistance of Bhimadev), *The Etymologies of Yāska*. Hoshiarpur, V.V.R.I., 1953.

Similarly Madhva (in h.l.) introduces eight different modifications (of which Brahman is the cause): *sṛṣṭi* (production), *sthiti* (existence), *saṃhāra* (destruction), *niyama* (control), *jñāna* (knowledge), *ajñāna* (ignorance), *bandha* (bondage) and *mokṣa* (salvation).

give us the full literal meaning of our *sūtra*: 'Brahman is that whence the origination, preservation and transformation of this World come.' Or, shorter: *Brahman is the sole and ultimate cause of the World.*

Up to this point virtually all of the numerous commentators on Bādarāyaṇa agree. The formal structure of the aphorism is accepted by all to be: 'Brahman is that from which all things have come forth, into which they will return and by which they are maintained.' The discrepancies arise when its material contents are investigated, for it is not altogether obvious what the meaning of the words is, what is behind this meaning and still less what lies beyond it.

Now clearly we are face to face with a definition of Brahman. At this point the discussion becomes more involved. Is it an 'essential' definition[17] of Brahman like those given in the *śruti* (Scripture or, rather, revelation), as for example, Being, Knowledge and Bliss, or Truth, Consciousness and Infinitude?[18] Or is it an 'accidental' definition,[19] in which Brahman is made known to us by means of a characteristic property by which we come to know the thing defined? One branch of Śaṅkara's school, e.g. Vācaspati Miśra, will say that it is of course only an external definition. Madhva, on the contrary, will say that it is essential, and his school will point out that to characterize Brahman as *ānanda* (beatitude) or as *kāraṇa* (cause) amounts to the same thing. Both are appropriate and at the same time inadequate: the debate continues.[20]

c) *Importance*

The importance of this text in Indian philosophy is well known. In a certain sense a whole history of Indian philo-

[17] *Svarūpalakṣaṇa*, where the proper 'form' of the thing is given.
[18] Cf. e.g. TU II, 1.
[19] *Taṭasthalakṣaṇa*, where only the shore or bank beside which the thing flows is given, i.e. a property—distinct of its nature—by which the thing is known.
[20] Cf. for instance R. P. Singh, *The Vedānta of Śaṅkara* (Jaipur, 1949), p. 293, where he says that 'the entire misunderstanding about the problem of creation in the Vedānta of Śaṅkara has its genesis in the thought that the Saguṇa Brahman is an ontological principle and the second sūtra undertakes to define the nature of this Saguṇa Brahman.'

sophy could be written on the basis of the *Brahma-sūtra-bhāṣyas*. If the *Brahma-Sūtras* can be said to represent the quintessence of the Vedānta, this second *sūtra* (the first is purely introductory) is a cornerstone on which rests a great part of Indian philosophical speculation.

The central position of this *sūtra* on Brahman, however, should not make us infer that the problem of Brahman is the starting-point of Indian speculation. It seems to be true that the first concern, at least of Vedāntic philosophy, is not Brahman, but *ātman*. In other words psychological priority does not belong to the problem of Brahman but to preoccupation with the Self. It is in the process of reflection upon the Self that a good part of Indian philosophy is led to discover the problem of Brahman,[21] and once this issue is raised it is impossible either to avoid it or to ignore its prime importance.

Although nowadays there is a tendency to emphasize experiential questions and practical issues, we cannot neglect the importance of purely theoretical problems when these are not disconnected from life. In point of fact the importance of our *sūtra* belongs not only to the past but also to the present.[22] We have here an example of a problem common to most philosophical schools. Further, the text is philosophically important in itself because it deals with three major metaphysical problems: the Absolute, the World and their mutual relationship. Its simplicity—though in it lie inherent risks of vagueness and syncretism in the text's interpretation—invites us to a much closer contact with the problem itself than would a text wrapped in complicated speculations or dependent on a fully developed philosophical system. Without these complications, which are brought into being by the commentaries, not only is contact with the problem itself easier and deeper, but so also is the contact, the encounter, between East and West.

[21] Cf. B. Heimann, *Studien zur Eigenart des indischen Denkens*, where the evolution of the concept of *ātman* is thoroughly studied.

[22] Cf. the enlightening article by T. R. V. Murti, 'The Two Definitions of Brahman in the Advaita, *Taṭastha-* and *Svarūpa-Lakṣaṇa*' in *K. C. Bhattacharya Memorial Volume*. Amalner, Indian Institute of Philosophy, 1958. Cf. also M. Hiriyanna, *Indian Philosophical Studies* I (Mysore, 1957); 'Definition of Brahman', pp. 98–103.

We have here an aphorism summarizing Upanishadic cosmology which presents the starting-point for theological speculation and offers a basis on which several philosophical traditions can engage in fruitful discussion. My purpose is not to analyse all the implications of the text or to follow its evolution throughout the history of Indian philosophy, but only to point out some metaphysical considerations that may prove of interest for a dialogue between East and West. Since the attitude of dialogue implies the wish to learn from the partner rather than to teach or to be victorious, I should like to stress certain points from one or other of the two traditions without reference to any specific philosophical system. This same text offers us a valuable complementary insight into a 'Western' problem, namely the cosmological argument for the existence of God. Finally, it will provide an introduction to one aspect of the Christian thematic of the Trinity, for this *sūtra* and the doctrine of the Trinity touch a common problem about which fruitful dialogue can take place. As Śaṅkara himself might say: 'When two things are compared they are compared only with reference to some particular aspect they have in common.'[23] If we fail to seek out such common ground all dialogue is futile and barren, for no dialogue is possible without a certain communion—of minds, of ideas, of aims, or at least of desire.[24]

3. ŚAṄKARA'S INTERPRETATION

I should like to begin with a reference to the commentary of the most illustrious philosopher of Advaita-Vedānta, because no *sūtra* is to be read without a *bhāṣya*, and because no text can be fully understood without a knowledge of the traditional understanding of it. Furthermore, Śaṅkara's commentary is a classical and authoritative one. Moreover, I have chosen Śaṅkara because the *prima facie* meaning of the *sūtra* seems to be at variance with the illustrious Vedāntic system of which he is the most famous exponent. For the text seems to suggest that God is the cause of this World and that the first step

[23] *Brahma-sūtra-bhāṣya* III,2,20; cf. also II,3,40.
[24] Cf. Aristotle, *Metaphysics* III,6 (10006 to 15).

towards knowledge of Brahman is precisely to know it as the originator of this World.

However, the text is more subtle than this. It does not say directly that Brahman is the origin, etc. of the World, but that it is 'that-from-which' the origin, etc. of this World proceeds. In other words, this World has an 'origin, etc.' and 'that-from-which' this 'origin, etc.' proceeds is Brahman. But let us go back to the text, following Śaṅkara's commentary[25] and taking into consideration also the commentaries on Śaṅkara's *bhāṣya* by Vācaspati Miśra[26] and Padmapāda.[27]

For Śaṅkara, *janmādi* stands for origination, preservation and dissolution,[28] because all other transformations or changes can be reduced to these three. *Yataḥ* denotes Brahman as cause,[29] as the omniscient and omnipotent cause[30] from which there is origination, preservation and destruction, or rather production, existence and dissolution.

Only in the Lord (Īśvara) can the World find its source, for neither atoms, nor a non-intelligent being, nor non-existence, nor a changing being can be the cause of this World. Moreover, the source cannot lie in the World's nature as such, since we see that the World only presents us with particular places, times and causes, while we are obliged to consider the World as a whole and find a ground for this whole. If the source lay in the World's nature, it would be possible by mere inference to arrive at the knowledge of Brahman, or we would immediately recognize this World as an effect of Brahman. The theologian Śaṅkara, followed here by Rāmānuja and almost all exponents of Indian philosophy, denies this explicitly, on the grounds that it would, on the one hand, endanger the transcendence and the supernatural

[25] Cf. *Brahma-sūtra-catuḥsūtrī*, ed. Pandit Har Dutt Sharma, Poona Oriental Series no. 70. Poona, Oriental Book Agency, 1940.

[26] *The Bhāmatī of Vācaspati on Śaṅkara's Brahmasūtrabhāṣya, Catuḥsūtrī*, ed. S. S. Suryanarayana Sastri and C. Kunhan Raja. Adyar, Madras, Theosophical Society Publishing House, 1933.

[27] Cf. *The Pañcapādikā of Padmapāda*, tr. into English by D. Venkataramiah, Gaekwad's Oriental Series, 107. Oriental Institute Baroda, 1948.

[28] *Janmasthitirbhaṅga* in h.l.

[29] *Yata iti kāraṇanirdeśaḥ*, ibid.

[30] *Sarvajñātsarvaśakteḥ*, ibid.

reality of Brahman (that cannot be reached by any worldly means) and, on the other hand, would render superfluous the whole *śruti* (Scripture, revelation), whose purpose is precisely to lead us to the knowledge and realization of Brahman.

'Knowledge of the real nature of a thing does not depend on the human intellect'[31]—'it depends on the thing itself.'[32] However, Brahman is a kind of 'thing' that transcends all our sense-knowledge, and therefore the meaning of this text is that Scripture alone reveals Brahman to our intellect with certainty. Śaṅkara quotes the famous text of Varuṇa answering his son Bhṛgu: 'That from which these beings originate, that by which, being originated, they live, and that to which they return; desire to know that: that is Brahman.'[33] And he ends his commentary by quoting what he calls the definitive (Upanishadic) text: 'From bliss—*ānanda*—alone these beings originate, by bliss, being originated, do they live, unto bliss do they return.'[34] Brahman is essentially omniscent cause, eternally pure, intelligent and free.[35]

It is well known that in order to defend the absoluteness of Brahman, Śaṅkara's followers were compelled to say that, properly speaking, it is not Brahman but Īśvara who is the cause of this World, Brahman being completely beyond any kind of relation with this World. Śaṅkara himself, in his *bhāṣya*, does not make a clear-cut distinction between Brahman and Īśvara, identifying rather the latter with the former.[36] Although in one passage he mentions the word Īśvara, he is in fact constantly speaking about Brahman, as also do the Sūtras.

It is an undeniable fact that Śaṅkara refers to Brahman as that from which the origin, preservation and end of this World proceed, and that he stresses the necessity of the Scriptures for the (conceptual) knowing of Brahman. Thus, any kind of

[31] *Na vastuyāthātmyajñānaṃ puruṣabuddhyāpekṣāḥ*, ibid.
[32] *Vastutantram eva tat*, ibid.
[33] TU III,1.
[34] TU III,6.
[35] *Nitya-śuddha-buddha-mukta-svabhāva-sarvajña-svarūpa-kāraṇa* . . ., ibid.
[36] Cf. Paul Hacker, 'Eigentümlichkeiten der Lehre und Terminologie Śaṅkaras: Avidyā, Nāmarūpa, Māyā, Īśvara' in *Kleine Schriften*, pp. 99ff.

cosmological argument for proving the existence of Brahman seems to be ruled out. Nevertheless, if we look closer at Śaṅkara's views, we discover that he does not discard sense-knowledge (and inference therefrom) in itself, but rejects it as a means of reaching Brahman. 'Brahman is not an object of the senses',[37] and 'by nature the senses have objects as their content and not Brahman'.[38] But he states further that 'the knowledge of Brahman culminates in experience and has for content an existent object'.[39] This 'intuition of Brahman'[40] which his school calls the Advaitic experience[41] is, together with Scripture, the means of valid knowledge (*pramāṇa*) of Brahman. Even reasoning reason, inference (*anumāna*), has its place as a 'means of confirming' the given-revealed-truth of the Vedānta.[42] We might summarize Śaṅkara's commentary as follows:

1. Brahman is the cause, i.e., the cause of the origination, preservation and dissolution of this World.
2. This cause cannot be inferred by any type of valid knowledge, for
3. This cause is not the object of sense-knowledge, but
4. It is the object of the Vedānta texts, and
5. It is discovered by a special experience: the Advaitic intuition.

The whole meaning of Śaṅkara's doctrine cannot be derived from a single commentary, but we may assume that he has stated his fundamental ideas on the subject, and that his

[37] *Indriyāviṣayaḥ*, op. cit.
[38] Ibid.
[39] *Anubhavāvasānatvāddhatavastuviṣayatvācca*, ibid.
[40] *Brahmasākṣātkāraḥ, Bhāmatī*, op. cit.
[41] *Advaitānubhava.*
[42] His *Advaita* chapter on the *Māṇḍūkyopaniṣad* is devoted to this problem: It is asked whether non-dualism (*advaita*) can be established only by scriptural evidence or whether it can be proved by reasoning as well. It is said in reply that it is possible to establish non-dualism by reasoning as well. Śaṅkara, *Māṇḍūkyopaniṣadbhāṣya* III,1. Cf. T. Vetter, 'Die Gauḍapādīya-Kārikās: Zur Entstehung und zur Bedeutung von (A)Dvaita' in *Wiener Zeitschrift für die Kunde Südasiens* XXII (1978), pp. 95–131.

utterances here do not contradict the rest of his convictions.[43] His views here are fundamental but perhaps not explicit enough about the nature of the cause, the manner in which it causes, and the nature of the effects.

We should not be too hasty however in drawing conclusions about Śaṅkara's viewpoint. First of all, we are not dealing primarily with him, so the present exposition is only partial; and second, though he explicitly accepts Brahman as cause of the World,[44] he does not in fact say that the effect of Brahman is the being of the World. Being cannot be caused, because there is no transit from being to non-being and vice versa.[45] Being is Brahman and Brahman alone. (Brahman is Being itself.) The effect is nothing but a particular determination of the cause itself.[46] This is not the place to enter into a detailed discussion of Śaṅkara's interpretation. In general, he makes the distinction between an ultimate and ontological level (*pāramārthika*) and an empirical and epistemological level (*vyāvahārika*). Accordingly, there are two forms of Brahman:[47] one without attributes and absolutely unrelated, the other with attributes. It is this latter which constitutes the 'cause' of the World. He does, however, in conformity with Scriptures,[48] strongly stress the unity of this twofold Brahman. I shall indicate my interpretation of this point in the last section of this study.

4. THE SŪTRA IN ITS CONTEXT

Leaving Śaṅkara aside for now, we turn again to the text itself and try to gain some insight into its possible meaning, independently of any particular Indian school, but not outside

[43] Let us only mention, to satisfy our conscience, the important passage BSBh II,1,14 essential for an understanding of his advaitic doctrine.
[44] Cf. BSBh II,1,34, answering the query that God cannot be the cause of the World on account of the injustices and sufferings of this World.
[45] Cf. BG II,16 and Śaṅkara's *Bhāṣya* on it, op. cit.
[46] Cf. BSBh II,2,17. Students of Indian Philosophy will recognize here the *satkārya-vāda* (theory of the effect—pre-existing—in the cause).
[47] Cf. BU II,3,1; MaitU VI,3.
[48] Cf. *Brahma-Sūtra* III,3,39, reconciling texts like BU IV, 2,22 (where the *ātman* really is said to be attributeless) with passages like CU VIII,1,1 (where Brahman assumes all kinds of determinations).

the spirit of Indian philosophy.[49] It can hardly be denied that one of the main purposes of the entire *Vedānta-Sūtras* is to declare that Brahman is the Absolute, the Supreme Principle, the Cause of everything, whatever the *nature* of this Brahman may be and whatever degree of reality this World may have. Furthermore, the first four *sūtras* constitute the scaffolding which supports the most authoritative interpretation of the Vedānta:

1. Desire to know Brahman;
2. Brahman as that from which the origin etc. of the universe proceeds;
3. Brahman as the source of Scripture;
4. Brahman is known to us through Scripture.

The dialectical process could be stated thus:

(1) The *Vedānta-Sūtras* as a summary of the whole *śruti* tell us that Brahman needs to be known, for this knowledge is the summit of wisdom, the injunction of revelation, and the meaning of this life. We therefore desire to know Brahman. Brahman is the object of our research. But in order that this desire should be authentic, we must somehow 'know' its object; that is to say, this Brahman that needs to be known and that we desire to know must already be in some sense 'known' to us, have some meaning for us. We must be able—though we may need help—to make some sense out of the first *sūtra*, and for that to be so the word 'Brahman' cannot be devoid of meaning. It is necessary therefore to point out what is meant by Brahman.

(2) This is the task of the second aphorism. This Brahman that we desire to know is that from which the production and so on of this World proceeds. In other words, what we desire to know is the *whence* of the origin, maintenance and dissolution of this universe and the end of all desires, though we do not yet know who or what it is. Moreover, we are not capable of 'knowing' it by ourselves. We just discover in ourselves the urge to know the origin of everything, the Prin-

[49] As a kind of reparation for not dealing with other great Indian philosophers let us quote only O. Lacombe, *La doctrine morale et métaphysique de Rāmānouja*, besides the already quoted commentaries of Rāmānuja and Madhva.

ciple, the Foundation of 'this'—i.e. of that of which we are aware when we happen to be free of the sway of worldly desires. At the culmination of this urge, at the furthest horizon of this desire, there is Brahman.

(3) But this Brahman is only known to us in its true aspect through the Scriptures—though this still indirect knowledge (*śabda* as a *pramāṇa*) is to be completed by direct experience of the 'object', i.e. Brahman. Only a revelation from him (or it) can unveil to us his (its) real nature. This is obvious for two main reasons: *first*, the Scriptures are there, telling us what Brahman is, and nowhere else do we find this information. *Second*, if we were capable of discovering the nature of Brahman through our mind or senses, Brahman would not be Brahman any more, but would belong to our human sphere: it would be a part of this World and not its Principle. This will now be the path along which the other *sūtras* can safely proceed.[50] What follows is not Scholastic subtlety but a strictly necessary procedure in order to 'save' the transcendence of Brahman, on the one hand, and our possibility of speaking about it, on the other. The mere dialectics of immanence—transcendence (i.e. to affirm that Brahman is also immanent) does not solve the problem, because we cannot reach any synthesis between the two.

5. THE BRIDGE TO THE TRANSCENDENT

We would like now to reflect on the general structure of the question, within its own problematic. I do not claim the authority of any *bhāṣyakāra* for the considerations that follow. It is well known, however, that, at least in Śaṅkara, the desire to know Brahman is aroused by the *śruti* itself. The anthropological dynamism that I am going to read in the text, and to interpret in an ontological way, is reduced in Śaṅkara to a purely epistemological process—that of super-imposition.[51] Even so the problem of the *naturale desiderium*—natural de-

[50] For the sources of the *sūtra*, cf. besides the already quoted TU the SU III,4; V,5; VI,16.

[51] *Adhyāsa*, cf. Śaṅkara's introductory chapter to the BSBh, *Adhyāsa-adhyāya*.

sire—for the Absolute occurs at another level. This is not a question of mere human desire, that thirst which is so thoroughly condemned by Buddha and criticized by both Christian and Vedāntic Scholasticisms, but rather a question of the ultimate dynamism of Being mirrored in that being which is conscious of it and whose consciousness already affects that selfsame dynamism.

(a) The Jñāna of the Jijñāsā

We may wholeheartedly accept with some Indian systems (or reject with others) that the desire to know Brahman is already a 'grace' or 'gift', and even that a certain 'knowledge' of Brahman itself is given to us either directly or through the Scriptures.[52] But this does not affect our problem, because in any case there is a difference between the *desire* to know Brahman and real *knowledge* of Brahman. The point of departure (desire) may contain the final stage (knowledge) potentially or in embryo, as it were, but obviously they are not the same. So even if the desire to know Brahman were not 'natural', but 'inspired', there would still be a difference between the *grace* of desiring and the *gift* of realization.

Thus, by one means or another, we have the desire to know Brahman. This desire is not the same thing as actual (non-dual) 'knowledge' of Brahman, yet it implies a certain concept of Brahman—a concept that somehow must be the bridge over which full realization of Brahman comes to us. It is, as it were, a thin thread that already unites us with Brahman, an ignition-point, a kind of identity or at least a communication, not to say communion, that grows and develops from *Brahmajijñāsā* to *Brahmajñāna*, from the desire to the knowledge. Yet there is a gap, there is no continuity between them.

What are the constituents of this desire? Is the formal object of the desire the same as that of the knowledge? In other words, what is the *jñāna* of the *jijñāsā*? What is the knowledge inherent in our desire to know? What do we actually know (of Brahman) when we desire to know (Brahman)? This point is of capital importance, for it is the

[52] Madhva interprets *atha*, the first word of the BS, in the sense of the grace of Vishnu.

connecting link between ourselves and Brahman, and also seems to be one of the points of contact between Indian and Western philosophy.

Our *sūtra* itself answers this question. We want to know Brahman, we already have the desire. This means, on the one hand, that we do not yet known Brahman as we *can* know it, for we still desire it. That is, we do not know what Brahman is, but have yet to learn. It is unknown to us in that we still *want* to know it. On the other hand, it implies that we have already discovered the importance of Brahman, the place it can and must have in our lives, and that we *know* it to be the terminal and even the formal content of our very desire.[53] The second *sūtra* therefore will have a constitutive tension and a transcendental meaning, since it is to take us from where we are and point out where we desire to be. It cannot give an essential definition of Brahman, because Brahman remains fully unintelligible as long as we are not yet Brahman, as long as we still desire it.[54] It can only give a dynamic description, a verbal but not unreal definition of Brahman. The answer to our quest will correspond to the intensity of our desire. It will be intelligible to the extent that we in our present state as desiring beings are capable of absorbing its meaning. It must be in tune with us and at the same time it must be open to the real 'definition' of Brahman. It must point out the real nature of Brahman, lead us towards the actual end of our desire, while starting from the (perhaps unreal or inauthentic) 'contents' of that desire. In a word, it must be a very peculiar answer if it is to fulfil the dialectical requirements of the problem it intends to solve.

This is the answer given by the *sūtra*: that Brahman that you want to know, that Brahman that you somehow surmise and yet have not fully realized, which you know only in your desire and as an object of desire (and not of knowledge), is *that* from which the origin of *this* comes forth, and *that* which

[53] Cf. the analogous problematics in the West: the Bible, Bernhard, Anselm, Pascal.

[54] *Sa yo ha vai tat paramaṃ brahma veda brahmaiva bhavati*: 'He who knows (sees) the supreme Brahman becomes Brahman himself.' MundU III,2,9. Cf. AV X,7,24.

maintains the very existence of *this*. *This* is: whatever you know, see or can imagine—indeed it is knowing, seeing, imagination and desire itself. Brahman is the cause of all that you call 'this', i.e., of the World.

You may not know the whole World, but you do know a part of it and can well imagine that others know different parts of it. *This*—the World—you somehow know. Now, the cause of *this*—the cause of the World in general and your world in particular, including yourself—is Brahman.

You know this World, or at least your part of it. But you know still more: you know, or understand at least, that this World must have an origin, that it probably had a beginning and seems to require upholding (preservation); in short, it seems to postulate a cause (a reason for being). You desire to know Brahman because the World that you know is not Brahman. Were the World the Absolute, you would not desire, you could not desire to know anything else. The very desire would have no meaning at all. As it is, however, knowledge of the World is accompanied by the necessity of knowing its origin; or, *in concreto*: in knowing an empirical 'thing', you recognize that it is what it is because it has its *ultimate* origin elsewhere, not in itself (in the World). You know this World as originated, requiring a foundation, a source, as being sustained in its present form and requiring an ultimate reason for being. You know this World as *this* and not precisely as Brahman because you discover in *this* an absence of ultimacy.

We do not yet presuppose anything about the nature of that ultimate cause, as for example whether it has to be outside, transcendent, or whether it can also be inside, immanent. We only say that the knowledge of a *thing* carries with it the awareness that it is not its own cause. In other words, the *sūtra* points out the contingency of this World, the metaphysical fact that this World still has room for a foundation, a source, an origin, an ultimate reason, a cause.

(b) Jñāna: Knowledge of the Contingent

Some may object that we do not know this contingency by ourselves, but that this knowledge is communicated, taught to us by the Scriptures of which our *sūtra* is an explanation.

That is to say, we could well know this World without even surmising that it is contingent. It would then be the *śruti* that tells us that the World has a cause and that this cause is precisely Brahman.

However this may be, it makes no fundamental difference to our main purpose, for the statement makes sense in itself and we are able—through the grace of the Lord or without it—to understand its meaning and to accept it either by ourselves or through the teaching of the Scriptures. Our intellect, alone or with the aid of revelation, is capable of understanding the non-contradiction of the fact that this World has a cause—the fact that this World is not an Absolute in itself, that our World has room for an origin, that it admits a sustaining ground, and so on. It is not against the nature of the World to have a foundation, a source, a cause, whereas it would be contradictory for the human intellect to admit that Brahman has a still higher cause, for in that case it would not be Brahman at all.

In other words, the fact of the contingency of the World is not inconsistent with the nature of the World. It is *first* a reasonable statement, whether true or not, whether natural or not, whether attained in fact by our reason alone or 'aided' by some higher illumination. *Second*, it must be true since it is neither unreasonable nor self-contradictory. If, for instance, the World *can* have a cause and has not, then it is unoriginated, uncaused, even though there is 'room' for such an origin or cause. If it can have an origin and has not, either this possibility remains open and real, or it is fulfilled by the World itself, which is then its own origin. In the first case the contingency of the World is already accepted, namely that this World does not have an origin in itself; in the second case an origin is recognized, namely the World itself.

One must be careful to avoid hurried deductions. The existence of God has not been proved—though the basis for such proof has been established—nor has anything been said about his essence. We have tried to show that the World either has its own cause in itself, or that its cause lies beyond itself. It is easy to see that the World cannot have its cause in itself because we recognize its contingency. If we examine the grammatical expression of our text, we note that this

World is not said to be an *idam* but an *asya*; not a *this* but an *of this*. The Genitive (*asya*) is a constitutive property of the things of this World. Beings are 'beings' and not Being, precisely because they are be-coming, because they are not properly a 'to-be', namely *as, einai, esse,* but *sat, ōn, ens, idam*, or, even better, in the Genitive: *sataḥ, ontos, entis, asya*. Beings are 'things', being*s* and not Being because they *belong* to Being; beings are not autonomous but are 'of', 'from', 'to', Being itself.[55] Even if the World were its own cause, there would still be a radical distinction between the *World* as cause and the (totality of the) *things* of the World as effect or caused. That is to say, whether God exists as a separate being or not, and whatever his nature may be, we have shown that the contingency—*ontonomy*—of things and the non-contingency of their possible ground have to be admitted rationally.

We have arrived, then, at the following conclusion: this World is not its own cause. This is a rational truth, whether or not we needed revelation to arrive at it, no matter what the nature of the cause or how this World might have proceeded from it—whether by creation *ex nihilo*, or by some process like *avidyā*, or by any other process whatsoever. The name of that from which the origin etcetera of this World comes forth is Brahman, whose nature is in principle revealed to us by the *śruti*. These are the two statements that complete the teaching of our *sūtra*.

(c) Jijñāsā: The Desire to Know

I have tried to show that the desire to know Brahman is not only a kind of knowledge of Brahman, but also that it implies the knowledge of the contingency of the World. Still, a very important existential problem in this connection remains: do we have a desire to know an *X*, a beyond, an ultimate, a 'Brahman' because we have discovered the unsatisfactoriness, the contingency of the World; or do this contingency and our dissatisfaction with it become noticeable because we have in us a compelling desire for Brahman, for an Ultimate, which is thus already 'known' (albeit 'through a glass darkly') to be

[55] Cf. R. Panikkar, 'Le concept d'ontonomie' in *Proceedings of the XIth International Congress of Philosophy* III, pp. 182 ff., Brussels, 1953.

real? Which comes first, the *knowledge* (of the contingency), or the *desire* (for Brahman)? I do not want to introduce here the pseudo-problem of the priority of knowledge over will, but should like to point out their intrinsic relationship and the existential character of Indian philosophy.

First of all, as is clear from the desiderative verbal form of the substantive *jijñāsā*, it is not a question of will, desire, impulse or the like, *as such*—as an independent faculty—but it is a *knowing* inclination, an appetite to *know*. Such a relation could not be better expressed than by the word *jijñāsā*: we have to ask ourselves whether it is a *desire to know* or a *'knowing' desire*, a desire *springing from knowledge*. Is it an extra-cognitive desire that impels us to know, or is it a knowledge that makes us desire? A longing to know or a further urge of the very knowledge? Obviously it is both. We have already tried to describe the cognitive contents of such a desire. We now turn our attention to the very nature of this desire, this *desiderative knowledge*.

The *sūtra* begins with the clear affirmation of such a desire: we have an urge to jump, as it were, over all the things of this World, using these very things as the springboard to transcendence. The intellectual contents of our desire may be very weak, the cognitive portion quite vague, but the felt urge may be strong enough to bring us to the very threshold of the goal. The very existence of the desire, whatever the proportion of cognitive contents, enables us to leave the realm of pure possibility and enter the sphere of reality. The cognitive contents only open to us the possibility, the non-contradiction, of there being a cause of the World. But the naked desire in itself is a real—one is tempted to say royal—road to the very end of this desire, to the reality of transcendence.

Even after this desire has undergone thorough examination on the part of epistemology and psychology, there remains an ontological factor which can only be interpreted as a perceptible 'point' of this transcendence itself, a point where the transcendence finds an echo, an answer. The ontological structure of this desire appears, then, as a certain communion with its end or goal. There is a yearning for Brahman not only because Brahman calls and manifests itself as desirable, so to speak, but also because that desire, that deep point where the desire transcends the bounds of epistemology and psychology, is already in communication, indeed in communion, with Brahman. Brahman is not only the goal ('object'), it is the very ground of this desire.

Our previous analysis of this desire showed us its cognitive contents, but it is the existential element that pushes us towards the goal. We have no need to contradict Śaṅkara when he says that this desire is aroused by the *śruti*, nor are we saying that it leads to fulfilment, which would be the extinguishing of the desire, but it is only an existential analysis of the desire that can cope with its irreducible singularity. Such a dynamic tendency of our being presupposes many things and is burdened with consequences—perhaps even an argument for the existence of God—but it is in the very desire that our own contingency is embodied. Not only could we not desire Brahman if we already knew ourselves to be it, or if the World were an Absolute, but this desire also reveals our peculiar nature as creatures. This desire cannot be described, only experienced, suffered. The ineffability of which Indian philosophy is so fond represents the inadequacy of our knowledge, especially with regard to ultimate truths, but also with regard to existence itself, even to received and created existence.

The starting-point for an argument for the existence of God, consequently, would be not so much the contents of a certain knowledge as the existential fact of a fundamental desire. At any rate it is neither simple knowledge nor pure desire, but the peculiar human element called *jijñāsā*: the urge to know and the desiderative knowledge all in one. If we forget either of these two poles, we lose sight not only of the Indian perspective but also of the possibility of an authentic philosophical endeavour.

(d) Rational and Natural Knowledge

Before we draw any conclusions from our analysis we have to consider the problem that we have been side-stepping as irrelevant to our first inquiry: the question of whether the human mind is able to arrive by itself at the above-mentioned conclusions, or not. Does the mind require the help of revelation, or are we dealing with a purely rational and natural truth? In the latter case we would be close to a cosmological argument for rational proof of the existence of a supreme principle.[56] Before proceeding further let us briefly recall some classical distinctions. First of all we should recall here the discussion about what is meant by 'human mind', taking into account the various concepts of mind (*manas, buddhi, citta*, etc.) of the different Indian schools. The basic problem is whether the 'human mind' as such is able to reach the Absolute. Vedānta would maintain, following the Upanishads, that the only 'organ' which is truly capable of knowing Brahman is the *ātman*—because ultimately it *is* Brahman.

Further, revelation, understood here as a divine disclosure to the human mind, may be needed either absolutely or relatively. If 'absolutely', the mind may require revelation because it is incapable even of surmising the existence—or incapable of understanding the essence—of a certain revealed truth. Revealed truth surpasses the power of our reason. If 'relatively', the mind may need revelation when the truth is not, as such, above the capacity of human intellect; but (a) we have *made use of* revelation to get to that particular truth, or (b) according to the nature of the truth, our intellect could only affirm its *possibility*, having no means of knowing its actual existence.

Revelation may also mean the existential disclosure of a divine Person, but for the present we do not need to take this into consideration. If God exists and we are from him, if Brahman is the cause of all that exists, then even the human mind and our natural 'lights' are a gift of God, are in him as a participation in his knowledge and, broadly speaking, are also organs of revelation. But when we speak of revelation we mean something special and somehow extrinsic, not given along with human nature as such. It seems beyond dispute

[56] This kind of approach is found in the Nyāya-Vaiśeṣika school; cf. G. Chemparathy, *An Indian Rational Theology. Introduction to Udayana's Nyāyakusumāñjali.* This problem is also closely linked with the whole discussion around the proof for the authoritativeness of a scripture (*āgamaprāmāṇyam*), into which we cannot enter here. Cf. however, G. Oberhammer, 'Die Überlieferungsautorität im Hinduismus' in *Offenbarung, geistige Realität des Menschen*, pp. 41–92.

that the full 'knowledge' of Brahman, the realization of its essence, is absolutely supernatural and requires therefore more than just the acceptance of an extrinsic 'revelation'.

The problem that remains is this: does the knowledge of Brahman, not in its essence, but simply as the cause from which the universe proceeds, require revelation? In other words, does the knowledge of the existence of a Supreme Principle, origin of this World, require revelation, or is it a natural truth? We will not discuss here whether God has in fact revealed this truth or not. We are more concerned with whether human reason can go beyond this World and discover the necessity of the existence of Brahman (that from which and in which the World has its existence), or whether reason must be content merely to acknowledge the possibility of the existence, the non-contradiction of a first cause, once this has disclosed itself.

The problem is thus narrowed down to an analysis of the power of our reason, the crucial point of our philosophical inquiry. To begin with, we should develop a full and proper epistemology,[57] but this would require an independent study. We will have to presuppose it and proceed using very common terms to meet the problem as it presents itself to us. In other words, what is the meaning of that *buddhi* (discriminative faculty) by means of which, so the Upanishad tells us, we can see the Supreme?[58] Obviously, sense-knowledge cannot transcend sense-objects and therefore cannot reach the existence of God, but human reason is not exhausted in sense-knowledge.

Every school of philosophy, even materialism, will accept that Man has a higher form of knowledge that could be called 'reason', whatever connections it may have with perception and sensation. But the mere recognition of reason does not lead to an immediate answer to our problem. Reason does not really transcend sense-knowledge but only organizes and

[57] Cf. Śaṅkara, BSBh II,4,6, for a short summary of the several knowing functions like *buddhi, manas, ahaṃkāra* and *citta*.

[58] Cf. KathU III,12. We have to decline a commentary on KathU III,3–13, which may perhaps be the Indian clue to the whole problem. Cf. also BG III,42, VI,21.

relates it.[59] Reason understood simply as a dialectical power of *anumāna* and *upamāna*, inference and comparison, is unable either to jump out of the World or to penetrate its depths in order to discover beyond and within it that supreme Principle that we call God or Brahman.

Have we any other mental faculty besides our reason? One observation may help to clarify an issue that jeopardizes the mutual understanding between philosophical systems of East and West, though to a certain extent it is merely a matter of vocabulary. The Indian concept of *buddhi*, which has been translated as 'reason', should be understood not in the sense of the Kantian *Vernunft*, but in the Scholastic sense of *intellectus*. Due to the Kantian impact on modern Indian philosophers, what lies beyond reason has been called either 'faith' or 'intuition'. 'Faith', then, is understood as knowledge of the suprasensible, or rather supra-worldly, based on authority or other external sources; 'intuition', on the other hand, is understood as supra-sensible experience. However, to avoid losing the thread of our discourse let us curtail semantic reflections and revert to our main inquiry.

The controversial point is whether or not there is a kind of 'knowledge' that reaches the trans-empirical level without being either sense-knowledge or that higher form of suprarational knowledge that penetrates into the divine reality as such. In other words, if 'reason' is by definition confined to the empirical sphere or reduced to the Kantian *Vernunft*, then in order to transcend this World we need another kind of knowledge. This would be some sort of divine realization given in experience. Certainly, this experience to be 'experienced' also requires a kind of higher organ (the *Vernunft* of the German mystics, the *buddhi* of the Kaṭha Upanishad, and ultimately the *ātman* as mentioned above). In that case, only 'faith' as an intermediate state, understood as an acceptance of the Scriptures, could help us bridge the gulf. But the gap will not be filled unless the immediate experience takes hold of us. In the West this position has been called 'fideism'. For such an attitude the very possibility of a cos-

[59] Cf. Śaṅkara's KenUBh II,1: 'It is possible to know only that which can be an object of the perception of the senses.'

mological argument is excluded, because only faith can reach the transcendent and reason by definition is unable to transcend the empirical level.

We must emphasize that this is not the traditional Indian attitude, principally because the clear-cut distinction between reason and faith as the West knows it (due to Christian influence) is foreign to Indian philosophy, where the problem arises differently. Yet, if our interpretation is not completely mistaken, our *sūtra* expresses a cognitive dynamism conducive to the discovery of the contingency of the World. I shall leave the question open as to whether this knowledge is *arthāpatti* (inference) or faith; nor shall I engage in discussion of the possible existence of a higher human 'intellect' by which Man discovers the existence of the transcendent without penetrating to its essence. At any rate it would not be difficult to show that reasoning reason itself is founded in a peculiar rational intuition. But can human reason intuit the contingency of the World?

Not just the *Brahma-Sūtras* but the whole of Vedānta and almost all Indian philosophy, including the so-called 'non-orthodox' systems, have in common an idea that presupposes such an insight in relation to the World: namely, that *this* World is not definitive, that it is not worth being attached to because it is not real Being or ultimate reality, because it is neither the Principle nor the End of Being (or even of the World itself). This presupposition is so widespread as to represent a true common denominator of the Indian spirit, and to query this presupposition or to try to prove it would seem strange indeed. It is considered to be the most elementary condition for the study of philosophy and for any intellectual—i.e., spiritual—endeavour worthy of the name.[60] About the positive nature of that Principle and its relation to the World there may be discrepancies, but *neti neti*[61] is virtually the starting-point of all Indian speculation, expressing as it

[60] Cf. only as a few instances: the various commentaries on BS I,1,1 (especially Śaṅkara's); Sāṃkhya Kārikā 1; Yoga-Sūtra II,16.

[61] It is well known that *na iti, na iti* ('not this, not this') is applied primarily to God. It is in fact the best description of Brahman. Cf. BU II,3,6; and also III,9,26; IV,2,4, the *neti* applied to the *ātman*.

does the absolute incomparability of God to the World. The experience, or we could say the conviction, of the contingency of the World is the background over against which the problem of reality is viewed, for by far the greater part of Indian philosophy.

On the other hand, this conviction is not and cannot be simply a conclusion derived from an empirical kind of inference. Rather, it is the result of a spiritual experience. The very beginning of the inquiry about Brahman, the desire to know it, implies not only existential dissatisfaction with this World, but also the most deep-rooted conviction of its contingency. Obviously, if the problem is viewed from such an existential perspective, the question of the 'rational' proof of the existence of God does not arise in the way it does in post-Cartesian thought and even in a part of Thomistic Scholasticism. Here it arises in congruity with the Medieval and Ancient metaphysical systems of Europe and is closely related to Old Testament teaching.[62]

For Indian philosophy 'reason alone' has but little meaning—and this for two reasons: 1. reason is not isolated from the rest of our human faculties, our human nature; and 2. it is not self-sufficient even in the highest forms of knowing.

1. If it is reason that discovers the existence of God, it is a reason incarnated in a human person who has reached some degree of purification, objectivity, freedom of will, and so forth.[63] Reason may be the instrument, but it is not effective unless it is properly used. It is the whole Man who uses it, and he will only use it properly when he is pure, detached, moral. 2. It may be that the light, the power, God has given to reason enables us to discover his existence, but Man has not, in fact, received *reason alone*. After all, 'reason' is an abstraction, though a very real one, and the Indian mind abhors its conversion into a hypostasis. To those who do not believe in God, the Indian tradition does not say: 'Inquire, think, try to investigate with your reason!' but rather: 'Do penance, gain perspective by detaching yourself from the

[62] For the biblical attitude of C. Tresmontant, *Études de métaphysique biblique* (Paris, J. Gabalda, 1955), p. 161, for instance.

[63] Cf. MundU III,1,8; KathU II,9;20; etc.

World, look for a spiritual master, search with your whole being. It is not your reason that is weak, it is you who are ill.'

If we still insist on the power of 'reason alone' to discover the existence of the supreme principle, Indian philosophy will say: either God exists, in which case reason is not *alone*, or God does not exist, in which case alone reason *is*. But then this solitary reason cannot prove that which does not, by hypothesis, exist.

The problem thus can only be posed as an epistemological hypothesis: what is the instrument by which we come to know of the existence of God? Among the various instruments reason undoubtedly has a special role, a very important one, for it makes intelligible the structure of the World—that it is contingent, that it is not its own cause. But at the same time, reason has a very weak role, because it can say almost nothing about the nature of this cause. Reason, says Indian philosophy, only functions in its proper place when it listens to the Scriptures and tries to work together with faith to find a basis for a higher understanding.

6. THE COSMOLOGICAL ARGUMENT

A proof for the existence of God may be elaborated from all that we have said so far, but the Indian mind does not see the necessity for it and prefers to consider God as the point of departure for its inquiry rather than as its point of arrival. That is why the characteristics of immanence have more appeal than those of transcendence. To look for God outside, as transcendence, seems almost a betrayal of the God inside. In India, the cosmological argument seems rather like a cosmological presupposition. It is not so much that the vision of this World would lead us to God, but rather the reverse: the desire to know God enables us to see this World from the proper perspective.

The Indian argument, if it exists at all, will not take the form: we discover that this World is contingent, *therefore* God exists as its cause (i.e. if we assume that contingency really needs a non-contingent foundation); but rather: *because* God exists, we discover the contingency of the World. It is not so much something that we have to discover as it is something that makes us discover the true nature of things. The Indian believer cannot put his faith aside when he deals with vital and ultimate problems.

This attitude may proceed from a *heteronomic* assumption and generate confusion between faith and reason, theology and philosophy. Heteronomy is the attitude which takes for granted the divine transcendence and the contingency of the World. Yet in reality it contains in embryo a vision of things that we may call *ontonomic*, which is more mature than the extremist *autonomic* conception of reality. Autonomy is the rational, reflective attitude which assumes that every being has its own independent law, whereas ontonomy overcomes the extreme opposition of these two views by an integrated vision of being. For the autonomic period of Western thought proofs of the existence of God are essential; without them everything collapses. This is not the case in a heteronomic culture and philosophy.[64] At this point an ontonomic evaluation of all proofs becomes necessary.[65]

On this point, we will only say the following: Any proof implies a starting-point A and a conclusion B, on the one hand, and the proof proper, which gives evidence of B under the assumption of A, on the other. It is obvious that the consistency (epistemologically, the certainty) of B cannot be greater than that of A, for A is the ground on which B rests. Now, to prove the existence of God out of the existence of this World and by means of our reason implies that we have more confidence in the proof itself and in the validity of our means

[64] This does not mean that there have been no such approaches in Indian philosophy, such as the Nyāya-Vaiśeṣika mentioned above. It would lead us too far to analyse the Nyāya-Vaiśeṣika method in the light of what has been said here. See e.g. G. Oberhammer, 'Zum Problem des Gottesbeweises in der indischen Philosophie' in *Numen*, vol. xii, fasc. 1, Jan. 1965, pp. 1–34; G. Chemparathy, 'Two Early Buddhist Refutations of the Existence of Īśvara as the Creator of the Universe' in *WZKS* 12–13, 1968–9 (Festschrift Frauwallner), pp. 85–100; id., *An Indian Rational Theology*, op. cit.

[65] In this sense the enormous amount of literature on the theme of the proofs of the existence of God should be understood and appraised. For the concepts of heteronomy, autonomy and ontonomy, cf. R. Panikkar, *Māyā e Apocalisse*, pp. 71ff.

of attaining it than we have in the existence of God. This is a well-known syllogistic rule.[66]

A real believer or one who has not made a sharp separation between faith and reason is existentially unable to have more confidence in his own reason or in sense-evidence than in God. He needs and wants no proof because it seems to him a kind of blasphemy (even if such proof has value in the cultural and philosophical state called *autonomous*). At most, he will accept that the function of reason is either to clarify the problem or to offer a certain proof for those who still need it; but basically it will seem to him a sort of academic experiment or a kind of play, like children imitating what adults do in the 'real' world. Let us see, then, how this 'experiment' proceeds.

One thing that I proposed earlier in this chapter remains to be considered: between the World and Brahman there is a relation of effect-cause. Between the higher knowledge of Brahman and empirical worldly knowledge, there is the rational, and in a sense also natural, knowledge of Brahman as the cause of this World, or perhaps more accurately, a knowledge of this World as something which leaves room for Brahman as its Principle.

Turning again to our *sūtra*, we could put the problem in these terms: Brahman *as such* is unknown and *as such* is not desired (*nil volitum quin praecognitum*). But there is a point of encounter between the transcendence of Brahman and the immanent World. It is an intermediate stage that we are not to hypostatize or to consider as substance since it is only a relation, an epistemic stop on our way to Brahman. Between the two points of reference, so to speak, i.e. below Brahman and above the World, we discover the origin, preservation, destructibility etc. of this World. On our way to Brahman we start from this earth and reach a middle point, namely the 'reason'—*ratio*—of this World: its origin, preservation etc. But this is not yet the end of the journey. In a way we have reached the cause of this World, as cause, but we have not yet reached it as Brahman (which is not exhausted in its function as cause of the World). The text tells us that this

[66] *Peiorem sequitur semper conclusio partem.*

cause is not only a cause, but also Brahman, for the knowledge of which other Vedāntic texts exhort us to leave behind all worldly ideas and categories. Brahman may indeed coincide with the cause of the World, but simply recognizing the cause as cause is not yet the ultimate knowledge. The latter is the knowledge of the cause not only as cause, but as Brahman.

We are now faced with two different problems: the first concerns our ascent from the World to its cause, and the second consists in recognizing that cause as Brahman, the Supreme, Unique and Transcendent. It goes without saying that these two progressive moments are not two separate entities but two phases of our spiritual itinerary. The intermediate stage is but a pause in our theological ascent.

(a) From the World to its Cause

What makes us transcend this World and approach its cause? Why are we not satisfied with this World but feel the compulsion to go beyond, to look for something else as its basis and foundation? Two groups of 'reasons' answer such a question: the first group concerns our knowledge of the World; the second group, the world of our knowledge.

Our knowledge of the World. We want to transcend the World and seek its cause because we discover that this World is contingent and does not have in itself the ground of its being, that it is not the ultimate reality. But our knowing faculties impel us towards an Absolute. Our knowledge stops nowhere short of Fullness of Being. Two almost antagonistic ideas are in operation here: on the one hand, the recognition of the contingency of the World; and on the other hand, the awareness that our very knowledge presupposes or postulates an Absolute. That is to say, the very constitution of our thinking power compels us to assert: either the World is an Absolute or the Absolute lies beyond the World. Moreover, this is so almost by definition of reason itself, because that from which our reason ultimately proceeds—or in which it ends as not having need of a further explanation or foundation—that is the Absolute. The only problem not resolved is that of the nature of this idea of the Absolute, about which our reason can say very little. In a word, we go beyond the World because our intellect compels us always to go beyond, except when it presupposes that there is nothing 'outside' the World. Whether or not such a presupposition has a logical justification or an ontological motivation is a problem we cannot here consider.

The world of our knowledge. We want to transcend the World because we discover that the World is not an Absolute. But why do we discover the World as contingent? We have already noted that we could postulate the World as the Absolute, but this would be only a dispute of words because that Absolute 'World' would not be the World that we see and experience. Hence the problem remains. Indian speculation might answer this as follows: we experience the World as contingent because it *is* contingent; we can suppose the existence of an ultimate cause because such a cause exists; and if we want to 'prove' such an existence it is because that very Existence leads us to desire to transcend the World and go to Itself. God himself is the cause of our desire and the motor of our rational dynamic. Thus, when we try to demonstrate the existence of God, we are presupposing it, for if he were nonexistent we would not even have the desire to go to him.

No doubt a logical mind will say that this, though it is beyond dispute, does not prove the existence of God since in fact the argument presupposes it. The typical Indian reply would be: 'I could accuse my interlocutor of falling into a vicious circle, because he *could not* question whether God exists or not if that God did not exist. If God did not exist, my interlocutor could not even exist, let alone question.' Here the disagreement and the agreement both appear clearly: one discovers God as the logical implication and ontological presupposition of the question about his existence; the other discovers God as the logical conclusion and ontological result of the question about his existence. Both trains of thought are correct, though not interchangeable, and both have the same formal structure: an insight into God's existence derived from the data of our actual experience. Both are means or mediatory ways rather than immediate intuitions: one discovers

God in the implications, the other in the conclusions.[67] We have used the name 'God' throughout in order to make the argument simpler, more vivid; but clearly we are still in the first stage of the recognition of a First Cause of the World.

The answer to our first question, then, would be: 'That which makes us transcend this World and approach its cause is God himself.' But *how* does this happen? Evidently by means of our reason, or our intellect, if we prefer this word. Again, how does God guide our intellect? Does he guide it with a special illumination or through the natural light of our actual intellect? We can surely answer that God avails himself of the natural light of reason as regards the discovery of that First Cause, because this truth is not beyond the limits of reason. We therefore leave aside the question of whether in fact God grants a special illumination to our cognitive faculty, or whether he simply lets our reason grasp it with the natural light proper to it: that is, whether the *śruti* arouses in us the knowledge about Brahman, or whether a special 'grace' is required.

(b) From the Cause to Brahman

i) *Excursus on Brahman.* Before we proceed further with our argument an Indological note must be inserted in order to avoid misunderstandings. To Hinduism, Brahman is not a person and consequently is not looked upon as a personal God but as the Absolute, and thus is identified with God only in the transpersonal sense expressed by the word Godhead. Yet, in order to understand this peculiar relationship (Brahman-God) in its proper context, it is necessary, *first*, to explain briefly some of the steps in the development of the concept of Brahman and *second* to specify in a more speculative way the reasons for the equivalence I am making between God and

[67] Well known is that East-West encounter between Socrates and a certain Indian philosopher. The latter asked for the subject-matter of Socrates' philosophy. 'Human life', replied Socrates. The wise man from India burst into laughter and asked how one could know human realities without knowing the Divine previously. And in fact Socrates' first disciple shared in the opinion of the Indian thinker already. Cf. Eusebius, *Praeparatio evangelica* I,8 (*apud* M. Schmaus, *Katholische Dogmatik* II [München, Max Hueber, 1954], p. 64).

Brahman which is in agreement with the usage of modern scholars, though my usage is not exactly identical in sense to theirs.[68]

The Vedas present Brahman mainly as a mysterious power inherent in sacrifice and in the sacred hymns and prayers (*mantra*), which fortifies the Gods and provides a kind of ground for the whole of existence. There are several approaches to this power which are not exclusively linked with sacrifice and ritual; e.g. in the Atharva Veda it is identified with the *skambha*, the *axis mundi* or support of the universe, and with the supreme Lord.[69] In the Brāhmaṇas Brahman is sometimes identified with Prajāpati, the Lord of Creatures.[70] In the Upanishads Brahman is intimately connected with the quest for a World-ground, a first principle. 'Brahman is called the goal.'[71] In various Upanishads the mystery of Brahman is approached through the Upanishadic method of successive correlations and identifications between cosmic and psychological realities, the culmination of which is the identification of *ātman* (the inner Self) with Brahman (the cosmic ground). At some of these stages Brahman is identified with life-breath,[72] food,[73] and with a whole series of step-by-step identifications given by the Chāndogya Upanishad.[74] Underlying all these is the idea of the All,[75] the Reality of all things,[76] the Real of the real,[77] the imperishable,[78] the One.[79]

[68] Cf. the Outline by R. E. Hume and the Introduction by S. Radhakrishnan to their translations of the Upanishads (S. Radhakrishnan, *The Principal Upaniṣads*). Cf. also G. G. Mukhopadhyaya, *Studies in the Upaniṣads*, pp. 44ff. About the concept of Brahman see L. Renou, 'Sur la notion de brahman' in *Journal Asiatique* 237 (1949), pp. 7–46; J. Gonda, *Notes on Brahman*. Utrecht, 1950.

[69] *Parameṣṭhin*, cf. AV x,7,17, etc.

[70] Cf. SB xi,2,3,1, etc.

[71] MundU ii,2,4.

[72] Cf. KausU iii,2; BU iii,9,9; vi,1,13 (CU v,1,13); etc.

[73] Cf. TU ii,2; iii,7–9; iii,10,6; MaitU vi,12–14; CU vii,9,2, etc.

[74] CU vii; the series is: name, word, mind, purpose, thought, contemplation, wisdom, energy, water, radiance, space, memory, hope, life.

[75] CU vi,12,3; BU i,4,10; PrasnU iv,10–11, etc.

[76] Cf. CU vi, 1,3–6.

[77] *Satyasya satyam*, BU ii,1,20.

[78] MundU ii,1,2; SU v,1; BU iii,8,8, etc.

[79] BU iii,9,1–9; MaitU vi,17; MandU 7.

Analysis would show that the goal of this search was absolute Being, not in an abstract sense, but closely related to experience. Now because the question of Being always starts from an analysis of beings, and beings in their mobility point towards their own non-existence, Brahman had also to encompass non-Being.[80] All these different approaches to Brahman can be said to point to the mystery of the Absolute.[81]

At this point, two important problems arise, the *first* of which is the relationship of Brahman with *ātman*. Although this important relationship does not directly concern our problem, it gives rise to an analogous question. *Ātman*, the term of the interior search, being the innermost spirit or Self in Man, came to be identified with Brahman, the ground of being.[82] Each is ultimate in its own sphere and, in a certain way, irreducible, one in the anthropological, the other in the cosmological realm. The discovery of this identity was one of the loftiest heights reached by Indian philosophy and the corner-stone of Advaita-Vedānta,[83] though it is impossible to enlarge upon it here.

Now this is not the only creative tension in Indian thought. The *second* problem, though less loudly and insistently discussed, is no less important than the first and just as full of vital consequences. This is the question of the relationship between Brahman and God. Both names stand for the same ultimacy, yet they seem to connote distinct functions. Brahman stands at the end of philosophico-theological speculation, at the limits of the intellect, or just behind it, being essentially immanent. God, on the other hand, is the end and object of human adoration and love. The two different names refer ultimately to one Unity, because our will and our intellect will not stop short of absolute Oneness, but the God of Man's worship cannot be just the foundation of being, the mere condition of existence—it has also to be a person, a subject, an 'I'.

[80] CU VI,2,1; TU II,7.
[81] Our references are not exhaustive, but are only meant as an introduction to the problem.
[82] Cf. BU II,5,19; IV,4,25; CU VIII,14,1, etc.
[83] Cf. O. Lacombe, *L'Absolu selon le Vedānta*.

What for simplicity's sake we here call 'God' has in the course of the development of Vedic-upanishadic religion expressed itself in various ways. Beside the so-called 'henotheistic' attitude of the Rig-Veda, the two symbols which have contributed most to the idea of one God are the Purusha of the late Vedic period[84] and Prajāpati, the Lord of Beings of the Brāhmaṇas. When the exuberant Vedic Gods withdrew discretely from the scene, both the uniqueness of God and the absoluteness of Brahman appeared. After the affirmation of Brahman in the oldest Upanishads in contradistinction to a plurality of Gods, there was a corresponding counter-movement in the Kaṭha, Muṇḍaka and Śvetāśvatara Upanishads in favour of one God.[85] Although very often the distinction between God and Brahman is not sharply drawn, God here appears different from Brahman and is even called its source.[86] We shall come back to this in connection with the concept of Īśvara.

Modern scholarship is still discussing this double problem.[87] Brahman is the Ultimate, but God would have no meaning if he also were not the Absolute and the Ultimate. Now their natures—if we may speak thus—appear to be very different. The one is abstract, general, all-pervading from below as it were, common to everything and the presupposition of every being; the other is concrete, personal, all-embracing, from above, as it were, calling to union, but yet transcendent, the end and goal of every being.

Indian speculation identifies God and Brahman even though their characteristics do not seem to coincide. After all, the attributes of the Ultimate are only conveyed to us by means of our mode of knowledge. Yet the same criticisms that may be levelled against a hurried identification between Brah-

[84] Cf. RV X,90 etc. Cf. J. Gonda, *Viṣṇuism and Śivaism*, esp. the chapter 'The Gods' Rise to Superiority', pp. 25–33.
[85] Cf. the wonderful description of the *puruṣa* in MundU II, 1,2. Cf. also SU I,8; V,5–6, etc.
[86] Cf. MundU III,1,3.
[87] Cf. S. N. Dasgupta, *A History of Indian Philosophy*, vol. i, pp. 42 sq., also R. D. Ranade, *A Constructive Survey of Upanishadic Philosophy*; J. Gonda, 'The Concept of a Personal God in Ancient Indian Religious Thought' in *Selected Studies*, vol. iv (Leiden, Brill, 1975), pp. 1–26.

man and *ātman* apply also to a facile identification of Brahman and God. I would like to make a further distinction of fundamental importance and attempt to throw some light on the problem.

a) *From an essentialistic point of view*, I would agree with the criticism stated above, which can be expressed in Western Scholastic terms as follows: if Brahman is somehow the *ens commune*, the quiddity of all beings, the universal substratum and the primordial condition of all things, it cannot be identified with the *ens realissimum*, the living God, source of all beings, absolute reality that is not only *in* everything but also *above* all things. This problem clearly demands an independent study, but the following observation may be made.[88]

Although we should beware of reducing metaphysics to anthropology, much less to psychology, we should recognize the close ties that exist between the three disciplines. Our mode of thinking, our methods of investigation, are conditioned not only by the nature of the object but also by the anthropological structure of the subject. It seems, then, that our research on the Absolute can have two different orientations, since the object one sees will differ according to the path one follows. The Upanishads are, from a metaphysical point of view, one of the masterpieces of human thinking in its search for the World-ground, for the foundation of the universe, for the 'truth of the real' (*satyasya satyam*). But the search can be conducted in two ways: we can look for the ground, the Absolute, the support; or we can look for the end, the ultimate goal, the summit. In other words we are constitutionally bound to search for that principle either below, among the understructures common to all beings, or above, as the end and culmination of everything. I am not here simply talking about immanence and transcendence, even though what I say may have a certain relation with these two categories. The ways of immanence or transcendence concern

[88] Cf. the philosophies of K. Jaspers, M. Heidegger, etc. Cf. also within Scholastic philosophy: 'In verità l'Essere ci si presenta sempre come il fondamento assoluto di tutti gli oggetti e come ciò, che non può essere ridotto ad og-getto.' J. B. Lotz, 'Mythos, Logos, Mysterion' in *Il problema della demitizzazione* (Roma, Archivio di Filosofia, 1961), p. 121.

the object, while here I propose to consider two different methods with which the subject, Man, can proceed in his search for Being. Let me describe these two methods of inquiry a little more closely.

One of them will proceed in general by searching for that which all things have in common, that in which they all share. Everything that is *is*, and this *being* is everything that is. Every being is a being because it is a part, or a manifestation (*vivartavāda*), or a transformation (*pariṇāmavāda*), of that *being*. That *being* is therefore the origin of all, because it is all; it is the source of all beings because it *is* all beings. All that *is* is nothing but that. Some Greek philosophers referred to this concept as prime matter; the Upanishadic philosophers used the word Brahman. Everything that *is* is only this substratum, because only this substratum is common to all things. This is truly the all and the ground of everything.[89] Whatever the form in which being presents itself, this form exists only in so far as it is Brahman, Being, the substratum of everything.[90] Man's thirst for unity and his psychological inclination towards immanence may be two important factors in this search for a World-ground as the common basis of every being.[91] There is also a certain feminine feature in this conception of Brahman as 'matrix' and womb of all that is.

The second procedure shows the opposite characteristics. Man's thirst for sublimity and his psychological orientation towards transcendence are the dominant factors here. What is sought is a principle of otherness rather than one of identity. A certain masculine emphasis is found in this conception of God as Father, Creator, Active Principle.

This second way involves the search for the ultimate not

[89] Cf. AV x,8,2. Cf. M. Eliade, *Yoga* (London, 1958), p. 115 *et passim*. On *skambha* in the AV cf. also the interesting remarks by E. A. Solomon, *Summaries of Papers, Submitted to the XX Session of the All-India Oriental Conference* (Bhuvaneswar, 1959), pp. 22–3.

[90] In the *maṇḍala* and *yantra* the central point (*bindu*) symbolizes the undifferentiated Brahman. Cf. M. Eliade, op. cit., p. 219; G. Tucci, *The Theory and Practice of the Mandala*. London, Rider & Co., 1961.

[91] Cf. the famous comparison of Gauḍapāda, Āgamaśāstra III,3,9, referring to the one space limited by several jars and reverting to the same space once the jars are broken (so it occurs with the *jīvas* and *ātman*).

from below but from above. What all beings have in common will be only the most common thing, namely, only an external resemblance which allows us to give the same name to similar things; but in fact each being is unique and there does not exist a common being or 'prime matter' in which all things share and by which they subsist.

The Ultimate that I am trying to describe is not merely transcendence; it is also origin, principle, cause—that otherness that sustains and produces all other beings. If Brahman is the *One*, God is the *Other*. The return of all beings to the Absolute is not considered as a dissolution of all individuality, as in the case of being merged in Brahman, but as a union with God, a resurrection of all things on earth, because the World-ground is not a subjacent and pre-existing identity, but a sublime communion that has to be reached.

The first way is particularly oriented towards identity, immanence, unity; the other is more conscious of difference, transcendence, otherness. Indian speculation for the most part is inclined to search for identity; Semitic speculation, on the other hand, characteristically emphasizes the uniqueness of each being and differences between beings. The first kind of mind, typically Indian, probes the depths of being to find the truth; the second kind of mind is directed upwards, looking for the truth in the most sublime heights. To be blind to differences is as one-sided as to be blind to identity. To maintain a balance between these two tendencies, to be as profound as it is sublime, to look as deep as it does high, is one of the functions of mature philosophy.

In a word, the conception of Brahman scarcely coincides at all with the conception of God; the two conceptions are almost as opposed as pure potentiality to pure actuality. We recognize of course that the Absolute transcends every conception, but even so our ideas about it are not irrelevant so long as we live in this temporal World.

Moreover, no two conceptions of the Absolute coming from different traditions will coincide. The Muslim and the Christian concepts of God, for instance, though they have many points in common, are essentially different because of the Christian idea of God as Trinity which makes room for the belief in Christ as Son of God. Within Christianity itself, the

Thomistic conception of God is different from that of Duns Scotus; Leibniz and Descartes differ, as will any other pair of thinkers from different schools of metaphysical thought. *A fortiori* the idea of Brahman is not the theistic notion of God.

b) *From a vital and existential point of view* both conceptions, that of Brahman and that of God, even if they are different, and even if one were wrong, point to the same reality (which is Being, ultimate Truth, the Absolute). That Brahman, which is considered as passive, non-active, sub-structural, and is recognized as the cause of this World, may not stand philosophical analysis, or it may, on the other hand, oblige one to revise one's conception of God; nevertheless it certainly points towards the same Reality that the other philosophical tradition calls 'God'. Similarly, that God which is seen as creator, active, transcendent, masculine, the provider responsible for this World, may not be impervious to thrusts of philosophical speculation, ancient or modern, and we may need thoroughly to revise our concept of his nature; still, the concept 'God' undoubtedly points towards the same Mystery that the other tradition calls 'Brahman'.

In fact if we try to penetrate the *res significata*, as Thomas Aquinas would put it, and reach that above-mentioned existential level which transcends all conceptions, we will find ourselves within that Absolute that constitutes the ultimate Reality and its Mystery. But one can only speak of it using words that may be understood differently by whoever hears them, depending on the person's cultural heritage. It remains certain, however, that the ultimate Reality is what is intended by the different concepts we have been discussing, even though these, as we have seen, may be inadequate. That Reality is never fully reached by any concept, because it is inexhaustible and concepts are limited, finite. Yet the infinitude of the ultimate Reality allows even 'misguided missiles' to hit the target ontologically.

For this reason I think we are entitled to counterbalance those philosophical divergencies that belong to the *essential* order and to proceed in our search after the nature and function of that ultimate Reality that the Indian tradition calls Brahman.[92] After all, it is from within a living tradition that we will contribute to its progress. This is valid for the Hindu as well as the Christian traditions.

Even on the purely theoretical plane, the problem is far from being resolved in favour of one position or the other. Even within Indian philosophy itself there is no little argument about the concept of Brahman, and it would be too arbitrary to define Brahman only as undiscriminated Being.[93]

Brahman is not only indeterminate fundament, immanent, unconscious; it is also the supreme consciousness, the transcendent.[94] The *jñānins* may have discovered Brahman and the *bhaktas* God; but then comes the discovery of the relation between Brahman and God, which in a certain sense is as important as the identification of *ātman* and Brahman. God who is conceived as personal, without the corrective of the concept of Brahman, threatens to become an anthropomorphic idol. The trans-personal Brahman, if deprived of the complementary vision of Brahman *as* God, may dissolve into a mere abstraction of the *ens commune*. I believe however that Indian wisdom offers immense possibilities of deepening the concept of the Absolute.[95] The famous Pascalian dichotomy between the God of the philosophers and the God of Abraham, Isaac and Jacob is precisely what Indian thought has always tried to overcome. The Upanishads long ago began discussing the problem of unification, which medieval Indian

[92] I would agree with the remarkable study of R. C. Zaehner, *At Sundry Times*, except perhaps in his disparaging interpretation of Advaita which he identifies with a monolithic monism. I think that Advaita Vedānta in spite of its monistic danger—only too real in many of its representatives—contains a deeper truth which should not be easily dismissed in favour of an unqualified theism. Christian trinity is something more than pure theism. God is there not just *one* Person, and yet is *one* God.

[93] Only too well known is the thematic between *saguṇa* and *nirguṇa* Brahman.

[94] Besides the former references, cf. TU II,6; CU III,12,6; KathU IV,9; VI,13; MaitU VI,22; MundU II,2,8; SU I,13; BU IV,4,20; KenU II, etc.

[95] Cf. O. Lacombe, *L'Absolu selon le Vedānta*; H. Jacobi, *Die Entwicklung der Gottesidee bei den Indern*. Bonn-Leipzig, Schroeder, 1923 N. Macnicol, *Indian Theism*; J. Gonda, *Viṣṇuism and Śivaism*.

schools of thought took up with renewed speculative vigour.[96] There could not be, in fact, one God for pious believers and another, a World-ground, for philosophers. Men cannot be satisfied with an amorphous Brahman: they also want a living Brahman, pure consciousness, perfect bliss and supreme Being—not as a kind of sum-total of all beings, but that which, though being in all, cannot simply be resolved into 'all beings'.[97]

Has Indian philosophy realized this synthesis? It is not my concern here to develop this kind of inquiry, but I may recall that within Christian philosophy even as great a theologian as Thomas Aquinas has not been completely successful in welding a union between the Aristotelian philosophical God (prime mover, ultimate cause, absolute Being without relation to the World) and the living God who cares for Man, loves the World to the point of sending the eternal Word, his only-begotten Son, to save it.

To sum up, we could say that Brahman and God are, as it were, *materialiter* the same reality, but *formaliter* different. They point to the same supreme reality, but from two different points of view. The description of the Absolute differs fundamentally: we cannot equate the two notions. Yet if we are aware of the double perspective described above, we shall understand that in spite of the differences, both languages are talking about the same. Since both intend to express the Absolute, there is an internal dialectic in each pointing towards the complementary aspect. The concept of Brahman needs the 'concrete' aspect, and this gives rise to the concept of Īśvara with its attendant problems. On the other hand it is not sufficient to consider God solely as supreme Lord, and this is where philosophical discussion of God comes in, and the problem of the 'God of the philosophers'. It may be that the ongoing, deepening inquiry into the nature of the Absolute is one of the most important results of the contemporary

[96] Besides different schools of Vedānta and Nyāya-Vaiśeṣika, mention should be made also of an important and rich school like Kashmir Śaivism, besides other Bhakti-schools. Cf. also J. E. Carpenter, *Theism in Medieval India*.

[97] Cf. the famous passage of the Gītā, BG IX,4–5; cf. also VII,12.

meeting of philosophies and cultures. To avoid misunderstanding, let me add that in any effort to illumine a relationship one is obliged to stretch the meaning of words up to their utmost limit. God and Brahman are not just two perspectives of the 'same thing', because both God and Brahman include the respective 'perspectives'. We can call 'them' two ways of speaking about the 'same' if we understand language as also belonging to the reality it 'speaks about'. In the final analysis I am not proposing a synthesis but suggesting an understanding.

ii) *The Last Step of the Argument.* Throughout the history of Indian philosophy we find arguments to prove that without the Scriptures the reality of Brahman cannot be 'known'.[98] In order to identify the cause of the World with the Absolute we need a further epistemological step. Even if most of the preceding arguments were accepted, they would not constitute a proof. The First Cause is somehow divine, but if God is to be something more than a Relation to the World, we must pursue the inquiry further. We have not yet proved that the cause of the World is single or that it has no equal with what we call 'cause' in the empirical World. I shall not linger on this point since I think that it could easily be answered using arguments similar to those already adduced. All empirical causes are either based on a single cause or derive from a unique and superior source, which might be called the ultimate cause.

The more serious question is whether this unique and supreme cause is identical to or different from the absolute and transcendent Brahman. The terms Cause of the World, Demiurge, prime Mover, Creator, divine Power, Īśvara—to use several names according to different philosophical conceptions—though not equivalent, are all expressions for the principle of the World, but not for the Absolute *as such.* All this is not yet Brahman, according to Vedānta, and, as our text tells us, Brahman is *that from which* the whole being of the

[98] Cf. Sara Grant, 'Śaṅkara's Conception of Śruti as a Pramāṇa' in *Research Seminar on Non-Biblical Scriptures*, pp. 340–59; Tilmann Vetter, 'Die Funktion von Zentralsätzen der vedischen Offenbarung im System Sarvajñātmans' in *Offenbarung, geistige Realität des Menschen*, pp. 121–32.

World proceeds. It remains to be seen whether this cause is absolutely identified with Brahman.

We know the principal philosophical reason for this: if without due discrimination we make Brahman responsible for the World, if we, as it were, tie Brahman to the World, then it appears difficult to maintain the transcendence, the absoluteness, of Brahman. A dependent Brahman, a relative Absolute, are contradictions in terms within the framework of an *ātmavādin* ontology. On the other hand, an absolute unrelatedness would make Brahman superfluous, if not inconceivable, and would contradict all that we have been saying so far (and our *sūtra* in particular). Nothing can be said about something that has no relationship to us and to the World in which we live.

Some of the Vedāntic and Thomistic schools have tried to avoid this risk by stating that the relation of God as First Cause to the World is not a *real* one, that the reality of the effect and its variations do not affect the simplicity and independence of the cause, that divine causality is precisely of a unique type that results in a dependence that is only one-sided. Actually this theory already transcends dualism and opens the door to an Advaitic answer; it is therefore the least vulnerable philosophical attempt.[99] The monistic attitude, on the contrary, tries to solve the problem by denying any kind of dualism that might mar the exclusive reality of Brahman, although by so doing it creates a new dualism.

In fact neither dualism nor pure monism can resolve this problem. Dualism opens a gap that it has difficulty afterwards in closing; monism oversimplifies the problem, 'throwing the baby out with the bath-water', eliminating the problem instead of solving it. This leads us to the almost inevitable paradox, formulated by nearly all theologico-philosophical schools in one way or another: identity and diversity coexist and are both real. The harmonious or rather non-contradictory synthesis of both perspectives is the touchstone of true metaphysics. First, then, let us describe the two opposing aspects of the problem.

[99] There is no need to recall that precisely this is the Thomistic position within Scholastic philosophy.

There is identity, because if Brahman, or God, or the Absolute—three concepts that for the time being we shall take as synonymous—is something more than an empty word, there cannot be anything outside of it. The First Cause is by definition the ultimate that our knowledge can formally conceive on the metaphysical plane. Either there is a First Cause and this First Cause is Brahman, or there is no First Cause at all. Or, vice versa, either Brahman is the First Cause or there is no Brahman at all. If both could stand separately side by side without any kind of relationship, Brahman would make no sense to us. It would not be the First Cause and would have nothing to do with the World or with the First Cause either. It could not even be considered transcendent; there would be no room for it, either epistemologically or ontologically. That is to say, all that we can ever come to know is contained in the First Cause: if we could go beyond it, it would no longer be the *first* cause. Moreover, all being is exhausted in the First Cause: a super-being is either another kind of being and so is included in the First Cause, or else it has a relationship with 'being', and this is contrary to our premise. In such a case, the First Cause would no longer be the First Cause, nor would Brahman be unrelated to that supposed First Cause.

There is diversity, on the other hand, because if the First Cause were only first Cause and nothing else—namely, 'also' Brahman—it would have only a kind of ontological priority with regard to worldly beings, but it would not be ontologically different from them: it would simply be their cause. This cause would be only the Lord *of* the World, but it would not be Brahman *in itself*. If the First Cause were not of a different nature altogether from the World, it could not have the characteristics of perfection, simplicity, independence and the like, such as are required for being the First Cause. If the First Cause were just the first link in a chain of causation, why stop there? What makes this particular link absolutely the first? What makes us suppose that there is no previous link? The only possible answer must deny the value of the metaphor and say that the First Cause is of a *different* nature than its effects and therefore *something more* than just a *first* cause. In other words, its being 'first' is not a numerical, but a transcendental quality. The nature of the First Cause is richer, transcending its causal function: it is of a special nature, has a side that eludes us and cannot be reduced simply to its being 'cause'. The First Cause *in itself* and not merely *qua* cause is Brahman. The reality that is the First Cause is not exhausted in its causal function. This is only its relation-to-the-World, to us: its knowable aspect. Its inmost being, its infinite transcendence, its hidden side is Brahman. Thus there is diversity between the concept of First Cause (as such) and the concept of Brahman. They are not the same, yet they refer to the same Supreme Reality. What is the nature of the identity and the difference between these two concepts? We shall try to clarify this point in the last paragraph.

First, however, it is necessary to elaborate a little more the answer to the question we started with; that is, how does one reach (if at all) the knowledge of Brahman out of the recognition of a First Cause? That would be the crowning step of the cosmological argument. We now have all the data necessary for the answer that we have been trying to find. In so far as the human intellect is capable of grasping the identity between the First Cause and Brahman, there will be employed a kind of cosmological argument. As far as it discovers diversity, the argument will remain inconclusive and will not be proven; it will remain 'ready' to accept a higher instance if this happens to present itself.

The structure of the argument has two parts, which can be stated in four propositions:

1. the World requires a foundation;
2. such a foundation must present itself as ultimate and distinct from this World;
3. this foundation exists at least in the measure that this World exists and our reason postulates it;
4. its nature lies beyond the capacity of our understanding, though we can affirm that it 'exists' and that it is 'distinct' from the World.

The third point shows that the argument has a weak side that needs an entire philosophy to defend it: to what degree *does* this World exist, and what power does our reason have to transcend it? Only from an existent can we infer another existent. Existence as such, the act of *existence*, is the mysterious link between God and the World. Whether the philosophy one has is the cause or the effect of accepting God and recognizing the validity of the argument given above is another problem which exceeds the limits of this study.

7. ADVAITA AND TRINITY

a) The Problem of Īśvara

I pass now to another aspect of this same problem of the identity and diversity between God and the First Cause, continuing in accordance with the spirit of this work, which seeks to be in conformity with the Indian inspiration without, however, alienating the West. The question is that of the relation between Brahman, the Absolute, the Transcendent, the Unknown-unknowable; and Īśvara, the Lord, the Creator, the personal God.

I have no intention, in the following, of subjecting Indian philosophy to criticism or of attributing to it things which it does not say; nor do I want to do violence to Christian theology. But I cannot rid myself of the quiet and humble conviction that we are facing here not only one of the deepest intuitions of Indian wisdom but also an analogous insight found in at least one aspect of the Christian dogma of the Trinity. The dogma of the Trinity presents itself as the unexpected answer to the inevitable question of a mediator between the One and the Manifold, the Absolute and the Relative, between Brahman and the World. This is in my opinion not just a Vedāntic problem but, in the ultimate analysis, one of other cultures also. The *Amr* of the Koran, the *Logos* of Plotinus and the *Tathāgata* of Buddhism, for example, arise out of similar needs in their respective traditions to find an ontological link between the two opposed and apparently irreducible poles: the Absolute and the Relative. However, before continuing with this theme, I would like to make a brief excursus on the subject of the Indian concept of Īśvara.

Īśvara (including also the names *īśa* and *īśāna*) is the Lord, the all-powerful God and point of convergence of the theistic tendencies of the Upanishads, supplanting and at the same time resurrecting the 'henotheism' of the Vedas.[100] One of the oldest Upanishads starts with the very word *īśa*: 'All this, whatever there is, is enveloped by the Lord.'[101] At this stage there is no clear distinction between the cosmic and the personal aspect of the godhead, between Brahman and Iśvara. In the later Upanishads like the Śvetāśvatara, the personal aspect becomes more prominent and the Lord is called the One God (*eka deva*).[102] But even there, where Īśvara has risen to the heights of supreme Lord, creator, ruler, protector, refuge,[103] he remains closely linked with other concepts like *ātman*, Brahman, Purusha, combining in himself the qualities of all of them.[104] He is Lord of time, he is both today and tomorrow.[105] From fear of him the wind blows, from fear of him the sun rises, and he is Lord over death.[106] The Upanishadic conception of Īśvara is so rich that here only a few of its facets can be mentioned.

The sacred text which has obviously had the greatest influence on both the philosophical and the religious development of the idea of God (independently of 'confessional' differences) is the Bhagavad Gītā, one of the three authoritative texts of Vedānta which together comprise the *prasthānatraya*. We may just note the following for our purpose: in the Gītā, the Lord (called variously Īśvara, Prabhu, Bhagavān, Puruṣottama and other names) reveals himself fully as a personal being,

[100] The term *īśvara* does not occur in the Rig-Veda (except for the participle *īśāna*, 'powerful, mighty') but there are a few references in the Atharva-Veda, denoting divine powers (e.g. AV XI,4,1 and 10; XIX,6,4; XIX,53,8; etc.). Cf. in general about the idea of *īśvara* or God, besides the above quoted literature: J. Gonda, *Die Religionen Indiens* I, pp. 264 ff.; id., 'The Concept of a Personal God in Ancient Indian Religious Thought', art. cit.; id., *Aspects of Early Viṣṇuism*; G. Oberhammer, 'Die Gottesidee in der indischen Philosophie des ersten nachchristlichen Jahrtausends' in *Zeitschr. f. kath. Theol.*, 89–4 (1967), pp. 447–57, and also M. D. Shastri, 'History of the Word Īśvara and its Idea' in *The Princess of Wales Sarasvati Bhavana Studies* vol. X (Benares, 1938), pp. 35–63.

[101] IsU 1.

[102] Cf. SU IV,11,ff.; VI,10 ff.

[103] Cf. BU IV,4,22; SU III,1 ff. etc.

[104] Cf. BU IV,4,15; SU III,7 ff.; MundU II,1,2 ff. etc.

[105] Cf. KathU IV,13.

[106] Cf. TU II,8.

identified with Krishna who is both transcendent and immanent. Here, in addition to all his attributes, his changeless nature, his powers, what is important is the stress which the Gītā lays on the activity of the Lord. Although he is eternally free and unattached to any work, he engages in the work of creation, preservation, destruction and salvation of the World.[107] The relation of Īśvara to Brahman is shown in an interesting passage where Brahman is called the womb in which the Lord plants his seed, hence he becomes the father of all beings.[108] The most conspicuous feature of the divine revelation of the Gītā is however the great love of God for his devotees and the loving surrender (*bhakti*) of the latter to their Lord.[109]

Since the Vedāntic conception of Īśvara has been influenced by Sāṃkhya and Yoga, mention may also be made of how the idea arises in the Yoga-Sūtras of Patañjali.[110] Patañjali mentions meditation on, or surrender to, Īśvara as one of the means of attaining the goal of Yoga.[111] Īśvara is then described as a particular Spirit (*puruṣa*) who is free from the influence of affliction (*kleśa*), action (*karma*) and its results;[112] he is omniscient, the Guru of all former Gurus and not limited by time.[113] The symbol expressing him is the mystic syllable called *praṇava*, OM.[114] The commentary of Vyāsa adds that the essential difference between a liberated soul and Īśvara is that Īśvara is eternally free and has never been bound.[115] Thus in classical Yoga Īśvara, though he has not been a central figure, has been accepted as a possible

[107] Cf. BG III,22–4; IV,13–14.
[108] BG XIV,3; cf. MundU III,1–3.
[109] Cf. the selected texts on 'God', '*Bhakti*' and '*Parā Bhakti*' in R. C. Zaehner, *The Bhagavad-Gītā* (Oxford University Press, 1969), pp. 453 ff. 437 ff., 446 ff.
[110] Cf. for instance, K. C. Bhattacharyya, *Studies in Philosophy*, Vol. 1, 'The notion of Īśvara', in chapter 5: 'Studies in Yoga Philosophy', pp. 317–26; G. Oberhammer, 'Gott, Urbild der emanzipierten Existenz im Yoga des Patañjali' in *Zeitschr. f. kath. Theol.* 86 (1964), 2, pp. 197 ff.
[111] *Īśvarapraṇidhānād vā*, YS I,23.
[112] YS I,24.
[113] YS I,25–6.
[114] YS I,27.
[115] Vyāsa Bhāṣya on YS I,24.

alternative approach, probably because there have been theistic schools which advocated devotion to him. He is, so to say, the ideal of the Yogī since he is eternally liberated and pure.[116]

The school of Nyāya-Vaiśeṣika, mainly as a counter-attack against the Buddhist refutations of Īśvara, developed a conception and rational proof of the existence of Īśvara and of his being a creator without relying on 'revelation'.[117] The only other classical system (*darśana*) in which Īśvara played a central role is of course Vedānta with its different subschools. We have already seen the position of Śaṅkara.[118] His followers were so keen to preserve the absolute purity and transcendence of Brahman and its total uncontamination by the World that they placed Īśvara in the realm of *māyā*, since it is he who is concerned with the creation of the World and hence gets involved in the cosmic play. This leads either to a practical dualism (between a *para* and *apara brahman*, *nirguṇa* and *saguṇa*, between *pāramārthika* and *vyāvahārika*) or to an illusionistic conception of Īśvara. Both Īśvara and the individual soul (*jīva*) are only superimpositions upon Brahman.[119] Yet, says Vidyāraṇya, 'because of its association with its power (*śakti*), Brahman itself becomes (appears as) Īśvara'.[120]

I cannot pursue here a consideration of the theistic schools

[116] Cf. G. Oberhammer, art. cit.

[117] Cf. G. Oberhammer, 'Zum Problem des Gottesbeweises in der indischen Philosophie' in *Numen* XII,1 (Jan. 1965), pp. 1–34; G. Chemparathy, *An Indian Rational Theology*, op. cit.

[118] See above, Brahman. *Parameśvara* has two forms, says Śaṅkara, one *nirguṇa* and another one *saguṇa* which does not attain the former: *dvirūpe parameśvare nirguṇaṃ rūpam anavāpya saguṇa evāvatiṣṭhanta* (in the two--formed supreme Īśvara, the *saguṇa* does not attain the *nirguṇa* form), BSBh IV,4,19. Cf. also P. Hacker, 'Eigentümlichkeiten der Lehre und Terminologie Śaṅkaras', art. cit.

[119] Cf. *Pañcadaśī* III,37.

[120] *Pañcadaśī* III,40. The reaction of a prominent twentieth-century Vedantin is interesting: 'Brahman and Īśvara have sometimes been called the higher and the lower god. The distinction is, to say the least, misleading, and probably the over-definite language of some of the systematizing scholiasts is responsible for it. No doubt there is a distinction between the *conceptions*. Yet Īśvara is not *in reality* different from Brahman.' K. C. Bhattacharya, *Studies in Vedantism*, p. 34 (quoted from G. G. Mukhopadhyaya, *Studies in the Upaniṣads*, op. cit., p. 75).

in which Īśvara obviously occupies the central position, under different names and in different forms, because there the situation changes. I could equally well take up a dialogue with one of these schools such as the Vaiṣṇava Pāñcarātra, the Śaiva Siddhānta or Kashmir Śaivism, which would in fact be somewhat easier, but since I have limited my problematic to Vedāntic theology, I shall now proceed to analyse the function of Īśvara in Vedānta in a very general way, without explicit reference to any particular one of its historical forms.

In spite of the fact of Brahman being the absolute and unique cause of the universe, there is still place for Īśvara for the following reasons.

1. Brahman is absolutely transcendent and in a sense beyond being and non-being. It is pure silence and utter nothingness, truly ab-solute, i.e. unrelated. It can thus perform no external function, and it is for this that the figure of Īśvara appears. To be sure, Brahman is often said to be pure being, consciousness and bliss: *sat, cit* and *ānanda*. Yet this *sat* is pure static being without relations; *cit* is such a pure consciousness that it is not consciousness *of* (anything—not even of itself); moreover, the *ānanda* of Brahman consists of a plenitude of self-sufficiency. In other words Brahman is devoid of relations, and it is precisely Īśvara who provides for them. Īśvara is existence, consciousness and bliss in the relational sense. He is, properly speaking, the re-velation of Brahman, the first issue, so to speak, of the unfathomable womb of Brahman. Īśvara is God.

2. Brahman cannot be a person, for if it were it would have to relate to others (things or persons), which would compromise its absoluteness. Īśvara is the personal aspect of Brahman, in whatever manner he may be conceived.[121]

[121] Any student of Indian philosophy will know the distinction of the Brahma-Sūtra between the impersonal—*apuruṣa-vidha*—and the personal—*puruṣa-vidha*—in the Godhead. Cf. also *para-brahma* and *apara-brahma*. Cf. against the oversimplification of R. Guénon identifying the supreme Brahma with Brahman and the non-supreme with Īśvara: *L'homme et son devenir selon le Védānta* (Paris, 1925), p. 105, the fact that Śaṅkara calls the first one also *Parameśvara*. Cf. several texts and explanation in O. Lacombe, op. cit., pp. 217 ff.

3. Brahman *as such* cannot be creator of the World, again because of its absolute transcendence. Īśvara, therefore, is that 'aspect' of Brahman responsible for the creation of the World.[122]

4. Brahman cannot be made responsible for the return of the World to its origin and its reality (which is Brahman itself). In other words, the *grace* of the Lord, the destruction of *māyā*, the realization of Brahman, constitute precisely the role and function of Īśvara. Īśvara is the Lord and the Guru.

5. Brahman without attributes (*nirguṇa*) may be spoken of with the following paradoxical formulations: Brahman is Brahman but does not know that it is Brahman. Thus, in a certain sense, Brahman *is* not. Īśvara is, undoubtedly, Brahman, and knows that he is Brahman. The souls of living beings, the *jīvas*, are Brahman, but do not yet know it. They will know it through the grace of the Lord (Īśvara), by means of their identification with him. The rest of the World, broadly speaking, is Brahman—there is nothing that is not Brahman, in so far as it *is*—but does not know this identity, nor has it any possibility of knowing it, except through successive transmigrations of 'things' into *jīvas*, of *jīvas* into Īśvara and thence into Brahman. There is no *real* mutation in the World (nothing that is not can come to be and nothing that *is* need become).[123] There is only a realization of what really *is*. Īśvara is the connecting link, the cause of this discovery, the God who acts and towards whom creatures aspire in response to his call.

6. Brahman is so immutable and unmanifest, beyond every capacity for action, that Īśvara has to take over its functions in relation to the universe and to souls. Even Īśvara, or rather Vishnu, is deemed to be too aloof; thus, when he needs to act in the World, he manifests himself in the *avatāras*, in the most diverse kinds of which he appears and descends to earth.[124]

[122] Again *kāraṇa-brahman* is distinct from pure Brahman and even from the immanent *ātman (kārya-brahman)* of the universe, which would rather be *Hiranyagarbha*.

[123] Cf. BG II,16, etc.

[124] Cf. G. Parrinder, *Avatar and Incarnation*.

7. Finally, Īśvara zealously preserves the transcendence—or immanence (which is the same thing in the sense of its inaccessibility)—of Brahman. Īśvara does all *for* and *as* Brahman and consequently is different from but identical to Brahman. Otherwise (if Brahman were not the ultimate) all the functions of Īśvara would be meaningless and without any *raison d'être*.

At this point the philosophical schools try to resolve this antinomy and to maintain this tension, even if they do not entirely succeed. Here we should like to give our own version of the *sūtra*. Like the mathematical problem of the three bodies, we have here three statements which can be considered almost indisputable.

1. There is Brahman, or God, or the Divinity as Absolute, without relation, immutable, unique, simple.

2. There is the World with all the variety of its beings, from Gods to gross matter, with all the attributes that do not pertain to Brahman: mutability, manifestation, multiplicity and so on.

3. There is a relation, 'x', which is cause, mediator or similar between Brahman and the World. This relation, cause, mediation, this 'x', is caught in the most profound dilemma: if there is no link, the dualism that this implies destroys both the concept of Brahman and that of the World: of Brahman, for there would then exist a second (the World) as ultimate as Brahman itself, and thence Brahman would no longer be Brahman. The World would no longer be the relative World, but would necessarily be self-sufficient, its own foundation, and thus also become an Absolute. Paradoxical as it may seem, dualism thus leads to the most monolithic monism. If there is no link between Brahman and the World, it is because only one of them exists: either the World, if we take this World as our point of departure (in which case we have no right, logically, to speak of 'Brahman' at all); or Brahman, if we take the Absolute as our point of departure (in which case there is no room for the 'World'). Either way it amounts to a bold statement that the Absolute is the relative and vice versa, with no distinction or qualification whatsoever. On the other hand, if there *is* a link of an ontological nature, there follows a monism that also destroys both Brah-

man and the World. This link would fetter Brahman to the World and make the World unchangeable, perfect; but also the World to Brahman, and thus all the imperfections of the relative would become shortcomings of the Absolute, become the Absolute itself.

The only dialectical escape would be to admit a kind of link which does not allow for a perfect communication between the two 'terms'. Otherwise the characteristics of one term have to be 'reflected' in the other and vice versa, and this 'reflection' would tarnish the very essence of what Brahman and the World are supposed to be. This amounts to saying that the link does not really link Brahman and the World. This is in fact what Śaṅkara and Thomas, among others, have maintained. But even the Advaitic or Thomistic answer that this 'link' is only 'real' from one side, and 'unreal' from the other, does not entirely resolve the difficulty.

It is precisely here, however, that we find the place of Īśvara as well as one of the functions of Christ, in spite of all the differences that can be found between them. A point of contact may well occur in the crossing of two lines, lines that are running in opposite directions and which resemble a cross rather than two parallel lines.[125]

(b) Christological Commentary

I now venture a new reading of *Brahma-Sūtra* I,1,2, one that will not be foreign to the Christian tradition and yet will not stray from the significance of the text itself. I would request, however, that the reader approach what follows with a sympathetic mind. We are not dealing with crystallized concepts or with complete systems of philosophy, but with a living reality, which concepts express only more or less adequately.

That from which all things proceed and to which all things return and by which all things are (sustained in their being) is God, but we detect two 'moments' in it: the 'first' is the invisible origin whence the source springs forth; the 'second' is *primo et per se* not a silent Godhead, an inaccessible Brahman, not even God

[125] I would recall that this study does not intend to give a new solution, but only to state the problem in the light of two different traditions. For a deepening into the problem itself the author may refer to his other works.

the Father, source of all Divinity, but in a very true sense Īśvara, God the Son, the Logos, the Christ.[126]

The *that* of our text is God, the Absolute, not a Platonic demiurge or a secondary divinity. It is the one source, the ultimate reality—yet it is distinct, for it is its 'expression',[127] its image,[128] its revealer.[129] We may assert that this *that* is a divine Person 'begotten' by God,[130] equal in nature[131] but distinct in his subsistence and personality.[132]

This Beginning and End of all things[133] has two natures, though they are not in the same mode or on the same level. It has two faces, two aspects as it were.[134] One face is turned towards the Divinity and is its full expression and its bearer.[135] The other face is turned towards the external, the World, and is the firstborn,[136] the sustainer,[137] the giver of the World's

[126] We shall refrain from developing this chapter into a complete *bhāṣya* and we adduce only some texts from Scripture which, without being exhaustive, may give an insight into the problem. For further references the following literature may prove useful: U. Lattanzi, *Il primato universale di Cristo secondo le S. Scritture*. Rome 1937; J. Bonsirven, *L'Evangile de Paul*. Paris, 1948; id., *La Règne de Dieu*. Paris 1957; E. Walter, *Christus und der Kosmos*. Stuttgart, 1948; F. Mussner, *Christus, das All und die Kirche*. Trier, 1955; F. Prat, *La théologie de Saint Paul*, 8th edn. Paris, 1923; O. Bauhofer, *Die Heimholung der Welt*. Freiburg, 1936; F. X. Durrwell, *La résurrection de Jésus, mystère de salut*, 3rd edn. Paris, 1954; E. Mersch, *La théologie du Corps mystique*, 3rd edn. Paris, 1949; J. Pinsk, *Hoffnung auf Herrlichkeit*. Colmar, 1942; A. Frank-Duquesne, *Cosmos et Gloire. Dans quelle mesure l'univers a-t-il part à la chute, à la Rédemption et à la Gloire finale*? Paris, 1947; A. Grillmeier, *Christ in Christian Tradition. From the Apostolic Age to Chalcedon*; id., *Mit ihm und in ihm. Christologische Forschungen und Perspektiven*.

[127] Cf. Heb. 1:3.

[128] Cf. 2 Cor. 4:4; Col. 1:15, etc.

[129] Cf. John 7:16; 12:45; 14:9.

[130] Cf. John 1:14,18; 3:18; 6:46.

[131] Cf. John 10:30; 17:11,21–2; 1 John 5:7.

[132] Cf. John 1:1; 7:29; 17:5.

[133] Cf. Rev. 1:8; 2:8; 21:6; Col. 1:17.

[134] Cf. Phil. 2:7; 2 Cor. 8:9; Heb. 2:14.

[135] Cf. John 1:2; 2 Cor. 4:4; John 6:57.

[136] Cf. Rom. 8:29; Col. 1:15, 18; Rev. 1:5.

[137] Cf. Col. 1:17; 2:10.

being.[138] Yet it is not two, but one—one principle, one person.[139]

One further remark, while remaining faithful to the text, will try to formulate a nuance that has been adumbrated, though not explicitly affirmed, by the famous *bhāṣyakāras*. This observation will stress two main points concerning the significance of 1) *that from which* and 2) *the origin etc.* in the text.

1) *Yataḥ*, 'from which', is one of the most appropriate words for the supreme principle,[140] and this for two reasons. That 'from which' the World derives is a pure 'whence', not only in relation to the World but also as such. This is to say that it is pure relation.[141] Its proper characteristic is to be a 'from which', hence in itself it is an 'originated', a 'begotten', and an 'expression', an 'image'. The Logos is in itself the full Word, the total manifestation of God the Father. It is in reality God from God, Light from Light.[142] That is to say that even its proper 'face', which mirrors the Divine, is distinct from its source, though its substantial identity is not thereby diminished; for the Logos receives the full divine nature that the Father has as the source of Divinity.[143] It is, furthermore, *that* from which the World comes forth, the Alpha and Omega from which all things take their being and in which all subsist. Though this tradition has not mixed the two orders, the natural and the supernatural, with their respective movements *ad extra* and *ab intra*, 'creative' and 'intratrinitarian', it

[138] Cf. Col. 1:16; 1 Cor. 8:6.
[139] Cf. John 8:18, 21, 25, 58.
[140] Cf. John 16:28.
[141] Cf. BS I,4,27, where Brahman means the *yoni*, the matrix, the source.
[142] Cf. *Symbolum Epiphanii* (Denz. 13); *Nicaeni* (Denz. 54), etc.
[143] Cf. the dogmatic expressions: '*Christus est verus Deus, Verbum Patris, idemque Patris Filius, ipsi consubstantialis, ab ipso non separatus, genitus non factus, unigenitus, unus de trinitate . . .*' ('Christ is true God, Word of the Father, likewise Son of the Father, one in substance with him, not separate from him, begotten not created, only-begotten, one from trinity . . .') in any Christian theology.

has maintained that the two orders, though different in their nature, come out of one and the same ultimate Act.[144]

The Vedāntic intuition that Brahman is transcendent, absolute and unrelated to the World and yet is the World's cause and Lord in Īśvara is something more than a mere rational working hypothesis or an expeditious way to account for the two unequal poles of the problem. It comes rather from an authentic theological inspiration transmitted by the rishis and conserved in the *śruti*. This is why we may be allowed to draw upon Scripture, even though we do not fully concur with all of the Tradition.

Here we have a case in point of the mutual fecundation of religious traditions to which I alluded in the previous chapter. It would appear that the discussion around the relation between *saguṇa* and *nirguṇa* Brahman could hardly resist the temptation of falling into either dualism or monism. If *saguṇa* Brahman is this-worldly, the gap remains unbridged—and thus the two orders are irreducible: dualism. If it is identical with *nirguṇa* Brahman the gap collapses—and thus the two orders are unified: monism. Similarly, if God is the Creator and the creation is real, there is mutual interdependence and dualism looms up. If the process is only an intra-divine adventure the creation has no consistency of its own and monism becomes inevitable.

Keeping in mind both the Indian problematic and the Christian tradition I shall now attempt to formulate this tension, using as points of reference the two main Advaitic schools.

The Īśvara of the Śaṅkara school is in fact almost completely turned towards the phenomenal order. He can still be called God, but is no longer identifiable with the Absolute,

[144] Cf. '*Deus enim cognoscendo se, cognoscit omnem creaturam . . . Sed quia Deus uno actu et se et omnia intelligit, unicum Verbum eius est expressivum creaturarum.*' 'For God, in knowing himself, knows everything that is created . . . And because God knows himself and knows all things in a single act of cognition, his unique Word is an expressing that embraces all things created.' Thomas Aquinas, *Sum. Theol.* I, q. 34, a. 3.

with Brahman.[145] This Īśvara is essentially *saguṇa*, yet somehow claims also to be *nirguṇa*. The divergence between Brahman and Īśvara is overstressed in order to save the absolute purity of the former.

The Īśvara of our interpretation does not belong to the world of *māyā* only. He is not only a creature, but equal to Brahman, though distinct in his form of existence as well as in his function *vis-à-vis* the World. Our *sūtra* really refers us to Brahman and not to a *māyā*-affected Īśvara, otherwise the gap would subsist and the problem would remain unsolved. Īśvara, then, is not merely *saguṇa* Brahman, or an emanation of it, or a mere 'modality' of the Godhead. The *sūtra* instead seems to indicate a way to what the Christian tradition calls God the Father through God the Son. It points to an Īśvara who, though being *saguṇa*, has not ceased to be *nirguṇa*. Perhaps this was in the mind of Bādarāyaṇa when he refused to give up the reality either of the World or of Brahman, though he was clear that they were not identical.[146]

The Īśvara of Rāmānuja, on the other hand, while endeavouring to overcome the same tension, tends to fall on the opposite side, so to speak, of the fence. He is Brahman, and his creation is the Body of the Absolute. In a way there is no break in continuity between him and the World. Both together form a whole, the one complete Brahman.[147] Here the identity tends to be overemphasized so that somehow Īśvara may save the reality of the World, or at least of the *jīvas*, the souls.

The Īśvara of our interpretation does not belong only to the world of the Godhead. He is not just a mere aspect of the Divine. He is really 'human', or rather worldly without ceasing to be divine. Our *sūtra* points towards a reality which not only connects the two poles, but which 'is' the two poles without permitting them to coalesce.

[145] Cf. Ram Pratap Singh, *The Vedānta of Śaṅkara* (Baroda, 1949), against the old commentators like Sureśvara and Padmapāda and the recent ones like S. N. Dasgupta and S. Radhakrishnan.

[146] Cf. BS I,1,21; I,2,8 ff., etc.

[147] And yet his idea of Man as *īśvarasyāṃśa*, as a part of Īśvara (cf. Śrībhāṣya II,1,15) could be interpreted as a glimpse of the problem of participation.

In the Christian language that I have been using in order to show how an encounter may take place, I would say that the Īśvara of our interpretation points towards the Mystery of Christ, who, being unique in his existence and essence, is as such equal to God.[148] He is not *the* God, but *equal* to him, Son of God, God from God. Moreover, he has a double nature, but these two natures are 'without mixture' and 'without change' and yet 'inseparable' and 'indivisible'.[149] He is more than a mediator, he is in a certain sense, as the 'whole Christ', the whole reality of the World, as far as it is *real*, i.e. as it is—or shall be, if we speak within the framework of time—incorporated in him, one with him, forming one Mystical Body. Thus Christ (Īśvara), one with the *real* World is—shall be, if we include time—one with God the Father so that God may be all in all and nothing remain beyond or beside or behind him.[150]

I cannot linger here in order to deal with all the functions of Īśvara, as I have interpreted him. I simply wanted to show that this interpretation responds to the requirements of the text and continues the problematic of Indian speculation. Nevertheless, this Īśvara remains mysterious and paradoxical. It requires faith—not blind credulity but a superior form of knowledge—to accept him, precisely because he is a living God and not simply an abstract mental hypothesis. Another way of saying the same is to affirm that the Advaitic experience is required to actualize this 'knowledge'. In point of fact mere discursive reason is unable to support the two horns of the dilemma without falling into contradiction.[151] So much for the *yataḥ*.

2) *Janmādi*, 'the origin, etc.': the Indian mind's thirst for eternity has sometimes caused commentators to overlook the double sense of the 'production etc.' of Īśvara. There is in

[148] Cf. MandU 6, a text that claims a commentary of its own regarding this very problem.
[149] Cf. these four famous qualifications of the Council of Chalcedon, Denz. 148.
[150] Cf. 1 Cor. 12:12; 15:28; Col. 3:8; Gal. 3:28; Rom. 12:5; Eph. 1:23.
[151] This is actually the crux of a great part of neo-Vedānta thought, i.e. that it tries to solve the conflicting statements of the texts by dialectics, whereas these are only meaningful in the light of a sapiental intuition.

fact a production and a conservation of the World as such that happens in a non-temporal, or 'eternal' way; and there is also the development or evolution of all these acts, happening concurrently with the temporal development of things. The Īśvara of our commentary fulfils both these functions: he is that from which being *is* in an 'eternal' way; and he is that towards which being tends or be-comes, within the temporal process. This double function of Īśvara, namely that of 'keeping the World in being' in time and 'out of time', is ultimately one, for there are not two worlds, one in eternity and another in time. It is precisely in order to avoid such a dichotomy that I have introduced the concept of *tempiternity*,[152] which attempts to express the non-dualistic intuition of what is otherwise seen as the double 'dimension' of time and eternity. The process is thus tempiternal. In order to make explicit this function of Īśvara it will be well, however, to describe its two 'moments'.

a) To imagine the non-temporal origin, production, preservation and destruction of the World, we may consider it as being already accomplished, as if every being had reached the end of time, and then suppress the temporal factor. But this is only an image, and we have to transcend imagination and even discursive thinking if we want a glimpse into the 'tempiternal' reality, which is more than mere non-temporality. In such a perspective there is nothing but God, a God that as the absolute 'I' has an eternal 'Thou', which is equal to him and which is nevertheless not a second, but always a Thou. This Thou, which is the Son, is the whole Christ, including the new heavens and the new earth: all beings participate in this Christ, find their place in him and are fully what they are when they become one with him, the Son. All that exists, i.e. the whole of reality, is nothing but God: Father, Christ and Holy Spirit. All that exists is nothing but

[152] Cf. R. Panikkar, 'El presente tempiterno. Una apostilla a la historia de la salvación y a la teología de la liberación' in *Teología y mundo contemporaneo* (Homenaje a Karl Rahner), ed. A. Vargas-Machuca (Madrid, Universidad Pontificia de Comillas, 1975), pp. 133–75; and id., 'La tempiternidad' in *Sanctum Sacrificium*, V Congreso Eucarístico Nacional (Zaragoza, 1961), pp. 75–93.

Brahman as *sat, cit* and *ānanda*, as being, consciousness and bliss, i.e. *sat* as the very support of all that in one way or another constitutes 'being'; *cit* as the spiritual or intellectual link that encompasses and penetrates the total reality; and *ānanda* as the perfect fullness that receives into itself and inspires all that is tending towards it. There are not two Brahmans: *nirguṇa* Brahman 'is' *saguṇa*, precisely when it *is*, in the same way that *śabda-brahman* is *parabrahman*, precisely when it is *said*.

b) *In time*: that is, in the temporal development of all beings that here on earth are pilgrim beings, things in the making, itinerant creatures, Īśvara is also that from which they come forth, to which they return and by which they are sustained. The growth of all things in time is nothing but a fuller realization of their being in Īśvara, says the Vedānta, and in Christ, as our *bhāṣya* discloses.[153] Whatever degree of reality this World may have, it is produced, sustained and attracted by this divine and human mediator, indicated in the Brahma-Sūtra.

Trinitas reducit dualitatem ad unitatem; 'the Trinity reduces dualism to unity', says Saint Augustine, who describes the final state of the World with the words, *et erit unus Christus amans seipsum*: there will be only one Christ loving himself[154]—not selfishly, needless to say, but because the Divinity in its fullness dwells bodily in him.[155] In him all things are summed up and the Spirit will quicken them with that life which flows out of the Father alone.[156]

To develop these ideas further by giving them an exhaustive treatment would require a full commentary (*bhāṣya*). Ultimately, we have but one comment to make: *that from which this World comes forth and to which it returns and by which it is sustained, that is Īśvara, the Christ.*[157]

[153] Cf. Eph. 1:10; 4:2–13.

[154] *In Epist. ad Parthos* (PL XXXV, 2055). We have to refrain here from adducing parallel conceptions, e.g. in Śaiva theology (the basic conception being that only Śiva can worship Śiva).

[155] Cf. Col. 2:9.

[156] Cf. 1 Cor. 12:6; Eph. 1:11; 4:6.

[157] Cf. John 12:32.

EPILOGUE

The burden of our discourse has been that many of Mankind's philosophical and religious texts contain a *sensus plenior*, a fuller meaning.[1] In using this expression, I am not intending to equate the Hindu tradition with the tradition of the Old Testament or to add that all finds fulfilment in Christianity. God provides for all his children, he guides their steps towards the new heavens and the new earth by means of the most diverse traditions of Mankind. We must refrain from rejecting a religious text or tradition—an attitude that has often proved fatal—simply because it does not accord with our already crystallized ideas or formulations. Only when we have arrived at the *res significata*, the reality, have we the right to exercise a pure critique, for only then can we reach a higher synthesis. Such a synthesis would utilize new and old elements (*nova et vetera*), letting what is superfluous fall by the wayside.

It may not be out of place to qualify the expression 'a fuller meaning' in the direction of a *sensus semper plenior*, an ever fuller meaning of sacred texts. The reader also belongs to the text,[2] and when the reader changes or comes at it from another perspective, the text may be capable of yielding another meaning also. There may be progressively a *sensus plenior* of any such text. The theory of the *sensus plenior* postulates an unfolding of both human consciousness and divine revelation. It is not the 'Christian', but the *new* meaning that may emerge that gives the fuller significance of a text. Further, the new meaning we find in our *sūtra* does not blur the differences between the two traditions, but permits a point of encounter and a possibility of mutual fecundation.

I have taken the risk of speaking of Christ all the time, and

[1] If our view is correct it may throw some light on the difficult theological problem of 'implicit faith', for it provides the implicit object of that faith and shows its development.

[2] Cf. R. Panikkar, 'The Texture of a Text: In Response to Paul Ricoeur', in *Point of Contact*, New York (April, May 1978), Vol. II, Nr. 1, pp. 51–64.

I have tried to avoid being misunderstood. I have not brought into play unnecessary polemics revolving around the use of this name. I might have spoken instead of the Logos or the Word, or of *śabda* or *vāc* or the like, or even of the Lord, which is somewhat better, culturally more neutral and thus more appropriately used in an encounter. Yet if the word Christ has been used it is not due to 'Christian imperialism' or any similar design, but for the reason given in the Introduction, namely, that Christ is the name Christians use to express this reality. My use of it, however, implies no monopoly on the name or any form of exclusivity.

Obviously, neither the author of the *Brahma-Sūtra* nor the commentators thought explicitly for a moment of Jesus Christ. Every one had at the back of his mind the goal of his devotion (*iṣṭa-devatā*). It is also an incontrovertible fact that the Christ in whom Christians believe cannot be simply equated with the Īśvara of the Vedānta. Christian theology has always tried, especially in more recent centuries (in the Patristic period things were different), to accentuate the differences between Christianity and the 'non-Christian' religions and to emphasize the newness of the Christian fact, both as revelation and as an ontological 'new creation'.[3] Without underrating all this, I venture two assertions which are complementary to our theme.

First, in the realm of philosophy: the role of Īśvara in Vedānta—which is postulated in order to explain the connection between God and the World without compromising the absoluteness of the former or the relativity of the latter—corresponds functionally to the role of Christ in Christian thought. It is precisely this correspondence that provides Indian philosophy with a locus for Christ and Christian theology for Īśvara. If we start with the historicity of Christ, essential though it may be, we are liable to be gravely misunderstood. Not only is the Christian concept of history somewhat alien to the Indian mind, but such a concept is in fact *a posteriori* to the incarnation of Christ. To admit the Christian idea of history, indispensable though it may be for an understanding

[3] Cf. the almost classical study of K. Prümm, *Christentum als Neuheitserlebnis*. Freiburg, Herder, 1939.

of the historical Christ, is to presuppose the Christian concept of Christ. We should not forget that the first philosophical interpretation of Christ begins with a discourse not on the 'flesh', but on the 'Logos' that became 'flesh'. Most philosophical misunderstandings about Christ and the incarnation, from the side of Indian philosophy, would disappear if Christian theology tried to speak of Christ in a way that might make sense to the partner in dialogue. However, to show how to proceed further in this dialogue—and much less how to decide upon its contents and results—cannot be within the compass of this essay.[4]

Second, using a certain theological language, one could speak of a historical action of divine providence that inspires Mankind in different ways according to time and place, and directs human life with all its components—including the philosophical and religious—towards its fullness, guiding Man and his ideas towards the ultimate end of history. None can claim to know the 'hour' of God, the concrete design of providence in the undetermined events of the human struggle on earth; but nobody can rightly object to the peaceful expression of a conviction.[5] Such a conviction is that Christ has always been at work everywhere—that he was present not only when God created all things, fixing the heavens and commanding the waters, but also when the Indian rishis composed and handed down the *śruti*—for God's wisdom (*sophia, śakti*) 'was delighted every day playing before God at all times, playing in the World, for her delight is to be with the children of Men'. However, in this sphere philosophy must be silent, and theology confess its own inadequacy.[6]

To avoid misunderstanding, let me cite in this connection two authorities. Whatever merit this work may have, it can take no credit for novelty. We could adduce many other authoritative instances, but these two must here suffice.

I have tried to do *mutatis mutandis* what the Christian Scholastics, especially St Thomas Aquinas, did with Hellenic wis-

[4] Cf. R. Panikkar, 'La demitologizzazione nell'incontro del Cristianesimo con l'Induismo' in *Archivio di Filosofia* (Padua, Cedam, 1961), pp. 243–66.
[5] Cf. Prov. 8:22ff.
[6] Cf. 1 Cor. 13:1–3.

dom in general and with Aristotle in particular. It would not be difficult to prove that I have treated our text more literally than Thomas Aquinas did Aristotelian thought.[7] The Aristotelian God could be neither a Creator nor a Father who loves his children. Further, Aristotle's conception of time was incompatible with the exigencies of the Christian Incarnation as understood by St Thomas and his day. Moreover, in speaking of St Thomas' treatment of Aristotelian thought I am not referring to specific moral problems such as slavery or particular Christian concepts such as grace, but to certain fundamental philosophical concepts which, despite being vastly different from those of Christian thought, St Thomas did not hesitate to use—and transform—commenting as he did on the 'Philosopher' *pro domo sua*.

It must be added at once that St Thomas was perfectly justified intellectually in so doing: he was not simply performing the academic work of an interpreter, but undertaking a theological mission of assimilation, namely an explanation of Christian truths by adoption of the Aristotelian framework conveniently transformed. He was not concerned with aseptic 'scientific' hermeneutics, but sought only the truth.[8]

Furthermore, St Thomas was following the traditional Christian line which is based on the assumption that the Christian seeks fullness of truth and that christianizing certain values (of Aristotelian philosophy in this case) does those values no harm, but rather clarifies them, makes them shine in a purer light. He considered that he was saying in his time what Aristotle would have wanted to say, not psychologically, perhaps, but ontologically, in so far as Aristotle tried to explain certain truths that are beyond words.[9] If the Christian

[7] '. . . One should not forget that even the elementary notions of physical substance, of matter and of form, above all of potency and act have not the same sense in Aristotle and in Thomas Aquinas, because his own notion of being is other than that of Aristotle.' E. Gilson, *History of Christian Philosophy in the Middle Ages* (London, Sheed & Ward, 1955), p. 709.

[8] '*Studium philosophiae non est ad hoc quod sciatur quid homines senserint, sed qualiter se habeat veritas rerum*', says Aquinas, commenting precisely Aristotle, *De Coelo* I,22.

[9] '*Sub verbis latent significata verborum*' is something that Saint Thomas never forgot. *Sum. Theol.* II–II, q.8, a.1.

Aristotle of Thomism were to contain more truth than the historical one, then we might even say that the true Aristotle is that of the thirteenth century.

I have said above *mutatis mutandis* for many reasons. The first that springs to mind is obviously not in my favour; I do not venture to compare my attempt at rethinking a non-Christian philosophy with the efforts of the Angelic Doctor, nor, as far as my person, contents of thought and method are concerned, can I presume to emulate even distantly the great Scholastic. But there is another reason which may give me an advantage. Seven centuries of human experience have made us aware of what St Thomas, impelled by his Christian urge, achieved—even though today not everything he said is acceptable. Nowadays, however, our perspective is different and we possess new tools. It is possible, certainly, that St Thomas thought he was reviving the historical Aristotle (though some very positive signs lead us to doubt it). We of our age are fully aware, in a way that he was not, of the exegetical, dialectical and philological planes. Thus my interpretation has a critical understanding of the Christian dynamism of 'establishing all things in Christ'.[10] Today we are critically aware that the Christian *a priori* of Christ being the unique Mediator and Christianity the true religion is embedded in time, space, culture and a particular human understanding. Furthermore, philosophical and theological consciousness would no longer approve of the *spolia aegyptiorum* method. That is, of the Christian right and duty to consider the earth and all human cultural values as being bequeathed to them in perpetuity by the Creator. Any Christian reflection today must reconsider its starting-point and, at the least, justify it in the human arena.

I would like to reiterate that in my opinion the 'discovery' of a Śaṅkara or a Rāmānuja is just as important for Christian theology today as the assimilation of Plato and Aristotle was in ages past.

Minutis minuendis I venture to think that such an attempt as mine could find inspiration, illumination and justification in

[10] Eph. 1:10.

the famous encounter of St Paul with the Men of Athens.[11] There, it will be recalled, there was a 'pagan' shrine to an unknown and nameless God, and Paul said that he was proclaiming that very God whom they, without knowing it, were worshipping.[12] Needless to say, it was not a zealous 'strategy' which led Paul to utter such memorable words and to adopt such an attitude. Rather, unveiling a true face of God, he did not proclaim *another* God. After saying, further, that God was not far from any of his listeners, for 'in him we live and move and are', he substantiated his bold statement with the saying of a Greek poet: 'For we are also his off-spring.'[13] Here there comes to mind the refrain of the great cosmological hymn of the Rig-Veda: 'What God shall we adore with our oblation?'[14] One of the possible meanings of the text is the mysterious character of the Godhead, which can never be fully grasped and hence is only fittingly approached by an open interrogation. What on the Areopagus was a dedication in the dative is here a question in the dative: God is the 'to whom?' of our search.

God is at work in all religions: the Christian *kerygma* does not proclaim a new God, but the *mirabilia* of God,[15] of which the Mystery of Christ hidden in God is the *alpha* and *omega*.[16] This very expression in fact is declaring that Christ is not yet 'finished', not 'discovered', until the 'last moment' or the 'end' has come. The process itself is still open-ended.

In the wake of St Paul we believe we may speak not only of the unknown God of the Greeks, but also of the *hidden Christ of Hinduism*—hidden and unknown and yet present and at work because he is not far from any one of us. St Paul had to fight on two different fronts in order to defend the Christian position. On the one hand the Jews, even when converted, tended to make Christianity into a reformed sect of

[11] Cf. Acts 17:16–34.

[12] ὃ οὖν ἀγνοοῦντες εὐσεβεῖτε, τοῦτο ἐγὼ καταγγέλλω ὑμῖν.

[13] An analysis of this γένος used by Aratus (*Phenomenes* 5) and repeated and accepted by St Paul should prove extremely fruitful and revealing.

[14] RV X, 121. Cf. R. Panikkar, *The Vedic Experience*, pp. 67–72.

[15] This is a recurrent theme of the Scripture; cf. Ps. 9:2; 25:7; 39:6; 70:17; 74:2; 97:1, etc; Ecclus. 42:17, etc.

[16] Cf. Eph. 3:9; Rom. 16:25, etc.

Judaism.[17] The Greeks, on the other hand, were inclined to absorb Christianity into a kind of gnosis or a variety of Greek wisdom.[18] In both cases the struggle was the same—against the attempt to minimize the figure of Christ and interpret it apart from the central mystery of the Trinity. Paul's reaction was to show how in Christ the mystery of God has been revealed, and how he—the *Pantocrator*, the cosmic redeemer, the beginning and end of all things, the only-begotten, the Logos—is at the same time Jesus, son of Mary, crucified by Men and risen from the dead so that he may sum up the whole of creation in himself and lead it back to God the Father, gathering together all the scattered pieces[19] of wandering humanity, of a Mankind which remains full of expectancy, because the children of God are still to be made known.[20]

Finally, I shall formulate a theological conclusion which is directly consequent upon this christological approach: the unity of Christ. Whatever God does *ad extra* happens through Christ. Thus, recognizing the presence of *God* in other religions is equivalent to proclaiming the presence of Christ in them, 'for in him all things subsist'.[21]

[17] Romans and Galatians are the main epistles in this struggle.
[18] Cf. 1 and 2 Cor.
[19] Cf. John 6:12.
[20] Cf. Rom. 8:19.
[21] Col. 1:17.

BIBLIOGRAPHY

Unless otherwise stated the place of publication is London.

I. CHRISTIANITY AND WORLD RELIGIONS

ALLEN, G. F., *The Theology of Mission*. SCM Press 1943.

ANDERSON, G. H. (ed.), *Asian Voices in Christian Theology*. New York, Orbis, 1976.

APPLETON, G., *Glad Encounter. Jesus Christ and the Living Faiths of Men*. Edinburgh House Press 1959.

AUBERT, R., *Problèmes de l'unité chrétienne*. Chevetogne, Editions de Chevetogne, 1952.

BACH, M., *Had You Been Born in Another Faith*. Englewood Cliffs, N. J., Prentice-Hall, 1961.

BARDY, G., *La conversion au christianisme durant les premiers siècles*. Paris, Aubier, 1947.

BARROWS, J.-H., *The World's Parliament of Religions*, 2 vols. Chicago, The Parliament Publishing House, 1893.

BAUHOFER, O., *Das Metareligiöse. Eine kritische Religionsphilosophie*. Leipzig, J. C. Hinrichs, 1930.

BECKMANN, J., *Weltkirche und Weltreligionen*. Freiburg, Herder, 1960.

BENZ, E., *Ideen zu einer Theologie der Religionsgeschichte*. Mainz, Akademie der Wissenschaften, 1961.

Das Christentum und die nichtchristlichen Hochreligionen. Eine internationale Bibliographie. Leiden, Brill, 1960.

BERGMANN, G., *Jesus Christus—oder Buddha, Mohammed, Hinduismus*. Gladbeck/Westf., Schriften Missionsverlag, 1966.

BHATTACHARYYA, H., *The Foundations of Living Faiths. An Introduction to Comparative Religion*, vol. i. Calcutta, University of Calcutta, 1938.

BOUQUET, A. C., *The Christian Faith and Non-Christian Religions*. J. Nirbet 1958.

BOYD, R., *An Introduction to Indian Christian Theology*. Madras, Christian Literature Society, 1969.

India and the Latin Captivity of the Church. The Cultural Context of the Gospel. Cambridge University Press 1974.

Khristadvaita. A Theology for India. Madras, Christian Literature Society, 1977.

BSTEH, A. (ed.), *Universales Christentum angesichts einer pluralen Welt* (Beiträge zur Religionstheologie 1). Mödling, St Gabriei, 1976.

BÜRKLE, H., *Einführung in die Theologie der Religionen.* Darmstadt, Wissenschaftliche Buchgesellschaft, 1977.

CARPENTER, J. E., *Christianity and the Religions of the World.* Boston, American Unitarian Association, 1904.

CLARKE, J. F., *Ten Great Religions. An Essay in Comparative Theology.* Boston, Houghton Mifflin, 1871.

CONGAR, Y. M.-J., *Divided Christendom, A Catholic Study of the Problem of Re-Union.* G. Bles 1939.

COOKE, G., *As Christians Face Rival Religions. An Interreligious Strategy for Community Without Compromise.* New York, Association Press, 1962.

COPELAND, E. L., *Christianity and World Religions.* Nashville, Convention Press, 1963.

CORNELIS, E., *Valeurs chrétiennes des religions non-chrétiennes. Histoire du salut et histoire des religions.* Paris, Cerf, 1965.

CRAGG, K., *Christianity in World Perspective.* Oxford University Press 1968.

CUPITT, D., *Christ and the Hiddenness of God.* Lutterworth Press 1971.

CUTTAT, J.-A., *Begegnung der Religionen.* Einsiedeln, Johannes Verlag, 1956.

The Encounter of Religions. New York, Desclée, 1960.

DANIÉLOU, J., *Introduction to the Great Religions.* Notre Dame, Ind., Fides, 1964.

The Advent of Salvation. A Comparative Study of Non-Christian Religions and Christianity. New York, Paulist Press, 1962.

Le mystère du salut des nations. Paris, Seuil, 1948.

DE LUBAC, H., *Le fondement théologique des missions.* Paris, Seuil, 1946.

DENISON, M. F., *The Religions of the World and their Relation to Christianity.* Cambridge 1852.

DERRICK, Ch., *Light of Revelation and Non-Christians,* New York, Society of St. Paul, 1965.

DEWICK, E. C., *The Christian Attitude to Other Religions.* Cambridge University Press 1953.

DUMONT, C. J., *Approaches to Christian Unity.* Darton, Longman & Todd 1959.

EVERS, G., *Mission—Nichtchristliche Religionen—Weltliche Welt.* Münster, Aschendorff, 1974.

FERRE, N. F. S., *The Finality of Faith and Christianity Among the World Religions.* New York, Harper & Row, 1963.

FLEMING, D. J., *Attitudes Towards Other Faiths.* New York, Association Press, 1928.

FORMAN, Ch. W., *Christianity in the Non-Western World.* Englewood Cliffs, N. J., Prentice Hall, 1967.

FORSTER, K., *Das Christentum und die Weltreligionen* (Kath. Akademie in Bayern). Würzburg, Echter Verlag, 1965.

FRANK, E., *Philosophical Understanding and Religious Truth*, 5th edn. Oxford University Press 1956.

FREYTAG, W., *The Gospel and the Religions. A Biblical Enquiry.* SCM Press 1957.

GALLOWAY, A. D., *The Cosmic Christ.* New York, Harper, 1951.

GARDET, L., *Expériences mystiques en terres non chrétiennes.* Paris, Alsatia, 1953.

GENSICHEN, H. W., ROSENKRANZ, G., VICEDOM, G. F., *Theologische Stimmen aus Asien, Afrika and Lateinamerika.* München, Chr. Kaiser Verlag, 1965.

GIRAULT, R., *Dialogues aux frontières de l'Eglise* (Coll. Spiritualité, 21). Paris, Economie et Humanisme, 1965.

GOWEN, H. H., *The Universal Faith. Comparative Religion from the Christian Standpoint.* Milwaukee, Morehouse, 1926.

GRANT, G. M., *Religions of the World in Relation to Christianity.* New York, Revel, 1894.

GRILL, S., *Vergleichende Religionsgeschichte und Kirchenväter.* Horn, 1959.

GRILLMEIER, A., *Christ in Christian Tradition. From the Apostolic Age to Chalcedon.* New York, Sheed & Ward, 1965.

Mit ihm und in ihm. Christologische Forschungen und Perspektiven. Freiburg, Herder, 1975.

HALL, Ch. C., *Christ and the Eastern Soul.* Chicago, University of Chicago Press, 1909.

HEISLBETZ, J., *Theologische Gründe der nichtchristlichen Religionen* (Quaestiones Disputatae 33). Freiburg, Herder, 1967.

HENRY, A. M., *Esquisse d'une théologie de la mission* (Coll. 'Foi vivante', série 'Parole et Mission'). Paris, Cerf, 1959.

HESSEN, J., *Der Absolutheitsanspruch des Christentums.* München, E. Reinhardt, 1963.

HILLMAN, E., *The Wider Ecumenism: Anonymous Christianity and the Church.* Burns and Oates 1968.

HOCKING, W. E., *Living Religions and a World Faith.* New York, Macmillan, 1940.

The Coming World Civilisation. New York, Harper, 1956.

HUME, R. E., *The World's Living Religions—with Special Reference to their Sacred Scriptures in Comparison with Christianity. An Historical Sketch*. New York, Ch. Scribner's, 1959.

JOLIVET, R., *Essai sur les rapports entre la pensée grecque et la pensée chrétienne*, 2nd edn. Paris, Vrin, 1956.

JUNG, M., NIKHILANANDA, Sw., SCHNEIDER, H. W., *Relations among Religions Today—A Handbook of Policies and Principles*. Leiden, Brill, 1963.

JUNGHEINRICH, H., *'Was ist Wahrheit?' Das Christentum und die Weltreligionen*. Frankfurt, Deutscher Bund für Freies Christentum, 1957.

JURGI, E. J., *The Christian Interpretation of Religion*. New York, Macmillan, 1952.

KARRER, O., *Das Religiöse in der Menschheit und das Christentum*. Freiburg, Herder, 1956.

KASPER, W. (ed.), *Absolutheit des Christentums* (Questiones Disputatae 79). Freiburg, Herder, 1977.

KITAGAWA, J. M., *Gibt es ein Verstehen fremder Religionen?* Leiden, Brill, 1963.

KLINGER, E. (ed.), *Christentum innerhalb und ausserhalb der Kirche* (Quaestiones Disputatae 73). Freiburg, Herder, 1976.

KÖNIG, F., *Christus und die Religionen der Erde*, 3 vols. Freiburg, Herder, 1961.

KRAEMER, H., *The Christian Message in a Non-Christian World*. New York, Harper, 1938.

Religion and the Christian Faith. Philadelphia, Westminster Press, 1956.

World Cultures and World Religions—The Coming Dialogue. Philadelphia, Westminster Press, 1960.

Why Christianity of All Religions. Philadelphia, Westminster Press, 1962.

LANCZKOWSKI, G., *Begegnung und Wandel der Religionen*. Düsseldorf-Köln 1971.

LEEUWEN, A. Th. Van, *Christianity in World History—The Meeting of the Faiths of East and West*. Edinburgh House Press 1964 (new edn 1966).

LOMBARDI, R., *The Salvation of the Unbeliever*. Burns & Oates 1956.

MACNICOL, N., *Is Christianity Unique? A Comparative Study of the Religions*. SCM Press 1936.

MANN, U. (ed.), *Theologie und Religionswissenschaft*. Darmstadt, Wissenschaftliche Buchgesellschaft, 1973.

MASURE, E., *Devant les religions non chrétiennes*. Lille, Ed. Catholicité, 1945.

MATHEWS, B. J. (ed.), *East and West—Conflict or Cooperation*. Freeport, N.Y., Books for Libraries Press, 1967.

MAURICE, F. D., *The Religions of the World and their Relation to Christianity*. Sould & Lincoln 1854.

MAURIER, H., *Essai d'une théologie du paganisme*. Paris, L'Orante, 1965.

McKAIN, D. W. (ed.), *Christianity—Some Non-Christian Appraisals*. New York, McGraw-Hill, 1964.

MENSCHING, G., *Die Religionen und die Welt. Typen religiöser Weltdeutung*. Bonn, Ludwig Röhrscheid, 1947.

NEILL, St. *Christian Faith and Other Faiths. The Christian Dialogue with Other Religions*. Oxford University Press 1961.

NEUNER, J. (ed.), *Christian Revelation and World Religions*. Burns & Oates 1967.

NORTHROP, F. S. C., *The Meeting of East and West*. New York, Macmillan, 1946.

OHM, Th., *Die Liebe zu Gott in den nichtchristlichen Religionen*. München, E. Wewel, 1950.

PANIKKAR, R., *Die Religionen und die Religion*. München, Max Hueber, 1966.

The Trinity and World Religions. Madras, Christian Literature Society, 1970. Rev. edn: *The Trinity and the Religious Experience of Man. Icon, Person, Mystery*. Darton, Longman & Todd 1973.

The Intrareligious Dialogue. New York, Paulist Press, 1978.

PARRINDER, G., *The Christian Debate. Light from the East*. Garden City, N.J., Doubleday, 1966.

PATHRAPANKAL, J. (ed.) *Service and Salvation. Nagpur Theological Conference on Evangelisation*. Bangalore, Theological Publications of India, 1973.

PATTON, W., *Jesus Christ and the World's Religions*. Livingstone Press 1937.

PERRY, E., *The Gospel in Dispute. The Relation of Christian Faith to Other Missionary Religions*. New York, Doubleday, 1958.

PHILIPS, Th., *The Grace of God and a World Religion*. The Carey Press, n.d.

PHILLIPPIDIS, L. J., *Religionsgeschichte als Heilsgeschichte in der Weltgeschichte*, Mitteilung an die XI. Deutsche Jahrestagung für Religionsgeschichte. Bonn 1952.

PRATER, S., *Das Christentum und die ausserchristlichen Religionen*. Dresden 1935.

PROSPER OF AQUITAINE, St, *The Call of All Nations* (Ancient Christian Writers, vol. xiv). Longmans 1952.

PRÜMM, K., *Der christliche Glaube und die altheidnische Welt*, 2 vols. Leipzig, J. Hegner, 1935.

RAHNER, K., *Schriften zur Theologie* V. Einsiedeln, Benziger, 1962.

REID, G., *A Christian's Appreciation of Other Faiths. A Study of the West in the World's Greatest Religions*. The Open Court 1921.

RETIF, A., *Foi au Christ et Mission d'après les Actes des Apôtres*. Paris, Cerf, 1953.

RIEDLS, J., *Das Heil der Heiden nach dem Römerbrief*. Wien, St. Gabriel, 1965.

ROSENKRANZ, G., *Der christliche Glaube angesichts der Weltreligionen*. Bern, Francke, 1967.

ROUSE, R. and NEILL, S. C. (ed.), *A History of the Ecumenical Movement 1517–1948*. S.P.C.K. 1954.

RUPP, G., *Christologies and Cultures. Toward a Typology of Religious Word-Views*. The Hague, Mouton, 1974.

ST. JOHN, H., *Essays in Christian Unity*. Blackfriars 1955.

SAMARTHA, St. J. (ed.), *Dialogue Between Men of Living Faiths*. Geneva, World Council of Churches, 1971.

SARTORY, Th., *Die ökumenische Begegnung und die Einheit der Kirche*. Meitingen bei Augsburg, Kyrios Verlag, 1955.

SCHLETTE, H. R., *Die Religionen als Thema der Theologie* (Quaestiones Disputatae 22). Freiburg, Herder, 1963.

Towards a Theology of Religions. Burns & Oates 1966.

Die Konfrontation mit den Religionen. Köln, Bachem, 1965.

Colloquium Salutis. Christen und Nichtchristen heute. Köln, Bachem, 1965.

SCHUON, F., *The Transcendent Unity of Religions*. Faber & Faber 1953.

SCHUSTER, H., *Der christliche Glaube und die Religionen der Völker*. Frankfurt, 1951.

SCHÜTTE, J. (ed.), *Mission nach dem Konzil*. Mainz, Matthias-Grünewald-Verlag, 1967.

SCHWEITZER, A., *Christianity and the Religions of the World*. Allen & Unwin 1923.

SECRETARIATUS PRO NON CHRISTIANIS (ed.), *Religions—thèmes fondamentaux pour une connaissance dialogique*. Rome 1970.

SIMON, G., *Auseinandersetzung des Christentums mit der ausserchristlichen Welt*. Gütersloh, C. Bertelsmann, 1930.

SINGH, H. J. (ed.), *Inter-Religious Dialogue* (Devanandan Memorial Volume), no. 3. Bangalore, CISRS, 1967.

SLATER, R. L., *Can Christians Learn from Other Religions?* New York, Seabury Press, 1963.

World Religions and World Community. New York, Columbia University Press, 1963.

SMART, N., *A Dialogue of Religions*. SCM Press 1960.

Reason and Faith. An Investigation of Religious Discourse, Christian and Non-Christian. Routledge & Kegan Paul 1958.

SMITH, W. C., *The Faith of Other Men*. New York, New American Library, 1963.

SPEER, R. E., *The Light of the World. A Brief Comparative Study of Christianity and Non-Christian Religions*. West Medford, Mass., United Study of Missions, 1911.

SPRINGER, Ch. R., *Christianity and Rival Religions*. Philadelphia, Fortress Press, 1966.

STOECKLE, B., *Die ausserbiblische Menschheit und die Weltreligionen* in *Mysterium Salutis* II, 1049–75. Einsiedeln, Benziger, 1967.

STOWE, D. M., *When Faith Meets Faith*. New York, Friendship Press, 1963.

THILS, G., *Propos et problèmes de la théologie des religions non-chrétiennes*. Paris, Casterman, 1966.

THOMAS, M. M., *Salvation and Humanisation. Some Crucial Issues of the Theology of Mission in Contemporary India*. Madras, Christian Literature Society, 1971.

TILLICH, P., *Christianity and the Encounter of the World Religions*. New York, Columbia University Press, 1964.

TODD, J. M., *Catholicism and the Ecumenical Movement*. Longmans 1956.

TOYNBEE, A. J., *An Historian's Approach to Religion*. Oxford University Press 1956.

Christianity among the Religions of the World. New York, Scribner, 1957.

VERENO, M., *Vom Mythos zum Christos*. Salzburg, O. Müller, 1958.

VICEDOM, G. F., *Die Mission der Weltreligionen*. Munich, Kaiser, 1959.

Die Weltreligionen im Angriff auf das Christentum. Munich, Kaiser, 1956.

The Challenge of the World Religions. Philadelphia, Fortress Press, 1963.

VILLAIN, M., *Unity*. Harvill-Collins 1963.

VISSER'T HOOFT, W. A., *No Other Name. The Choice Between Syncretism and Christian Universalism*. Philadelphia, Westminster Press, 1963.

WARREN, M. A. C., *The Relationship between Christianity and Other World Religions*. Prism 1966.
WATTS, A. W., *The Supreme Identity. An Essay on Oriental Metaphysics and the Christian Religion*. New York, Pantheon, 1950.
WITTE, J., *Die Christusbotschaft und die Religionen*. Göttingen, Vandenhoek & Ruprecht, 1936.
ZAEHNER, R. C., *At Sundry Times*. Faber & Faber 1958.
Christianity and Other Religions. New York, Hawthorn Books, 1964.
The Catholic Church and World Religions. Burns & Oates 1964.

II. HINDUISM AND CHRISTIANITY

ABHEDANANDA, Sw., *Why a Hindu Accepts Christ and Rejects Churchianity*, 11th edn. Calcutta, Ramakrishna Vedanta Math, 1965.
ABHISHIKTANANDA, Sw., *Hindu-Christian Meeting Point Within the Cave of the Heart*. Bombay, Institute of Indian Culture, 1969.
Saccidananda. A Christian Approach to Advaitic Experience. Delhi, ISPCK, 1974.
The Further Shore. Two Essays: Sannyasa and the Upanishads, an Introduction. Delhi, ISPCK, 1975.
AKHILANANDA, Sw., *Hindu View of Christ*. New York, Philosophical Library, 1949.
AMALORPAVADASS, D. S., *L'Inde à la rencontre du Seigneur*. Paris, Ed. Spes, 1964.
(ed.), *Research Seminar on Non-Biblical Scriptures*. Bangalore, National Biblical, Catachetical and Liturgical Centre, 1974.
ANDERSON, G. H., (ed.), *Christ and Crisis in Southeast Asia*. Friendship Press 1968.
ASHBY, P. H., *History and Future of Religious Thought, Christianity, Hinduism, Buddhism, Islam*. Englewood Cliffs, N. J., Prentice Hall, 1963.
The Conflict of Religion. New York, Scribner's, 1955.
ASIRVATHAM, E., *Christianity in the Indian Crucible*. Calcutta, Y.M.C.A., 1955.
BALLANTYNE, J. R., *Christianity Contrasted with Hindu Philosophy*. James Madden 1859.
BARLAGE, H., *Christ Saviour of Mankind. A Christian Appreciation of Swami Akhilananda*. St Augustin, Steyler Verlag, 1977.
BENZ, E., *Indische Einflüsse auf die frühchristliche Theologie*. Wiesbaden, F. Steiner, 1951.
BOUQUET, A. C., *The Christian Faith and Non-Christian Religions*. J. Nirbet 1958.
CAVE, S., *Hinduism or Christianity. A Study in the Distinctiveness of the*

Christian Message (The Haskell Lectures 1939). Hodder & Stoughton 1939.

CHAKKARAI, V., *The Cross and Indian Thought*. Madras, Christian Literature Society for India, 1932.

CUTTAT, J.-A., *Asiatische Gottheit—Christlicher Gott. Die Spiritualität der beiden Hemisphären*. Einsiedeln, Johannes, n.d.

DANDOY, G., *L'ontologie du Vedānta*. Paris, D.D.B., 1932.

Catholicism and National Cultures. Calcutta, Light of the East no. 27, 1939.

DAS, Bhagavan, *Essential Unity of All Religions*. Madras, Theosophical Publishing House, 1955.

DEWICK, E. C., *The Christian Attitude to Other Religions*. C.U.P. 1953.

EIDLITZ, W., *Die indische Gottesliebe*, Freiburg, Walter, 1955.

Der Glaube und die heiligen Schriften der Inder. Freiburg, Walter, 1957.

EMMANUEL, A., *La Bible et l'Inde. Clartés convergentes*. Paris, A. Maisonneuve, 1933.

FARMER, H. H., *Revelation and Religion. Studies in the Theological Interpretation of Religious Types*. New York, Harper, 1954.

FARQUHAR, J. N., *The Crown of Hinduism*. O.U.P. 1913.

FORMAN, C. W., *A Faith for the Nations*. Philadelphia, Westminster Press, 1957.

FREYTAG, W., *The Gospel and the Religions*. Scon 1957.

GARBE, R., *Indien und das Christentum. Eine Untersuchung der religions–geschichtlichen Zusammenhänge*. Tübingen, J. C. B. Mohr, 1914.

HEIMANN, B., *Indian and Western Philosophy*. Allen & Unwin 1937.

HEINRICHS, M., *Katholische Theologie und asiatisches Denken*. Mainz, M. Grünewald, 1963.

HUSAIN, J. A. M., *A Christian's View of the Vedanta*. Tiruchirappalli, CTS, 1957.

HUTTEN, K., *Die Bhakti-Religion in Indien und der christliche Glaube im Neuen Testament*. Stuttgart, W. Kohlhammer, 1930.

JOHANNS, P., *Vers le Christ par le Vedānta*, 2 vols. Louvain, D.D.B., 1932.

La pensée religieuse de l'Inde. Paris, Vrin, 1952.

KRÄMER, A., *Christus und Christentum im Denken des modernen Hinduismus*. Bonn, L. Röhrscheid, 1958.

KRAUSE, W., *Die Stellung der frühchristilichen Autoren zur heidnischen Literatur*. Wien, Herder, 1958.

LACOMBE, O., *Chemins de l'Inde et philosophie chrétienne* (Coll. 'Sagesse et Cultures'). Paris, Alsatia, 1956.

LE SAUX, H., see ABHISHIKTANANDA.

MASURE, E., *Devant les religions non chrétiennes*. Lille, Ed. Catholicité, 1945.

MELZER, F., *Indische Weisheit und christliche Erkenntnis*. Tübingen, Der Leuchter, O. Reichl Verlag, 1948.

MONCHANIN, J., LE SAUX, H., *Ermites du Saccidānanda. Un essai d'intégration chrétienne de la tradition monastique de l'Inde*. Paris, Casterman, 1956.

OHM, Th., *Asiens Nein und Ja zum westlichen Christentum*. München, Kösel, 1960.

OTTO, R., *West-östliche Mystik*, 2nd edn. München, C. H. Beck, 1929.

Indiens Gnadenreligion und das Christentum. Gotha, L. Klotz Verlag, 1930.

PANIKKAR, R., *Kultmysterium in Hinduismus und Christentum*. Freiburg, K. Alber, 1964.

Le mystère du culte dans l'hindouisme et le christianisme. Paris, Cerf, 1970.

Die vielen Götter und der eine Herr. Weilheim, Obb., O.W. Barth, 1964.

Kerygma und Indien. Zur heilsgeschichtlichen Problematik der christlichen Begegnung mit Indien. Hamburg, H. Reich, 1967.

Māyā e Apocalisse. L'incontro dell'Induismo e del Cristianesimo. Roma, Abete, 1966.

Misterio y Revelación. Hinduismo y Cristianesimo. Madrid, Marova, 1971.

PARRINDER, G., *Avatar and Incarnation*. Faber & Faber 1970.

PLOTT, J. C., *A Philosophy of Devotion. A Comparative Study of Bhakti and Prapatti in Viśiṣṭādvaita and St. Bonaventura and Gabriel Marcel*. Delhi, Motilal Banarsidass, 1974.

PRABHAVANANDA, Sw., *The Sermon on the Mount According to Vedanta*. Allen & Unwin 1964.

RADHAKRISHNAN, S., *Eastern Religions and Western Thought*, 2nd edn. Oxford University Press 1940 (reprinted 1951).

REGAMEY, P., *Die Religionen Indiens* in *Christus und die Religionen der Erde*, vol. III (pp. 73–227). Freiburg, Herder, 1951.

SAMARTHA, S., *Hindus vor dem universalen Christus. Beiträge zu einer Christologie in Indien*. Stuttgart, Evangelisches Verlagswerk, 1970.

SCHOMERUS, H. W., *Indien und das Christentum*, 3 vols. Halle-Saale, Bachhandlung des Waisenhauses, 1931–3.

Die indische theologische Spekulation und die Trinitätslehre. Berlin-Lichterfelde 1919.

Indische Erlösungslehren. Ihre Bedeutung für das Verständnis des Christentums und für die Missionspredigt. Leipzig, Hinrichs, 1919.

Indische und christliche Enderwartung und Erlösungshoffnung. Gütersloh 1941.

SCHWEITZER, A., *Indian Thought and its Development*. New York, Holt, 1936. 2nd edn: Boston, Beacon Press, 1957.

SINGH, S., *Preface to Personality. Christology in Relation to Radhakrishnan's Philosophy* (Indian Research Series, no. 9). Madras, 1952.

SLATER, T. E., *The Higher Hinduism in Relation to Christianity*. Elliot Stock 1903.

URQUHART, W. S., *Theosophy and Christian Thought*. Boston, Pilgrim Press, 1922.

VÄTH, A., *Im Kampf mit der Zauberwelt des Hinduismus*. Bonn, Dümmler, 1928.

WOLFF, O., *Christus unter den Hindus*. Gütersloh, Verlagshaus G. Mohn, 1965.

III. HINDUISM AND VEDĀNTA

BHATTACHARYA, K. C., *Studies in Philosophy*, 2 vols. Calcutta, Progressive Publishers, 1956–8.

CARPENTER, J. E., *Theism in Medieval India*. Williams 1921.

CHEMPARATHY, G., *An Indian Rational Theology. Introduction to Udayana's Nyāyakusumāñjali*. Vienna, Publications of the De Nobili Research Library, 1972.

DANDEKAR, R. N., *Some Aspects of the History of Hinduism*. Poona, University of Poona, 1967.

DASGUPTA, S. N., *A History of Indian Philosophy*, 5 vols. C.U.P. 1951–5 (reprinted in India by Motilal Banarsidass).

DE SMET, R. V., *The Theological Method of Śaṅkara* (Diss. ad Lauream). Rome, Pont. Univ. Gregoriana, 1953.

DEUSSEN, P., *Das System des Vedānta nach den Brahma-Sūtras des Bādarāyana und dem Kommentare des Çaṅkara über dieselben*. Leipzig, Brockhaus, 1883 (4th edn 1923).

Die Sūtras des Vedānta. Leipzig, Brockhaus, 1887.

The Philosophy of the Vedānta. Calcutta, S. Gupta, 1957.

FARQUHAR, J. N., *An Outline of the Religious Literature of India*. Millford 1920.

FRAUWALLNER, E., *Geschichte der indischen Philosophie*, 2 vols. Salzburg, O. Müller, 1953–6.

GHATE, V. S., *Le Vedānta, études sur les brahma-soutras et leurs cinq commentaires* (*thèse*). Paris 1918.

Le Vedānta. Paris, Geuthner, 1930.

GONDA, J., *Die Religionen Indiens*, 2 vols. Stuttgart, Kohlhammer, 1960–3.

Aspects of Early Viṣṇuism. Utrecht, 1954. 2nd edn. Delhi, Motilal Banarsidass, 1969.

Change and Continuity in Indian Religion. The Hague, Mouton & Co., 1965.

Viṣṇuism and Śivaism. A Comparison. London University (School of Oriental and African Studies) 1970.

GUENON, R., *L'homme et son devenir selon le Vedānta*. Paris, Les Editions traditionnelles, 1941.

HACKER, P., *Kleine Schriften*, ed. L. SCHMITHAUSEN. Wiesbaden, F. Steiner, 1978.

HEIMANN, B., *Studien zur Eigenart des indischen Denkens*. Tübingen, J. C. B. Mohr, Siebeck, 1930.

HIRIYANNA, M., *Outlines of Indian Philosophy*. Allen & Unwin 1956.

The Essentials of Indian Philosophy. Allen & Unwin 1949.

Indian Philosophical Studies. Mysore 1957.

ISHERWOOD, C., *Vedanta for Modern Man*. Allen & Unwin 1952.

KUMARAPPA, B., *The Hindu Conception of Deity*. Luzac 1934.

LACOMBE, O., *L'Absolu selon le Vedânta*. Paris, P. Geuthner, 1937.

La doctrine morale et métaphysique de Râmânouja. Paris, A. Maisonneuve, 1938.

MACNICOL, N., *Indian Theism*. O.U.P. 1915 (reprint: Delhi, Munshiram Manoharlal, 1968).

MADHVA, *Brahmasūtrabhāṣya*, ed. RADDI RANGACHARYA. Poona, 1926.

MEHTA, P. D., *Early Indian Religious Thought*. Luzac 1956.

MUKHOPADHYAYA, G. G., *Studies in the Upaniṣads*. Calcutta, Sanskrit College, 1960.

MURTY, K. S., *Revelation and Reason in Advaita Vedānta*. Waltair, Andhra University, 1959.

OBERHAMMER, G. (ed.), *Offenbarung, geistige Realität des Menschen*. Wien, Publications of the De Nobili Research Library, 1974.

(ed.), *Transzendenzerfahrung, Vollzugshorizont des Heils*. Wien, Publications of the De Nobili Research Library, 1978.

PANIKKAR, R., *The Vedic Experience. Mantramañjarī*. Darton, Longman & Todd 1977.

RADHAKRISHNAN, S., *Indian Philosophy*, 2 vols. Allen & Unwin 1923–7.

History of Philosophy Eastern and Western, 2 vols. Allen & Unwin 1952–3.

The Hindu View of Life. Allen & Unwin 1927.

The Principal Upaniṣads. Allen & Unwin 1953.

The Brahma Sūtra. Allen & Unwin 1960.

RĀMĀNUJA, *Śrībhāṣyam*. New Delhi, Govt of India, 1967.

The Vedānta-Sūtras with Rāmānuja's Śrībhāṣya, tr. G. THIBAUT (SBE vol. 48), 2nd edn. Delhi, Motilal Banarsidass, 1966.

RANADE, R. D., *A Constructive Survey of the Upanishadic Philosophy*. Poona, Oriental Book Agency, 1926.

Vedanta the Culmination of Indian Thought. Bombay 1970.

RENOU, L., *L'hindouisme*. Paris, P.U.F., 1951.

The Destiny of the Veda in India. Delhi, Motilal Banarsidass, 1965.

RENOU, L., FILLIOZAT, J., et al., *L'Inde classique*, 2 vols. Paris, Payot, 1947–53.

ŚAṄKARA, *Works of Śaṅkarācārya*, vol. III: *Brahmasūtra with Śaṅkarabhāṣya*. Delhi, Motilal Banarsidass, 1964 (reprint of Poona edn 1927 ff.).

The Brahmasūtra-Shaṅkara-bhāshyam with the commentaries Bhāshya-Ratnaprabhā, Bhāmatī and Nyāyanirṇaya of Shrīgovindānanda, Vācaspati and Anandagiri, 3rd edn, ed. MAHADEV ŚASTRI PANSIKAR. Bombay, Nirnaya Sagar Press, 1934.

The Vedānta-Sūtras with the Comm. by Śaṅkarācārya, tr. G. THIBAUT, Pt. 1–2, SBE vols. 34, 38. ( ) Delhi, Motilal Banarsidass, 1962 (reprint of London edn 1904).

SHARMA, B. N. K., *The Brahmasūtras and their Principal Commentaries*, 2 vols. Bombay, Bharatiya Vidya Bhavan, 1971–4.

SIAUVE, S., *La doctrine de Madhva*. Pondichéry, Institut Français d'Indologie, 1968.

La voie de la connaissance de Dieu (Brahmajijñāsa) selon l'Anuvyākhyāna de Madhva. Pondichéry, Institut Français d'Indologie, 1957.

SIRCAR, M. N., *The System of Vedantic Thought and Culture*. Calcutta, University of Calcutta, 1927.

TAGORE, R., *The Religion of Man*, 4th edn. Macmillan 1953.

ZAEHNER, R. C., *The Bhagavad-Gītā*. O.U.P. 1969.

ZIMMER, H., *Philosophies of India*, ed. J. CAMPBELL. Routledge 1952.

GLOSSARY

Unless otherwise indicated the words are of Sanskrit origin.

adhyāsa superimposition, false attribution (of the relative on the Absolute, etc.)
Advaita non-duality, a non-dualistic philosophical view of reality, not to be confounded with monism
aham I, the absolute I
ahaṃkāra ego-sense, individual self-centredness, selfishness
ajñāna ignorance
ānanda joy, bliss, beatitude
antaryāmin the inner guide, the Self leading from within
anumāna inference, one of the 'means of knowledge' (*pramāṇa*)
arthāpatti implication
asya 'of this' (Gen.)
ātman the Self
ātmavāda doctrine accepting the existence of the Self
avatāra 'descent', incarnation of Vishnu in animal or human form
avidyā ignorance
avyakta unmanifest
bandha bondage
Bhagavān 'the blessed One', the Lord
bhakta devotee, believer
bhakti love of God, devotion, surrender
bhāṣya commentary
bhedābheda philosophy of difference-and-non-difference (between God and the World)
bindu 'drop', point, cosmological principle
Brahman the Absolute, the World-ground
buddhi intellect, discriminative faculty
cit consciousness, spirit
citta thought, mind
Cosmotheandric (Greek) the tri-unity of World, God and Man
darśana vision, world-view, philosophical system
dharma universal cosmic law, order, religion
doxa (Greek) glory
dvaita duality, dualism as a philosophical system
ens commune (Latin) common being, the abstract idea of being common to all beings
ens realissimum (Latin) absolutely real being (God)
ex nihilo (Latin) (creation) out of nothing
extra ecclesiam nulla salus 'there is no salvation outside the Church'

filioque (Latin) trinitarian controversy between Latin and Greek theology, the former assuming that the Spirit is brought forth both by the Father 'and the Son'

Guru master, teacher

Hiraṇyagarbha 'the Golden Germ', cosmological principle in the Veda, later identified with the creator (Brahmā)

Homeomorphism (Greek) theory used in Comparative Religion for discovering functional equivalences in two or more religions

idam 'this', the World

iṣṭadevatā (*iṣṭadeva*) the 'chosen' deity for worship, the personal form of God

Iśvara, *īśa* the Lord, God

janmādi origin etc.

jijñāsā desire to know, thirst for the liberating knowledge

jīva the individual soul

jñāna knowledge, higher wisdom

jñānin the wise, sage

kaivalya 'isolation', aloneness

kāraṇa cause

karma act, action, accumulated result of past actions

kenosis (Greek) annihilation, self-denial (of Christ)

kerygma (Greek) message, proclamation (of the Word of God)

kleśa affliction, impurity of the soul

manas mind

mantra verse of the Veda, sacred word, prayer

māyā divine power, power of illusion, World-illusion

mokṣa liberation, salvation

mumukṣutva the desire for liberation

naiṣkarmya inactivity, action free from desires

nāma-rūpa name and form, the constituents of the relative World

neti neti 'not so, not so', referring to the ultimate reality or the Self which can be expressed only negatively

nirguṇa (Brahman) without attributes

nirvāṇa extinction, liberation (mainly in Buddhism)

Orthopraxis (Greek) right action

Pantocrator (Greek) the Ruler of the All, designation of Christ and also of God

paramā gati supreme goal

pāramārthika the ultimate level, the ultimately real

Parameśvara the supreme Lord, God

pariṇāmavāda doctrine of creation as transformation (of the Cause into the effect)

pramāṇa means of valid knowledge

praṇava the sacred syllable OM

prasthāna starting-point, source

prasthāna-traya the three authoritative texts of Vedānta (Upaniṣads, Bhagavad Gītā, Brahma-Sūtra)

Purusha (*puruṣa*) original, archetypal Man, Person

Puruṣottama the supreme Person

ratio (Latin) reason
res significata (Latin) the intended reality
ṛṣi sage, seer (of the Veda)
śabda Word
saccidānanda Brahman as Being (*sat*), Consciousness (*cit*) and Bliss (*ānanda*)
saguṇa (Brahman) endowed with qualities
śakti divine power, creative energy of the God, conceived in female form
saṃhāra dissolution, destruction (of the World at the end of a cosmic period)
sampradāya tradition, religious system and community following one tradition
saṃsāra worldly existence, transmigration
saṃskāra 'sacrament', rites sanctifying the different stages of human life
sanātana dharma 'eternal religion', self-designation of Hinduism
sat Being
satkārya-vāda doctrine of creation according to which the effect (the World) is pre-existing in the Cause
sensus plenior (Latin) fuller meaning (of a scripture)
skambha pillar, support of the universe
sophia (Greek) wisdom
sṛṣṭi creation, emanation
śruti 'that which has been heard', revelation of the Vedas, authoritative Scriptures of Hinduism
sthiti maintenance, preservation (of the World)
sūtra lit. 'thread', short aphorism
svarūpalakṣaṇa essential definition
taṭasthalakṣaṇa accidental definition
Tempiternity (Latin) unity of time and eternity
upamāna comparison, one of the 'means of knowledge' (*pramāṇa*)
vāc the Word, speech, a sacred principle in the Veda
Vernunft (German) intellect, intelligence
Viśiṣṭādvaita doctrine of 'qualified non-dualism', represented by Rāmānuja
vivartavāda doctrine of creation according to which the World is an illusory manifestation
vyāvahārika worldly reality, relative level

INDEX OF SUBJECTS

INDEX OF NAMES

INDEX OF SCRIPTURES QUOTED